European Governance After Nice

What is the impact of institutional reform implemented by the Nice Treaty on European Governance? What should be done to enhance democratic legitimacy in the EU?

This book provides an up-to-date guide to understanding the European Union as an international institution. The contributors not only describe its functions, but also suggest reasons why it works the way it does. Analysing the pressures to which the EU is subject and its relationship with the member states, they consistently provide a comprehensive backdrop against which to discuss the various effects of the Nice Treaty.

Globalisation has led to enormous changes in the international environment which, in turn, have demanded institutional reform of the European Union in the form of the Nice Treaty. *European Governance After Nice* scrutinises how, and to what extent, the treaty will contribute to the solution of existing problems, examining both its positive effects and its limitations. The reforms within the EU are examined through a number of disciplines – political science, law and economics – in order to express the full extent of the different effects of the Nice Treaty on non-member as well as member countries. The contributors suggest that the threat of varying exchange rates in the future, when the Treaty has an expansionary effect on economic scale, will lead to a deepening interdependence between the excluded countries.

Koji Fukuda is Professor of International Administration at Waseda University, Tokyo and is on the Board of Directors of the Japan Association of EU Studies. **Hiroya Akiba** is Professor of Economics at Waseda University, Tokyo.

Waseda/RoutledgeCurzon international series

Series editor: Koichiro Agata

Books in the series

Convergence of Telecommunications and Broadcasting in Japan, United Kingdom and Germany
Edited by Koichiro Agata and Kiyoshi Nakamura

Nicholas of Cusa
A medieval thinker for the modern age
Edited by Kazuhiko Yamaki

Symbiosis of Government and Market
The private, the public and bureaucracy
Edited by Sadao Tamura and Minoru Tokita

European Governance After Nice
Edited by Koji Fukuda and Hiroya Akiba

European Governance
After Nice

Edited by Koji Fukuda and Hiroya Akiba

Routledge
Taylor & Francis Group

LONDON AND NEW YORK

First published 2003 by RoutledgeCurzon

Published 2018 by Routledge
2 Park Square, Milton Park, Abingdon, Oxon OX14 4RN
52 Vanderbilt Avenue, New York, NY 10017

First issued in paperback 2018

*Routledge is an imprint of the Taylor & Francis Group, an informa
business*

Typeset in Baskerville by Wearset Ltd, Boldon, Tyne and Wear

British Library Cataloguing in Publication Data
A catalogue record for this book is available from the British Library

Library of Congress Cataloging in Publication Data
European governance after Nice : between the present and the
future of the European Union / edited by Koji Fukuda and Hiroya
Akiba.
    p. cm. – (Waseda/RoutledgeCurzon International series)
1. European Union. 2. Treaty on European Union (1992) 3.
European cooperation. 4. Europe–Economic integration. 5.
European–Politics and government–1989– I. Fukuda, Kåoji, 1953– II.
Akiba, Hiroya, 1945– III. Series.
    JN15 .E854 2003
    341.24′22–dc21

                                                            2002152853

ISBN 13: 978-1-138-99360-0 (pbk)
ISBN 13: 978-0-7007-1717-0 (hbk)

Contents

Figures

Tables

Contributors

Hiroya Akiba is Professor of International Economics at Waseda University, Japan. Dr. Akiba has published numerous articles in professional journals including the *American Economic Review, Journal of Post-Keynesian Economics, Ricerche Economishe, Economics Letters, Journal of International Economic Integration, Journal of Socio-Economics, Public Finance, Asian Journal of Economics, International Economic Journal.*

Koji Fukuda is Professor of International Administration at Waseda University, Tokyo. Dr. Fukuda is a member of the Board of Directors of the Japan Association of EU Studies. He was a Research Fellow at the College of Europe in Brugge (1992–3). He has written a number of journal articles and is the author of *The Administrative Structure and Policy Processes in the European Communities* (Seibundo, Tokyo, 1992); "La coopération réglementaire en Europe et au Japon," Cinquieme conference ECSA-WORLD, Bruxelles, 2000.

Tomoko Hikuma is a full-time lecturer at Niigata Seiryo University. She teaches social policy and international social welfare. She graduated from the London School of Economics (M.Sc.). Her current interests include the welfare state, globalization, social rights, and core labor standards in Japan and Europe. Her recent work has focused on "core labor standards" and the WTO, EU social policy, and Central Europe in transition.

Takayuki Ito is Professor of Comparative Politics at the School of Political Science and Economics, Waseda University, Tokyo. His publications include "Slavistik und Osteuropakunde in Japan," *Osteuropa*, 1983, No. 5; (ed.) *Facing Up to the Past. Soviet Historiography under Perestroika* (Slavic Research Center, Sapporo, 1989); "Eastern Europe: Achieving Legitimacy," in Gilbert Rozman, Seizaburo Sato and Gerald Segal (eds) *Dismantling Communism: Common Causes and Regional Variations* (Johns Hopkins University Press, Washington, 1992).

Tamio Nakamura is Associate Professor of Law at the Institute of Social Science, the University of Tokyo. Dr. Nakamura is a member of the Board of Directors of the Japan Association of EU Studies. His publications include *The Decline of Parliamentary Sovereignty: Constitutional Change in Britain Since its Accession to the European Community* (University of Tokyo Press, 1993); "Constitutional Features of the APEC Process: A Voluntary Approach to Regional Integration," *Journal of Social Science*, vol. 52, no. 2, pp. 147–67, 2000.

Takao Suami is Professor of Trade Law and EU Law at Waseda University. He is a member of the Board of Directors of the Japan Association of EU Studies. He has thirteen years' practical experience as an attorney in Belgium as well as Japan. He studied law in Japan, the USA, and Europe. He is a graduate of Katholieke Universiteit Leuven in Belgium. He specializes in competition law, trade law, and basic theories of community law.

Noriko Yasue is Professor of International Organizations and EU Studies at Ritsumeikan University, Japan. She is an author of *The Birth of European Citizenship, Starting from Maastricht*, 1992 (in Japanese) (Maruzen, Tokyo, Japan, 1992); "The EU Integration and French Parliament – The Amsterdam Treaty and Article 88-4 of French Constitution," in A. Ishikawa (ed.) *The Actualities and Development of the EU Law* (in Japanese) (Sinzansha, Tokyo, Japan, 1999).

Preface

What is the impact on institutional reform from the Nice Treaty on European Governance? How does it change in reform? What should be done to enhance democratic legitimacy in the EU? Institutional reform of the European Union was necessary because of the changes in the international environment due to globalization, and institutional changes caused by the challenges of enlargement.

What are the effects of the Nice Treaty on non-member countries in terms of variations in exchange rates in the future, when the Treaty actually has an expansionary effect on the economic scale and, also, a deepening effect on the interdependence of non-member countries? In what ways might the future of European integration be influenced by the globalization of systems of structures which affect Europe.

The purpose of this book is to examine how, and to what extent, the Nice Treaty will contribute to solutions to the existing problems, and also to try to find both its positive meanings and its limits.

This book considers the transformation of European Union governance from the viewpoints of political science, law, sociology, and economics.

Most of the chapters contained in this volume were first presented at a symposium on "The Transformation of European Governance: European Integration after Nice," held at Waseda University on May 16, 2001. It was organized by the Institute for Research in Contemporary Political and Economic Affairs, Waseda University and supported by the European Union, Delegation of the European Commission in Japan, during the EU–Japan Friendship Week 2001. A few more chapters were specially commissioned for this volume to enhance the completeness of the project.

We have sought to fulfill three objectives: first, to provide an up-to-date guide to the European Union as an institution, describing its functions; second, to explain why it works in the way that it does, analyzing the pressures to which it is subject to and its relationship with the Member States;

third, to examine how, and to what extent, the Nice Treaty will contribute to solutions of existing problems, and to try to find both its positive meaning and its limits.

Koji Fukuda and Hiroya Akiba
School of Political Science and Economics,
Waseda University, Tokyo.
January 2003

Acknowledgments

This publication is the result of a symposium on "The Transformation of European Governance: European Integration after Nice," held at Waseda University on May 16, 2001. We are particularly grateful to the Institute for Research in Contemporary Political and Economic Affairs, Waseda University and the European Union, Delegation of the European Commission in Japan during the EU–Japan Friendship Week 2001. The editors would like to thank all of the individuals who proposed papers for inclusion in the conference. The authors are drawn from four universities and different academic backgrounds, covering international relations, law, economics, international administration, sociology, and comparative politics. The editors would also like to thank Malcolm Cambell, Senior Publisher, and Ms Rachel Saunders, Editor, RoutledgeCurzon.

This work was supported by the Waseda University Grant for Joint Research 99B-037, as well as a the Waseda University Academic Publications Subsidy in the fiscal year 2002.

Abbreviations

ACP	African, Caribbean, and Pacific Countries
ASEAN	Association of South-East Asian Nations
ASEM	Asia–Europe Meeting
CAP	Common Agricultural Policy
CCEE	Countries of Central and Eastern Europe
CDU/CSU	German Christian Democratic Union/Christian Social Union
CFSP	Common Foreign and Security Policy
CIP	Covered Interest-rate Parity
COPA	Confederation of Professional Agricultural Organizations
COR	Committee of the Regions
COREPER	Committee of Permanent Representatives
CSCE	Conference on Security and Cooperation in Europe
DG	Directorate General
EAEC	European Atomic Energy Community
EAGGF	European Agricultural Guidance and Guarantee Fund
EC	European Community
ECB	European Central Bank
ECOFIN	Council of Economic and Finance Ministers
ECOSOC	Economic and Social Committee
ECSC	European Coal and Steel Community
ECU	European Currency Unit
EDC	European Defence Community
EDF	European Development Fund
EEA	European Economic Area
EEC	European Economic Community
EFTA	European Free Trade Association
EIB	European Investment Bank
EMS	European Monetary System
EMU	Economic and Monetary Union

EP	European Parliament
EPC	European Political Cooperation
EPP	European People's Party
ERDF	European Regional Development Fund
ERM	Exchange Rate Mechanism
ESCB	European System of Central Banks
ESF	European Social Fund
EU	European Union
IGC	Intergovernmental Conference
IMF	International Monetary Fund
JHA	Justice and Home Affairs
MEP	Member of the European Parliament
NATO	North Atlantic Treaty Organisation
NTB	Non-Tariff Barrier (to trade)
OECD	Organisation for Economic Cooperation and Development
OJ	*Official Journal of the European Communities*
PHARE	Poland and Hungary: Aid for the Restructuring of Europe
PPP	Purchasing-Power Parity
QMV	Qualified Majority Voting
SEA	Single European Act
SEM	Single European Market
TEC	Treaty establishing the European Community
TEU	Treaty on European Union
UIP	Uncovered Interest-rate Parity
UN	United Nations
UNCTAD	United Nations Conference on Trade and Development
UNICE	Union of Industrial and Employers' Confederations of Europe
VAT	Value Added Tax
WEU	Western European Union

Part I

Reform of the European Union

1 The direction of the European constitution after the Nice Treaty

Tamio Nakamura

A basic question

The European Union Member States passed through four treaty negotiations in fifteen years, the first being the Single European Act (1986), followed by the Maastricht Treaty (1992), the Amsterdam Treaty (1997) and the most recent being the Nice Treaty (2001). In this process of transforming their relations with the Union, the Member States made clear their overall change of emphasis from building a single economic market to building a civil society. To use the symbolic phrases of the Treaty of the European Union (TEU) and the Treaty of the European Community (TEC), the change is from completing 'an area without internal frontiers' (Art. 14 TEC) to establishing 'an area of freedom, security and justice' (Art. 29 TEU). Thus, the activities of the EU now extend from agriculture and the introduction of a single currency to police cooperation and the progressive framing of a common defence policy. In this process, the original EEC also dropped 'Economic' from its name to become the European Community, which would provide the general foundation of the Union, and the EC acquired some power to act in socio-political fields including culture, education, environment and public health.

However, the institutional arrangements for the new polity have not yet found their final form. In normative terms, the Amsterdam Treaty acknowledges at least three different modes of governance depending on the fields of activities (the so-called 'three pillars'); and although the Union is supposed to be served by 'a single institutional framework' (Art. 3 TEU), different sets of institutions and subordinate bodies serve each pillar. (The Nice Treaty will not change these general arrangements.) Admittedly, the major institutions, including the European Council, the Council of Ministers, the Commission and the European Parliament, are indeed used for all EU activities. However, the Court of Justice has its unconditional and obligatory jurisdiction only for the activities of the EC

(Art. 46 TEU);[1] and the powers and obligations that those major institutions have in relation to each other differ pillar by pillar.[2] In the second (Common Foreign and Security Policy) and third pillars (Police and Criminal Justice Cooperation), the Council is at the centre of decision-making, whereas in the first pillar (the EC), the triangle of the Council, the Commission and the European Parliament check and balance each other in making decisions. When we look at the de facto picture of governance in the EU, many empirical studies[3] state that various modes of governance have grown within the EC system, depending on issues or economic sectors; whether, and to what extent, we should recognise those de facto arrangements as *de jure* as well as a different matter.

Therefore, a basic institutional and constitutional question for the emerging polity is whether the current normative institutional configuration is not only efficient and effective but also appropriate and legitimate to fulfil the broader socio-political aims of the Union, and if not, how it is to be modified. The EU Treaty indicates fundamental values relevant to the assessment of institutional legitimacy: in particular, the principles of liberty, democracy,[4] respect for human rights, the rule of law (Art. 6 (1) TEU), the ideal that decisions are taken as closely as possible to the citizen (Art. 1 TEU) and respect for the national identities of the Member States (Art. 6 (3) TEU). The concern for national 'identity' can be rephrased as the wish to retain national 'autonomy', for the purpose of this chapter. These fundamental values are the values for the citizens of Europe as well as for the Member States. Thus, we should assess EU institutional reforms from the viewpoint of citizens as well as the Member States, in the light of those fundamental values.

Since the intergovernmental conference (IGC) for the Nice Treaty focused on institutional reforms of the EU, it is important to ask whether its results would ensure the fundamental values that the EU upholds, and whether the approach taken by the IGC was appropriate in reforming EU institutional arrangements in the light of the overall civil shift of its aims and activities since the 1990s.

The limited agenda and outcomes of the Nice Treaty

It was clear from the beginning that the Nice IGC would not seek a radical reform of EU institutional arrangements. The agenda for the IGC, though gradually expanded as the conference went on, assumed that the extant institutional arrangements and their mutual legal relations ('the institutional balance') should, in principle, be maintained. The Amsterdam Treaty had specified the major topics of negotiation in a limited way: the size and composition of the Commission, the weighting of votes in the

Council and the possible extension of qualified majority voting. These 'Amsterdam leftovers' formed the core issues of the IGC throughout,[5] and the primary aim of these reforms was set by the Member States in terms of efficiency: to ensure effective and efficient decision-making after the enlargement to east and south Europe.[6] The Member States had feared that, unless the issues left pending in Amsterdam were resolved, decision-making in the Union (particularly in the Council) might be paralysed when the eastern and southern candidate countries accede to the Union, and bring its total up to twenty-seven Member States. Although the enhancement of democratic legitimacy in EU governance has been widely discussed in public since the 1990s, the Member States merely presented the legitimacy of the Nice negotiation in rather result-oriented, technocratic terms: their aim was to reach 'a balanced outcome that can be politically defended, ... understandable to and acceptable also by the public in the Member States'.[7]

Many outcomes are indeed explainable in terms of efficiency. The Member States' urgent concern was the efficacy of decision-making in the Council after the enlargement. Thus, they decided to switch from unanimous voting to qualified majority voting, on several topics of legislation:[8] as a consequence, they reweighted their votes to correspond more closely with their respective populations (Table 1.1). The Member States also allowed the most populous states, in return for ceding their right to appoint second Commissioners, to increase their political influence in the Council in another way instead. Specifically, abolishing second Commissioners was linked to the introduction of a new discretionary condition attached to qualified majority voting in the Council: the Member States in the majority should represent at least 62 per cent of the total EU population, although this condition only comes into effect if a Member State demands it ('the 62 per cent rule'). This rule will work only in favour of the most populous Member States (especially for Germany, in the Union of twenty-seven states).

These dexterous manoeuvres in the Council voting system, however they may use the concept of 'population', do not as such enhance the democratic legitimacy of the Council's decision-making in relation to the citizens of Europe, nor do they promote public accountability of Council decisions. This is because the Minister who casts his/her vote in the Council is, in normative terms, accountable only to his/her national parliament, and it is the legal and political relationship between the Minister and the national parliament under the national constitution that formally determines the level of democratic control of the voting behaviour of the Minister in the Council. Weighting of votes according to the population or the 62 per cent rule may, in practice, have some persuasive effect on

Table 1.1 Distribution of votes and seats in the major EC institutions

Member States Candidate States	Population (000)	Population points	Weighted votes		Seats in European Parliament	
			EU27	EU15 (2005~)	EU27 (change)	EU15 (at present)
Germany	82,038	169	29	29	99 (±0)	99
UK	59,247	123	29	29	72 (−15)	87
France	58,966	123	29	29	72 (−15)	87
Italy	57,612	120	29	29	72 (−15)	87
Spain	39,394	82	27	27	50 (−14)	64
Poland	38,667	80	27	–	50	–
Romania	22,489	47	14	–	33	–
The Netherlands	15,760	33	13	13	25 (−6)	31
Greece	10,533	22	12	12	22 (−3)	25
Czech Republic	10,290	21	12	–	20	–
Belgium	10,213	21	12	12	22 (−3)	25
Hungary	10,092	21	12	–	20	–
Portugal	9,980	21	12	12	22 (−3)	25
Sweden	8,854	18	10	10	18 (−4)	22
Bulgaria	8,230	17	10	–	17	–
Austria	8,082	17	10	10	17 (−4)	21
Slovakia	5,393	11	7	–	13	–
Denmark	5,313	11	7	7	13 (−3)	16
Finland	5,160	11	7	7	13 (−3)	16
Ireland	3,744	8	7	7	12 (−3)	15
Lithuania	3,701	8	7	–	12	–
Latvia	2,439	5	4	–	8	–
Slovenia	1,978	4	4	–	7	–
Estonia	1,446	3	4	–	6	–
Cyprus	752	2	4	–	6	–
Luxembourg	429	1	4	4	6 (±0)	6
Malta	377	1	3	–	5	–
Total	481,179	1,000	345	237	732	626
Qualified majority		62%	255	169		
Blocking minority		38%	91	69		

the citizens of Europe in relation to voting outcomes, but in normative terms it has nothing to do with the level of control by the peoples' representatives over the governments' collective execution of powers at European level. The Member States' interest at the IGC, therefore, lay mainly in improving the efficiency and effectiveness of Council decision-making amongst themselves, rather than the development of a democratic decision-making system more accountable to their citizens.

The IGC was also concerned with, first, the Commission's integrity, and, second, its efficiency. Regarding the first concern, in March 1999, just before the IGC started, the Santer Commission had resigned en bloc because of some Commissioners' grave irregularities. Second, a simple increase of the number of Commissioners with each accession in the near future would render the Commission too large a body to decide policy matters efficiently. As to the Commission's reform, the Member States' response was mainly to give the formal status of *primus inter pares* to the Commission President:

a   while the President is nominated by the Council of Heads of State or Government, the other members of the Commission are nominated by the ordinary Council of Ministers (New Art. 214 (2) TEC);
b   the President is given the sole right to organise the internal workings of the Commission (New Art. 217 (1), (2) and (3) TEC);
c   the President can require a member of the Commission to resign after obtaining the approval of the College (New Art. 217 (4) TEC).

These reforms concerning the Commission President might suggest, at first sight, the Member States' expectation of much stronger leadership by the President in exercising the power of the Commission given by the EC and EU Treaties. However, the Member States' expectations for the role of the Commission remain ambiguous because the normative ideal indicated by the Treaty and the actual understanding by the Member States on the role of the Commissioners seem to be fundamentally different.

The Treaty provides that the members of the Commission 'shall be chosen on the grounds of ... [their] independence [being] beyond doubt' and they 'shall, in the general interest of the Community, be completely independent in the performance of their duties' (Art. 213 (1) and (2) TEC). Yet the Member States at the IGC linked the issue of the reduction of the size of the Commission (in particular, eliminating second Commissioners) and the issue of reweighting of votes in the Council; this linking suggests much about each country's influence in the decision-making. The outcome of the negotiation was to keep 'one Commissioner for one state' until the Union grows into twenty-seven states, which reveals how much the Member States (especially the smaller states) are determined to retain their influence, at least in appointing their own national members to the Commission, for some time in the future. The Member States' persistent wish to retain their 'national' Commissioners in this way is at odds with the ideal of the 'independence' of the Commissioners. This outcome will hardly improve the efficiency or effectiveness of the decision-making in the Commission: there will be between fifteen and twenty-six Commissioners (i.e. no fewer, or more, members than at present) working collegially for some time to come after all. The only hope for more efficiency lies with the President's leadership and ability in personnel management.

The normative implication of this outcome is, at best, that the Commission is indeed expected to serve both for the general interest of the Community and for the national interest of each Member State, rather than the former only. If that is the case, there remains a reform option, for instance, to reduce the number of Commissioners to below that of the number of the Member States, for the sake of the efficiency and independence of the Commission's decision-making, while providing explicitly in the Treaty for the duty of cooperation between the Commission and the Member States in carrying out the Commission's tasks of policy formation and implementation.

Apart from the reforms of the Council and the Commission, some of the other outcomes of the IGC relate squarely to the enhancement of democratic legitimacy in EU decision-making, especially in law-making, in relation to the citizens of Europe: the reallocation of seats in the European Parliament in a manner more proportionate to the population of the Member States (Table 1.1) (though the total increase in number of the Members of the European Parliament may reduce efficiency in its decision-making); extension of the 'co-decision' and the 'assent' procedures; and giving the European Parliament an equal standing with the Council, the Commission and the Member States before the Court of Justice under Articles 230 and 300 (6) TEC procedures.[9]

The critical issue of 'horizontal' law-making and democracy

However, the Nice IGC left unsolved some serious institutional and constitutional problems that have been emerging in the EU since the 1990s. One of the most serious is the 'horizontal' (cross-sector, economic and non-economic) coordination problem in law-making. Because of its expanding competence to act for non-economic values such as those involved in public health, environment and internal or external security, the EU as a whole (or even within the EC) now more frequently faces issues that cut across many policy fields and require the balancing of various economic and non-economic interests.

Let us take the Biotechnology Patent Directive 98/44[10] as an example. The Directive aims at facilitating the free movement of biotechnology inventions in the internal market and at promoting the stable development of the European biotechnology industry by harmonising national patent laws as to the patentability of biotechnology inventions. The Directive is relevant to such policy fields as 'free movement of goods' (Part III,

Title I, TEC), 'research and technological development' (Title XVIII, TEC), 'industry' (Title XVI, TEC) and, importantly, respect for human rights (Art. 6 TEU) and ethics in general. Indeed, the controversy before and after its adoption centred on the ethical aspect of the legislation: whether and to what extent the sequence of a gene, especially a human gene, should be considered as an 'invention' (not a 'discovery') and patentable. It was also widely feared that technical processes of human cloning or genetic modification of human beings or organs might be claimed as 'inventions' for commercial use if there were no clear limits to patentable inventions from an ethical point of view.

Judging by the criterion of efficiency, the legislative process of the Directive was by no means efficient: it took ten years to legislate (1988–98), and three years to confirm the validity of the Directive (1998–2001), thus taking thirteen years in total to settle the matter, at least at the EU level. The implementation at national level is still under way. It is fair to note, however, that to judge the thirteen years solely on the criterion of efficiency is unbalanced because the issue raised in the Directive has grave social implications and requires serious democratic discussion at European level; in particular a harmonisation Directive such as this is meant to bind the Member States as to its legal result (i.e. in this case, conditions of patentability of biotechnological inventions). Therefore, democratic discussions in the European legislative process should be at least equivalent to those in national parliaments and sufficient to replace parliamentary discussions at national level.

Because of the predominantly 'economic', and sector-by-sector 'vertical' traditions of the Community's institutional practice and law-making, the legislative process concerning this Directive was haphazard, although its end result was acceptable, in improvising a political solution for a legislative gap in EU polity. To illustrate the unsettled and shaky situation concerning EU law-making for 'horizontal' matters, let us for a moment turn to the legislative history of this Directive.

When the Commission published its initial proposal based on Art. 100a [now with modification, Art. 95] TEC in 1988, few provisions in the proposal indicated the ethical limit to the patentability of biotechnology inventions. This aroused strong opposition in the European Parliament. It stayed for several years at the stage of its first reading, since Art. 100a TEC at that time stipulated the 'cooperation' procedure, which did not give the Parliament a formal right to reject the proposal. The Maastricht Treaty came into force (1993) during that period, which changed the legislative procedure under Art. 100a into 'co-decision'. This procedure gave the Parliament a formal right of rejection, and, despite the efforts to save the proposal at the Conciliation Committee under the co-decision procedure, the Parliament rejected the heavily amended proposal in 1995. Nine months later, again on the basis of Art. 95 TEC, the Commission submitted a second proposal, which contained clearer clauses on the ethical limit to the patentability of biotechnology inventions. The Commission this time set up its own advisory group on the ethical implications of biotechnology to discuss the issue independently of the European Parliament. In 1996, the group gave an affirmative opinion to the second proposal.[11] Eventually, both the Council and the European Parliament approved the proposal by majority votes in 1998.

Then, however, the Netherlands brought an action to annul the Directive in the Court of Justice. The Dutch Parliament had expressed opposition to genetic manipulation involving humans, animals and plants, and to the issuing of patents for the biotechnological products liable to promote such manipulation. The Dutch government had voted against the adoption of the Directive in the Council in vain and now brought an annulment action at the request of the national parliament. One of the Netherlands' arguments was that the patentability of isolated parts of the human body provided for by the Directive reduced living human matter to a means to an end, undermining human dignity. In its judgment on 9 October 2001, the Court rejected every plea made by the Netherlands, although it recognised the fundamental right to human dignity and integrity as a general principle of Community law, which, according to the Court's assessment, was sufficiently protected by the Directive.[12] Meanwhile, the European Parliament set up a Temporary Committee on Human Genetics in December 2000 to discuss possible legal controls on biotechnology from various perspectives, in cooperation with the Council of Europe, which adopted a Convention (1997) and a Protocol (1998) on biotechnology and human rights.[13] Thus the debate goes on.

The history related in this chapter, especially the Netherlands' lawsuit at the last stage, implies, first, the ineffective coordination between the Member States in the Council of the EC/EU on horizontal matters. Indeed, the current formation of the Council, sector by sector, who new number 16,[14] has posed a serious problem of overlap, or worse, contradictory decisions among the various sectoral Councils. More fundamentally, the Council formations are largely based on the EC/EU Treaties' policy divisions that scarcely touch on non-economic, socio-political matters. There is no Council for social justice and human rights, for example. Thus such social and civil concerns, as displayed by the Netherlands, do not receive as much discussion as other economically motivated concerns in the Council and in the subordinate preparatory bodies; still less is there room for such concerns to be integrated into the Council decision-making process in all fields of EU activities.

Although the General Affairs Council, whose usual members are the foreign ministers of the Member States, should have been in the position of coordinating various sectoral Councils and political concerns, it can hardly fulfil such a role consistently since the issues involved are increasingly complex and sensitive and often require detailed technical discussions in each relevant policy field. The three-pillar structure worsens the situation. For instance, potentially overlapping Councils such as the justice, home affairs and civil protection Council (in the EC pillar) and the third-pillar Council on police and criminal justice cooperation have separate preparatory and advisory bodies of their own. There is no overarching coordination body between the pillars, except the European Council. Thus, according to the Committee on Constitutional Affairs of the European Parliament, the sectoral Councils now refer 'important matters' more frequently to the European Council for a decision.[15] The same Committee also points out that, after the introduction of the Economic and Monetary Union, the Ecofin Council increased its practical independence from the other Councils, developing its autonomous preparatory procedure.[16]

It is true that many of the practical reforms suggested by the Trumpf/Piris Report (March 1999) were approved by the Helsinki European Council (December 1999), including reducing the number of the sectoral Councils (from twenty-two to sixteen), by integrating some of them, and separating the agenda of the General Affairs Council into 'horizontal' issues and the issues of external relations.[17] However, one-and-a-half years later, the Council's Secretary-General Report (June 2001) admitted that the reforms implemented after Helsinki appeared to 'have only marginally strengthened the authority and impact of the General Affairs Council on horizontal matters'.[18] In short, the institutional arrangement of policy coordination between the various Councils is becoming weaker at present, and does not correspond to the changing nature of the Union.

The legislative history of the Biotechnology Patent Directive indicates, second, the shaky guarantee of democracy by the European Parliament: namely, the problem of various kinds of legislative processes provided for by the EC/EU Treaties, according to legal base. In the Netherlands' lawsuit, the Italian government, which intervened on the Netherlands' side, argued that the correct legal base for the Directive should have been Art. 157 TEC (in the Maastricht and the Amsterdam Treaty), in which case the European Parliament could have given only a non-binding opinion to the Council under the 'consultation' procedure, which would have been worse for parliamentary democracy than the 'cooperation' procedure under the ex-Article 100a TEC. It was a matter of chance in the case of the Biotechnology Patent Directive that the Maastricht Treaty changed the relevant procedure into 'co-decision' while the European Parliament was strategically staying its first reading under the 'cooperation' procedure. Thus, depending on the choice of legal base, which will lead to different legislative procedures in many instances, legislation for 'horizontal' matters may enjoy the European Parliament's democratic sanction, fully (in the 'co-decision' procedure), or less (in the 'assent' or 'cooperation' procedures), or least of all (in the 'consultation' procedure). To enhance the democratic legitimacy of EC/EU legislation, it is necessary to go beyond the institutional dimension in providing for the legislation's legal bases, not according to policy field, but according to the nature of legislation: that is to say, whether or not it is a basic piece of legislation in which important interests may be compromised. Depending on the degree of its importance, rather than the identification of 'the main objective' (i.e. the most relevant policy-sector in the Treaty), the procedure should be either 'co-decision', 'assent' or 'consultation'.

Third, it is also important to note that the debate over the Biotechnology Patent Directive was and is carried out on the assumption that the citizens of Europe and the Member States share some kind of ethical values. Indeed, the Netherlands successfully made the Court of Justice declare the existence, at least, of the fundamental right to human dignity and integrity as a general principle of Community law. However, to describe the present situation more cynically, 'horizontal' EU laws are being made without structured discussion based on solid social values recognised as such among the citizens and the Member States of Europe. It is a tradition of the Member States' constitutionalism, in contrast, that the basic social values commonly shared among citizens are (more or less explicitly) guaranteed legally and politically under the name of 'human rights and fundamental freedoms'. The Union still lacks this dimension, and is responding on an *ad hoc* basis as the specific need appears. The establishment of its advisory group on the ethical implications of biotechnology by the Commission, or of a Temporary Committee on Human Genetics by the European Parliament, are *ad hoc* institutional responses to the lack of a civil dimension to the EU polity. It is important to go further by re-adjusting the institutional arrangements and practices comprehensively to reflect in their discussions such basic social and civil values as the EU upholds; and also, to guarantee more structured discussion, it is crucial to make those fundamental social values of the Union clear. The importance of the Union's Charter of Fundamental Rights is obvious in this connection.

Fourth, there is another institutional and constitutional problem highlighted by the Biotechnology Patent Directive case. That is the issue of the distribution of power between the Community/Union and the Member

States: the issue of autonomy. The issue can emerge as an institutional issue or a substantive issue of powers given to the Community/Union under the EC/EU Treaties. The Netherlands in the case discussed earlier also argued that it was a substantive issue: it argued that the Council and the European Parliament had lacked the power to legislate on that subject under Art. 100a TEC because (a) the national patent laws of the Member States were originally made in accordance with a separate, non-EC, international treaty on patents (the Convention on the Grant of European Patents, 1973), and hence the issues that the Convention dealt with should lie, in principle, within the jurisdiction of the Member States, and (b) because the diversity of the Member States' national patent laws was not, in fact, likely to hinder free movement of biotechnological inventions in practice. The Netherlands was also concerned that the Directive would pre-empt a policy decision by the national parliament on the ethical limitation to the patentability of biological inventions. If we put a similar concern in institutional terms, the argument would be (a) that there are no appropriate fora in the EU that gather various representatives of major interests to discuss 'horizontal' issues with profound social implications intensively and comprehensively, sufficient to replace the democratic debates held at national parliaments; and (b) that there is little effective democratic control over the national governments' behaviour in the Council either.

To approach the issue of division of power between the EC/EU and the Member States in a substantive way, by listing the matters for the jurisdiction of the EC/EU and the matters reserved for the Member States, would hardly bring stable solutions for the Union, which is facing more and more complex 'horizontal' issues. Even matters of national jurisdiction may, on occasion, need united European responses to global forces (e.g. protection of the diversity of European culture). A better approach would be to guarantee such fora and procedures that would enable at least both the Member States and the representatives of citizens of Europe to debate those complex issues effectively, between State and State, between the representatives of the citizens, and between those two groups.

It is important to realise that guaranteeing democratic debate at a European level is also a matter of national constitutional arrangements. One example is the electoral system of the European Parliament. Currently each Member State has its own electoral system for European Parliament elections, and the democratic representativeness of the Members of the European Parliament depends largely on those national legislations. Another example is the national constitutional and political arrangement of the national parliament's power to control the executive government on European issues. So far, national constitutions have tended not to treat

EC/EU matters as domestic issues but as being in the category of foreign relations in general. Thus, in normative terms, some national governments are open to only limited scrutiny by their parliaments on EC/EU decision-making.[19] However, the current EU is dealing with issues that have serious social implications, which used to be national issues. Thus, it seems imperative to make specific arrangements within national constitutions to enhance political control of national parliaments over the executive governments on EC/EU matters.

Towards mutual formation of democratic polity

Thus, we reach a wider perspective on the institutional and constitutional arrangements of the Union. That is the perspective to regard both the Member States' national constitutions and the Treaty-based common-law constitution of the EU as complementing each other to form the Constitution of the Union.[20]

This may sound at odds with the traditional doctrine of Community law, which stresses its 'independence' vis-à-vis national law. It is an axiom that the EEC (now EC) Treaty of 1957 created a 'new legal order' in international law; that the Member States have limited their sovereign rights for the benefit of this order; and that the subjects of this order are not only the Member States but also their nationals.[21] It is also well established that this order is an independent and superior source of law in each Member State, capable of imposing duties and conferring rights on individuals directly and in precedence over conflicting laws of the Member States.[22] The reach and effect of this primacy of Community law are now fundamental: the law of the EC takes precedence over any law, including constitutional provisions and practices, of the Member States.[23] A Member State that contravenes Community law is also obliged to remedy its wrongdoing, otherwise it might face financial sanctions by means of actions brought by the European Commission under Articles 226 and 228 TEC, or by means of a state liability action instituted by any individual who experienced an adverse effect as a result of a manifest and grave breach of Community law by the Member State.[24] The limitation of sovereign rights is being imposed on the Member States 'in ever wider fields'.[25] In some fields, Community legislative competence has been found to be exclusive where the Member States are deprived of their autonomous right to act.[26]

Despite this remarkable development of independence in its legal nature and its processes of law-making and law interpretation, the 'new legal order' is largely dependent on the institutions of the Member States, especially in the implementation phase.[27] In most fields of Community action, it is the Member State institutions that are obliged to make and execute their own laws in accordance with EC law, or execute directly effective Community legal instruments, and make adjudications based on Community law and national law relevant to the full implementation of Community law. The national courts are formally linked with the European Court of Justice (and will also be linked with the Court of First Instance as a result of the Nice Treaty) under the 'preliminary reference' procedure (Art. 234 TEC) so that the national courts are obliged to play dual roles as national and European judicial branches.

Even in the law-making phase, a large part of the Community legislative competence is concurrent with the Member States', and the Member States retain their power to act in so far as their action does not contravene the existing Community law written or unwritten, such as 'general principles' of law and rules 'inherent' in the establishing Treaties. Only certain matters have been found to be definitely exclusive to the Community after all. In some fields, including 'culture' and 'public health', the Community competence is clearly limited: there is no Community law-making that would involve any harmonisation of the laws and regulations of the Member States (e.g. Art. 151 (5) TEC). Thus, in short, shared competence and institutional dependency on the Member States are also the features of the 'new legal order', and the normative picture of dependency deepens as we turn to the third pillar (cooperation in police and criminal justice) and the second pillar (common foreign and security policy including defence) of the EU.

Therefore, a wider perspective does fit in the normative as well as the factual picture of the current EC/EU. What limited the outcome of the Nice IGC in terms of enhancing the democratic legitimacy of the EU lies in the Member States' limited perspective of not just efficiency,[28] but more fundamentally of one-sidedness: the Member States negotiated the Nice Treaty as if their national constitutions were unalterable, regarding EU institutions and procedures as the only permitted variables on the way to achieving their perceived goals. However, to complete essential reforms in order to create a more democratic and effective EU governing system, the discussion should extend to the coordinated modifications of the Member States' constitutions, or at least constitutional practices, as well as the revision of the EU Treaty, since both constitutional systems have now become mutually dependent and complementary in ever-wider fields. Indeed, what happened during the ratification process of the previous EU Treaties in the 1990s illustrates the point: the *ex post facto* modification of the Maastricht Treaty to reflect specific Danish concerns after the negative result of the Danish referendum, and the revision of essential parts of the French national constitution in the wake of the Maastricht and Amsterdam Treaties.

Conclusion

The transformation of the character of the Union towards civil polity has reached such a stage that democratic decision-making can only take place with future EU Treaty revisions coupled with national constitutional re-adjustments, carried out in coordination with all Member States. A discourse limited to the revision of the Treaties between the Member States, however much one may call it 'basic' or 'constitutional', would touch on only one side of the problem; the other side, which should not be neglected, is the reform by each Member State of its own constitutional system so that the latter would reinforce the Union's basic missions of rule of law, democracy and protection of individual freedom and fundamental rights. In conclusion, a wider perspective should be taken, to regard both the Member States' constitutions and the Treaty-based common-law constitution of the EU as complementing each other, to form the Constitution of the Union. This should provide the basis to revise each constitution at a national level as well as at the European level to enhance the common basic values of the Union.[29]

Notes

1 See Albors-Llorens (1998).
2 See de Witte (1998); Devuyst (2000).
3 For example, Wallace and Wallace (2000); Kohler-Koch and Eising (1999).
4 What kind of 'democracy' is envisaged for the new polity is a moot point on which the present chapter does not discuss in depth. On this issue, see Weiler (1999), Chapter 8.
5 Later some other specific institutional questions were added to the list, including the allocation of seats in the European Parliament, reforms of the Court of Justice, the Court of First Instance and the Court of Auditors. The Member States also agreed to discuss enhanced cooperation later in June 2000. See Galloway (2001).
6 Council of the European Union, 'Efficient Institutions after Enlargement: Options for the Intergovernmental Conference' (Finnish Presidency Report on 7 Dec. 1999) Doc. 13636/99, p. 2.
7 Ibid.
8 For further details, see Galloway (2001), Chapter 5.
9 The reform of the European Courts, which I do not discuss here, is considered elsewhere in this volume.
10 European Parliament and Council Directive 98/44/EC of 6 July 1998 on the legal protection of biotechnological inventions, OJ 1998 L 213/13.
11 Opinion of the Group of Advisors on the Ethical Implications of Biotechnology to the European Commission, No. 8: Ethical Aspects of Patenting Inventions Involving Elements of Human Origin (25 Sep. 1996).
12 Case C-277/98, Netherlands v. Parliament and Council [2001] ECR I-(not yet reported) (9 Oct. 2001), paras 70–7.
13 Convention for the Protection of Human Rights and Dignity of the Human Being with regard to the Application of Biology and Medicine (Euro Treaty

Series no. 164, signed in 1997); Additional Protocol to the Convention for the Protection of Human Rights and Dignity of the Human Being with regard to the Application of Biology and Medicine, on the Prohibition of Cloning Human Beings (ETS no. 168, signed in 1998).

14 Bulletin EU 4-2000, point 1.9.1. Until April 2000, there used to be as many as twenty-two sectoral Councils. The Helsinki European Council in December 1999 endorsed the reduction.

15 The European Parliament, Committee on Constitutional Affairs, Report on reform of the Council (2002/2020 (INI)) A5-0308/2001 ('Poos Report' on 17 Sep. 2001)

16 Ibid.

17 European Council, Presidency Conclusions in Helsinki, 10 and 11 December 1999 (SN 300/99) Annex III: An Effective Council for an Enlarged Union.

18 Report from the Secretary-General/High Representative to the European Union: Preparing the Council for Enlargement, Part II, para. 10 (Doc. Nr. 9518/01).

19 See Norton (1996).

20 See Pernice (1999); compare with Piris (1999).

21 Case 26/62, Van Gend en Loos [1963] ECR 1.

22 Case 6/64, Costa v. ENEL [1964] ECR 585.

23 Case 106/77, Simmenthal [1978] ECR 629; Case C-213/89, Factortame [1990] ECR I-2433.

24 Cases C-6 and 9/90, Francovich [1991] ECR I-5357; Case C-46/93, Brasserie du Pêcheur [1996] ECR I-1029.

25 Opinion 1/91 EEA [1991] ECR I-6079.

26 For example, externally: Case 22/70, ERTA [1971] ECR 263; internally: Case 804/79, Commission v. UK [1981] ECR 1045.

27 See Rometsch and Wessels (1996); Ibanez (1999); Pappas (1995).

28 The Prodi Commission shares the same limited perspective in its White Paper on European Governance (2001).

29 Cf. Schwarze (2001) describes the interaction of national and European constitutional law in factual terms.

References

Albors-Llorens, Albertina (1998) 'Changes in the Jurisdiction of the European Court of Justice under the Treaty of Amsterdam.' 35 Com. Mkt. L. Rev. 1273–94.

Devuyst, Youri (2000) 'The European Union's Constitutional Order? Between Community Method and Ad Hoc Compromise.' 18 Berk. J. Int'l Law 1–52.

European Commission (2001) *A White Paper on European Governance.* Luxembourg: Office for Official Publications of the European Communities.

Galloway, David (2001) *The Treaty of Nice and Beyond.* Sheffield: Sheffield Academic Press.

Ibanez, Alberto J. Gil (1999) *The Administrative Supervision and Enforcement of EC Law: Powers, Procedures and Limits.* Oxford: Hart Publishing.

Kohler-Koch, Beate and Rainer Eising (eds) (1999) *The Transformation of Governance in the European Union.* London: Routledge.

Norton, Philip (ed.) (1996) *National Parliaments and the European Union.* London: Frank Cass.

Pappas, Spyros A. (ed.) (1995) *National Administrative Procedures for the Preparation and Implementation of Community Decisions.* Maastricht: European Institute of Public Administration.

Pernice, Ingolf (1999) 'Multilevel Constitutionalism and the Treaty of Amsterdam: European Constitution-Making Revisited?' 36 Com. Mkt. L. Rev. 703–50.

Piris, Jean-Claude (1999) 'Does the European Union Have a Constitution? Does It Need One?' 24 Eur. L. Rev. 557–85.

Rometsch, Dietrich and Wolfgang Wessels (eds) (1996) *The European Union and Member States: Towards Institutional Fusion?* Manchester: Manchester University Press.

Schwarze, Jürgen (ed.) (2001) *The Birth of a European Constitutional Order* Baden-Baden: Nomos.

Wallace, Hellen and William Wallace (eds) (2000) *Policy-Making in the European Union*, 4th edn. Oxford: Oxford University Press.

Weiler, Joseph H.H. (1999) *The Constitution of Europe*. Cambridge: Cambridge University Press.

de Witte, Bruno (1998) 'The Pillar Structure and the Nature of the European Union,' in Ton Heukels *et al.* (eds), *The European Union after Amsterdam*. The Hague: Kluwer, pp. 51–67.

2 Euro and exchange rate stability

Hiroya Akiba

Introduction

In January 1999, a common currency, the euro, was introduced to eleven member countries of the EU. Although the euro had previously been used in conjunction with each member's own national currency, starting from January 2002, the euro was the only currency used within these countries. In December 2000, it was agreed to conclude the Treaty of Nice, to ratify it within the calendar year of 2002 and to have it take effect in 2003. Within the Treaty, it was agreed that middle and eastern European countries would join the EU as new member countries, starting hopefully from 2005.

The main points in the Treaty of Nice are summarized briefly as follows:

i   To limit the Commission to one member per Member State, effective in 2005;
ii to allow qualified-majority voting for decisions that previously required unanimity;
iii to allocate the weighting of votes for Member States for qualified majority;
iv to require a minimum of eight Member States to allow for the possibility of "close cooperation"; and
v   to limit the number of seats in the European parliament to a maximum of 732 and to allocate them between Member States and candidate countries.

One of the important implications of the Treaty is that the EU agreed to look ahead to the future enlargement of the European Union and made some structural changes to make such enlargement possible. From the standpoint of economics, the expansion of the EU means the expansion of economic scale, which in turn makes for an even stronger and larger economic player in the world. If the euro was the only currency to be used in the EU from 2002, as was scheduled, the exchange rates of the euro against the national currencies of non-member countries such as the USA or Japan would be significantly affected in several respects. The way in which the exchange rates of stronger currencies is determined, how they vary and respond to shocks, and through which channels they are fed back to each of their respective national economies are quite different in scale from those exchange rates of weaker currencies in smaller countries.

A related issue surrounding the exchange rate fluctuation is the long-disputed problem of the so-called "uncertainty hypothesis." That is, since the advent of generalized float in the spring of 1973, exchange rates have been much more volatile than anticipated. Because exchange rate volatility means variability of costs of international trade for traders when the contracts are denominated in currencies other than their own, it is expected to discourage international trade. This is the uncertainty hypothesis, which states that exchange rate uncertainty decreases the volume of trades because of an increase in the marginal cost of trade (see Levich 1985; Akiba 1990; Arize 1997; McKenzie 1999 for a survey).

In order to avoid an anticipated loss due to a fluctuation of the exchange rates, both exporting and importing firms operating under imperfect competition will be likely to adjust their prices by less than the full change in the exchange rates. For example, importing firms may lower their profit margins to absorb part of the exchange rate change, thereby passing-through only part of the appreciation to the importer's prices. Likewise, exporting firms may increase their profit margins, and thereby passing-through only part of the appreciation. By keeping the home (foreign) currency prices constant, the pass-through rate is said to be a 100 (0) percent when the exporter's price in terms of foreign (home) currency rises by the same rate as the appreciation.

A related measure of international price differential is the import price penetration index. This is defined as $1 + (\Delta P_M - \Delta P_D)/\Delta S$, where P_M and P_D is the import price and the domestic market price respectively, in terms of home currency, and S is the spot exchange rate, defined as the units of foreign currency per unit of home currency. This is considered a special case of incomplete import pass-through. Under the assumption that the domestic and imported products are homogeneous, the index represents a measure of trade obstacles for imports in a wider sense. The index takes the value of more than one if trade obstacles for imports shrink as the exchange rate appreciates.

Another related measure of international price differential is the pricing-to-market index for exports. It is defined as $(\Delta P_D - \Delta P_X)/\Delta S$, where P_X is the export price in terms of the home currency. This is also considered to be a special case of incomplete export pass-through. Export firms are assumed to sell to more than one market with different prices; this is known as third-degree price discrimination (see Marston 1990; Hooper and Marquez 1995 for survey; Feenstra and Kendall 1997; Kumakura 2000).

Thus, it is very clear that fluctuation of exchange rates between currencies of a rapidly growing economic zone (the EU) and an outside country (for example, Japan) will have unique characteristics, and hence significant impacts on economies outside of the EU. This chapter focuses on the effects of fluctuation of the euro's exchange rate on outside economies. We approach the analysis of those effects from an international finance aspect of economic integration.

Approaching the implications of economic integration from this standpoint has a long history of research, which reached its culmination almost half a century ago. A seminal contribution to the integration literature is Viner's (1950) *The Customs Union Issue*, in which he clarified that the formation of a customs union involves two fundamental effects: a change in the source of imports from a lower-cost non-member country to a higher-cost member country; and a change in the location of production from higher-cost domestic producers to lower-cost producers in the member countries. Viner labeled the former the "trade diversion" effect and claimed that the effect reduces welfare, simply because it effectively insulates international trade with non-member countries. He called the latter the "trade creation" effect and argued that the effect raises welfare. Thus, Viner's analysis shows that a customs union is formed if, and only if, the latter (trade creation) effect is greater than the former (trade diversion) effect (Viner 1950; Kowalczyk 2000).

Viner's model was criticized from the neoclassical, demand-oriented approach, which states that the gains from trade should be evaluated by the community utility for welfare function (Lipsey 1960; see also Kojima 1999). The theory of customs union has since been examined from various aspects, such as direct static gains, general equilibrium aspects, dynamic effects, etc.[1]

Even though a customs union is formed because it fulfils Viner's criterion in a static situation, it is not clear whether it could attain the gains from trade in a dynamic situation among participating countries (Ethier 1998; Kojima 1999). Furthermore, it is far from clear as to whether such an economic integration has desirable effects on non-member countries, simply because such an integration is nothing but a second-best policy from the standpoint of worldwide welfare.

This chapter works with these theoretical developments of customs unions from real economic aspects, but focuses on the effects of monetary disturbances in the EU on non-member countries. As the Treaty of Nice stipulates the expansion of the EU, the euro will be adopted by an even larger integrated region in terms of economic scale. Thus, the euro will be even stronger against other national currencies, as it is supported by a larger real economy, the EU. The purpose of this chapter is to examine the effects of the exchange rate between the even stronger euro against a currency of a non-member country.

The organization of this chapter is as follows. First, statistical facts about the major exchange rates and the euro/dollar rate are presented. The second section constructs a simple open economy model to analyze the effects of monetary shocks on the volatility of the exchange rate by clearly distinguishing capital substitutability and mobility. The third section focuses on different degrees of asset substitutability, followed by the discussions on the policy implications. Finally, there is a conclusion.

Statistical facts

The Third Asia–Europe Meeting (ASEM 3) was held in Seoul, Korea in October 20–21, 2000. The Chairman's Statement, consisting of thirty-three items, was made public as "ASEM III Documents & Speeches." In the sixth item, under the subtitle of "Developments in the Two Regions," it was stated:

> Leaders welcomed the introduction of the euro and noted that it will contribute to greater exchange rate stability in the international monetary system.

This purely political statement was quite ambiguous from an economics point of view and gave rise to at least three important questions. First, the statement did not mention *what* exchange rate. From the standpoint of exchange rate economics, the exchange rate should be made clear: bilateral or multilateral; nominal or real; effective or real effective; short-run or long-run, and so on. Second, it is totally unclear what the word "stability" actually means. It is also not clear whether it refers to short-term or long-term characteristics. Because the exchange rate is nothing but a relative price of two national "monies," it should fluctuate to adjust for changes in demand for and/or supply of currencies under a floating exchange regime. Finally, and most importantly, it is totally beyond an economist's comprehension that the existence of the euro will "contribute" somehow to enhance exchange rate stability. If such an economic mechanism for a currency to "contribute" to stability in fact existed, one of the most important yet difficult financial problems in our present and future world would be solved. Unfortunately, our accumulated knowledge at present tells us that the matter is not as simple as this political and wildly optimistic statement would suggest.

To illustrate these points, the historical data in Table 2.1 are used to calculate descriptive statistics before and after the launch of the euro in January 1999. The exchange rates utilized for statistical comparison are the Yen/US dollar and the Deutsche Mark/US dollar rates. The descriptive statistics are thus summarized in Table 2.1.

Several important implications can be deduced from the table. First, the sample standard deviation of the yen/dollar exchange rate declines after the launch of the euro; but, second, that of the DM/dollar rate rises for the same sample period. Furthermore, third, the same characteristics are observed from the coefficient of variation. Thus, if we define the "stability" of the exchange rate by the standard deviation, or equivalently the coefficient of variation, the two major exchange rates have different and opposite implications; while the yen/dollar exchange rate is stabilized after the launch of the euro, the DM/dollar exchange rate is destabilized for the same sample period. Therefore, the notion of the leaders of the ASEM III cited at the outset of this section – that is, the introduction of the euro will contribute to greater stability in the international monetary system – turns out to be quite misleading.[2] In addition, fourth, we find

Table 2.1 Statistical facts

	Period	Yen/US$	DM/US$	US$/euro
μ	before	126.02	1.7502	–
	after	111.20	1.9996	0.985
σ	before	1.89	0.013	–
	after	1.17	0.032	0.016
max/min (%)	before	114.23/113.70 (26.9)	1.848/1.673 (12.9)	–
	after	121.53/102.09 (19.0)	2.326/1.711 (36.0)	1.144/0.841 (36.0)
CV	before	0.015	0.007	–
	after	0.011	0.016	0.016

Notes
before = before the launch of euro (Jan., 1997–Dec., 1998).
after = after the launch of euro (Jan., 1999–Feb., 2001).
μ = the sample mean.
σ = the sample standard deviation.
max/min = the maximum and the minimum values.
CV = the coefficient of variation.
Data are the nominal interbank rates, observed at the end of month.

that the fluctuation of the dollar/euro rate measured by the coefficient of variation is as large as that of the DM/dollar rate, and is 45 percent larger (more unstable) than the yen/dollar exchange rate for the same sample period.

After due consideration of these statistics, it is imperative to distinguish and closely examine two characteristics about international asset transactions that are supposed to strongly influence exchange rate volatility. One is the asset mobility and the other is its substitutability. The launch of the euro means that exchange rates between countries that adopted the euro do not exist by definition.[3] This signifies that there is no exchange risk at all, and because of its risk-free characteristic, capital mobility between them is expected to be higher. However, it remains to be seen whether capital mobility between the EU and the non-member countries is getting higher or lower.

The second consideration is much more subtle, and in fact the problem of capital substitution has not been appropriately treated and rigorously analyzed in open economy macroeconomics with only a few exceptions. When the foreign exchange markets are turbulent, capital moves swiftly in large quantities, so that an exchange rate is likely to overshoot its long-run equilibrium value. Under such circumstances, it is not clear whether the degree of exchange rate overshooting is higher or lower under higher or lower capital "substitutability." In the next section, an open economy model is constructed to examine the effects of monetary disturbances by clearly distinguishing between those two characteristics of international asset transactions.

The model

Preliminary

In order to analyze the effects of the Treaty of Nice and the euro, we have to consider capital mobility and its substitutability separately for their effects on the exchange rate. As the Treaty of Nice stipulates the expansion of the European Union to include countries of central and eastern Europe, deregulation within the expanded EU is expected. As a result of deregulation, higher capital mobility within member countries, and also with non-member countries, will be expected. Thus, it can be argued that the exchange rate will be destabilized as a consequence of higher capital mobility.

In addition to higher capital mobility, higher capital substitutability will also be likely. Since no exchange risk exists, because there are no exchange rates within member countries that adopt the euro, substitutability will definitely be higher within those member countries. However, it is not clear whether substitutability is higher or lower for capital transaction with non-member countries.

Because assets are substituted for each other so as to equalize the expected rate of return adjusted for risk and transaction costs, it can be expected that changes in the exchange rate are greater as assets are more easily substituted (and mobile) between member and non-member countries. As a consequence, under highly mobile situations, it is expected that the higher the substitutability, the more likely it is that the exchange rate overshoots the equilibrium value. Or, conversely, the lower the substitutability, the more likely that the exchange rate will be temporarily undershooting.

Unfortunately, capital (asset) substitutability has not, with few exceptions, been distinguished clearly from capital mobility in the open-economy macroeconomics literature.[4] The reason for this lies in the simple fact that a version of interest rate parity can be shown to hold without considering capital substitutability under an assumption of "perfect" capital mobility. However, it is quite doubtful in reality that capital moves "perfectly," i.e., with infinite speed between countries, so that the proposition of "perfect" capital mobility has only been a hypothesis to be tested empirically.

The assumption of "perfect" ("extreme" in Mundell's (1963) original terminology) capital mobility is logically justified by such facts as the deregulation of international capital movement initiated by the IMF, and thus has been imposed in the so-called Mundell–Fleming model. To ascertain its practical validity, at least two methods for an empirical test have been proposed.[5] Unfortunately, they have arrived at opposite conclusions and hence conflicting implications for capital mobility. First of all, Feldstein and Horioka (1980) hypothesized that the association between saving and investment should be low if international capital is freely mobile. However, they arrived at the so-called Feldstein–Horioka puzzle that implies low international capital mobility because of an empirically high saving–investment association across OECD countries (for a comprehensive survey of the literature, see Coakley *et al.*, 1998).

The second test is more conservative, depending on regressions of interest rate parity due originally to Keynes (1923). According to interest rate parity, free international capital flows lead to the convergence of expected rate of return on financial assets denominated in different currencies, a situation of infeasibility of arbitrage profits. In general, the covered interest-rate parity (CIP) hypothesis has been shown to be empirically valid, if the interest rates are associated with claims that differ only in their currencies of denomination.

However, the uncovered interest-rate parity (UIP) hypothesis may also be valid but undetectable for many reasons such as risk premiums, peso problems, simultaneous bias, incomplete information with rational learning, rational speculative bubbles, and so on (Isard 1995: 88). Huisman *et al.* (1998), using exchange rates for fifteen countries against the pound sterling for the period of January 1979 until March 1996, showed that the rejection of UIP is not as severe as is commonly found and that it almost holds perfectly in periods when the forward premiums are large.

These empirical evidences imply that capital is highly mobile internationally so as to equate (appropriately adjusted) expected rate of returns across countries. Thus, the two main methods of empirical tests of capital mobility gave rise to different conclusions, one immobile, the other mobile. In contrast, capital substitutability has not been as well modeled and analyzed as capital mobility. The model presented next should, therefore, fill the gap in theoretical terms.

A simple open model

In this part of the chapter, we construct a simple model of a small, open economy that operates under flexible exchange rates. The model is inspired by Delbecque (1989) and Gazioglu (1996), but closer in spirit to Levin's (1994, 1999) version of Dornbusch's (1976) overshooting model.[6] This constant output model assumes instantaneous adjustment in the good sector and money market, and perfect foresight exchange rate expectations. There is one traded commodity, the price of which is fixed in the world market. The model is succinctly summarized by the following set of equations.

$$(1-\gamma)y = \mu - \sigma r + ca + \epsilon w, \qquad \epsilon, \gamma \in [0, 1] \tag{2.1}$$

$$m - p = -(1/\beta)r + \theta y \tag{2.2}$$

$$da/dt = ca \tag{2.3}$$

$$a^d = \rho[r^* + (de/dt)^e - r] - e + b \tag{2.4}$$

$$da/dt = \alpha[\{\rho(r^* + (de/dt)^e - r) - e + b\} - a] \tag{2.5}$$

$$e = p - p^* \tag{2.6}$$

$$w = \omega_1 b + \omega_2 m + (1 - \omega_1 - \omega_2)a - (\omega_1 + \omega_2)e \tag{2.7}$$

where the Roman characters are variables, and the Greek characters are parameters. All variables except r are defined by the natural logarithm. The superscript e denotes the expectations and the asterisk is the foreign counterpart of the corresponding variables. $y =$ real output; $e =$ the exchange rate (defined as units of domestic currency per unit of the foreign currency); $r =$ the domestic interest rate; $ca =$ real balance of trade; $p =$ the domestic price level; $a =$ the real stock of foreign assets held in the home country; $m =$ the money stock; $b =$ the stock of domestic bond; and $w =$ the net wealth.

Equation 2.1 represents the goods market where y, the aggregate output, is the sum of domestic absorption and the foreign trade balance. The former, the domestic absorption, is assumed to consist of consumption that depends on real output and also on net wealth and investment. The marginal propensities to consume (MPC) are γ and ϵ. It is assumed that not only each MPC, but also their sum is restricted within a unit interval.

Equation 2.2 is a standard money market equilibrium equation where the demand depends on the interest rate negatively and aggregate output positively.[7] It is assumed that domestic residents neither hold foreign currencies nor foreign bonds for a purely speculative purpose.

Equation 2.3 specifies that the balance of trade is financed by changes in foreign financial assets. From the balance of payments identity, this equation must hold identically in the absence of international transfer payments.

Under an assumption that the foreign and domestic bonds are imperfect substitutes, equation 2.4 shows that the stock demand for foreign assets, relative to the domestic ones, depends on the differential between their expected rate of return, $r^* + (de/dt)^e - r$. The parameter ρ is assumed to vary inversely with investors' degree of risk aversion, and thus measures risk tolerance, $\rho \in [0, \infty)$. In a limiting case where investors are risk neutral $(\rho \to \infty)$, asset holders regard domestic and foreign bonds as perfect substitutes, i.e. $r^* + (de/dt)^e = r$. This implies, as is well-known, in absence of arbitrage (Akiba 1997).

It is assumed that disequilibrium in holdings of foreign assets is eliminated over time through a stock adjustment scheme as specified in equation 2.5. The underlying and implicit assumption behind it is that the adjustment costs prohibit instantaneous adjustment of foreign asset holdings. The positive parameter, α, represents the speed of adjustment (capital mobility) in the international asset market. In the limiting case where adjustment costs are negligible, the speed of adjustment is sufficiently swift or instantaneous $(\alpha \to \infty)$, ensuring that the stock demand for foreign assets is always kept equal to its supply.

In order to make our analysis tractable and keep it as simple as possible, purchasing-power parity (PPP) is assumed as in equation 2.6 to link the domestic and foreign price levels. Assuming that the latter is constant and normalized at unity, PPP implies that we can identify the domestic price level with the exchange rate, $p = e$.

The nominal net wealth, W, is assumed to consist of three assets, a stock of money (M), a domestic bond (B) and a foreign bond (A). Thus, $W = M + B + EF$, where E stands for the nominal exchange rate. Taking the logarithm, and approximating it to yield $w' = \omega_1 m + \omega_2 b + (1 - \omega_1 - \omega_2)(e + a)$, where $w' \equiv \ln(W)$, ω_1 and ω_2 are the initial shares of M and B in the net wealth, respectively. Subtracting e from both side yields $w \equiv w' - e$, the real net wealth, as shown in equation 2.7.

The working of the model

Setting $da/dt = 0$ and $de/dt = 0$ in equations 2.4 and 2.5 results in the following two equations:

$$\left[\frac{\alpha - \epsilon(1 - \omega_1 - \omega_2)}{\alpha\rho}\right]a + \left[\frac{\alpha + (\alpha\rho + \sigma)\beta + \epsilon(\omega_1 + \omega_2)}{\alpha\rho}\right]e = Q_e \qquad (2.8)$$

$$[\sigma\beta + \epsilon(\omega_1 + \omega_2)]e - \epsilon(1 - \omega_1 - \omega_2)a = Q_a \qquad (2.9)$$

where:

$$Q_e \equiv \frac{[\epsilon\omega_2 + (\alpha\rho + \sigma)\beta]m + (\alpha + \epsilon\omega_1)b}{\alpha\rho} +$$

$$\left\{r^* - \frac{[1 - \gamma + (\alpha\rho + \sigma)\beta\theta y - \mu]}{\alpha\rho}\right\} \qquad (2.10)$$

$$Q_a \equiv (\alpha\beta + \epsilon\omega_2)m + \epsilon\omega_1 b + [\mu - (1 - \gamma + \sigma\beta\theta)y] \qquad (2.11)$$

Equations 2.8 and 2.9 can be solved for the steady-state values of e and a. One can easily check that the steady state equilibrium exists and is unique under the assumed restrictions on the parameters.

The dynamics of the model are described by the system of equations 2.3 and 2.4, and the local stability of the system can be examined by linearly approximating them around the neighborhood of the equilibrium values, e_0 and a_0. The approximation yields:

$$
\begin{bmatrix} \dfrac{de}{dt} \\[2ex] \dfrac{da}{dt} \end{bmatrix} = \left(\begin{array}{cc} \dfrac{\alpha + (\alpha\rho + \sigma)\beta + \epsilon(\omega_1 + \omega_2)}{\alpha\rho} & \dfrac{\alpha - \epsilon(1 - \omega_1 - \omega_2)}{\alpha\rho} \\[3ex] \alpha\beta + \epsilon(\omega_1 + \omega_2) & -\epsilon(1 - \omega_1 - \omega_2) \end{array} \right) \begin{pmatrix} (e - e_0) \\[2ex] (a - a_0) \end{pmatrix} \quad (2.12)
$$

The determinant of the coefficient matrix of equation 2.12 is shown to be negative, if $1/\beta$, the semi-elasticity of the demand for money with respect to the interest rate, is greater than or equal to unity. Assuming this sufficient condition implies that the stationary equilibrium is unstable, characterized by a saddle point (Sanchez *et al.*, 1988: 493) (see the phase diagram in Figure 2.1). In Figure 2.1, capital mobility is defined as being "high," if, and only if, $\alpha > \alpha^*$, where α^* is defined by:

$$
\alpha^* \equiv \epsilon(1 - \omega_1 - \omega_2) \tag{2.13}
$$

It can be easily checked that, for $\alpha > \alpha^*$ ($<\alpha^*$), the slope of the $de/dt = 0$ locus is negatively (positively) sloped in the e–a plane.

In the following, equations 2.8 and 2.9 are utilized to show the effects of an expansionary monetary shock on the equilibrium values of e and a. Differentiation of equations 2.8 and 2.9 with respect to m yields:

$$
\frac{\partial e}{\partial m} \bigg|_{de/dt=0} = \frac{(\alpha\rho + \sigma)\beta + \epsilon\omega_2}{\alpha + (\alpha\rho + \sigma)\beta + \epsilon(\omega_1 + \omega_2)} > 0 \tag{2.14-a}
$$

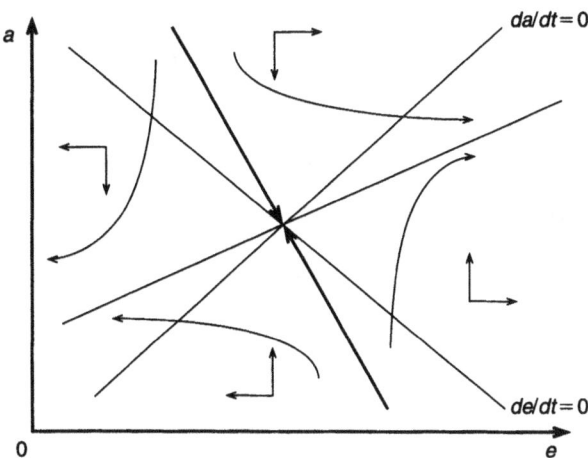

Figure 2.1 Phase diagram.

$$\frac{\partial e}{\partial m}\bigg|_{de/dt=0} = \frac{\sigma\beta + \epsilon\omega_2}{\sigma\beta + \epsilon(\omega_1 + \omega_2)} > 0 \qquad (2.14\text{-b})$$

Thus, both loci shift rightward in the *e–a* plane after the expansionary shock, but the shift is smaller than unity. However, it can be observed that $(\partial e / \partial m)_{da/dt=0} = 1$ if $\epsilon\omega_1 = 0$. $\epsilon\omega_1 = 0$ is satisfied if there is no wealth effect in consumption ($\epsilon = 0$), or there is no domestic bond ($\omega_1 = 0$), or both. $\alpha = 0$ is satisfied if capital is immobile internationally. It can also be confirmed that $\lim_{\alpha \to \infty} (\partial e / \partial m)_{de/dt=0} \to 1$, which means that perfect capital mobility brings about the same effect as $\alpha + \epsilon\omega_1 = 0$. Thus, it is demonstrated that long-run non-neutrality is brought in through substitution between domestic money and bonds, and the wealth effect (Delbecque 1989).

Because it is not clear which of the shifts shown in equation 2.14-a and 2.14-b is greater, a natural benchmark is to assume that they are the same. Equalizing them yields the benchmark rate of substitution:

$$\rho^* \equiv (\sigma\beta + \epsilon\omega_2)[\sigma\beta + \alpha(1-\beta)]/\alpha\beta[\epsilon\omega_1 + (\alpha - \sigma)\beta] \qquad (2.15)$$

Because 2.14-a is shown to be increasing with ρ, while equation 2.14-b does not depend on ρ, it can be inferred that, after an expansionary monetary shock, $a > (<) a_0$ for $\rho > (<)\rho^*$ (see Figure 2.2). In other words, the real stock of foreign assets is larger (smaller), the larger (smaller) the degree of asset substitutability.

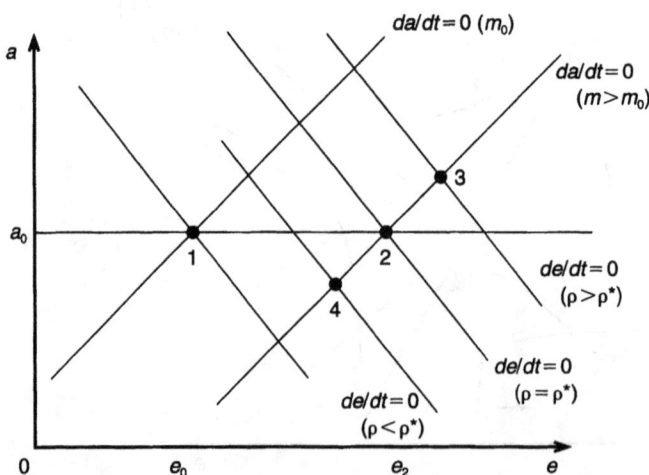

Figure 2.2 Expansionary monetary shock and asset substitutability.

Effects of asset substitutability

This section demonstrates that the situations are quite different under different assumptions of asset substitutability after a monetary expansion. Our focal point, of course, is how the exchange rate responds differently to monetary disturbances under different substitutability. It is assumed that capital is highly mobile, $\alpha > \epsilon(1 - \omega_1 - \omega_2)$, so that the $de/dt = 0$ locus is negatively sloped in the e–a plane.

Assuming first that $\rho > \rho^*$, where ρ^* is defined in equation 2.15. The new equilibrium point is given in point 3 in Figure 2.2 after a monetary expansion. The adjustment process can be followed in detail in Figure 2.3.

It can be observed that this country first jumps to point m_3 after the monetary expansion, and then moves gradually toward point 3 on the stable arm. Thus, it is clear that the exchange rate overshoots the new long-run equilibrium value, e_3.

The second case to examine is the effects of monetary expansion in the opposite case of low capital substitutability, the situation depicted at point 4 in Figure 2.2. As drawn in Figure 2.4, the country first jumps to point m_4 in Figure 2.4 after the monetary expansion, and it moves gradually toward point 4 afterward along the stable arm. Thus, the exchange rate movement is relatively smooth except for the initial jump (actually "undershooting"). This undershooting (Levin 1999) is shown to be more likely when international asset substitution is low. But mobility is high in our model.

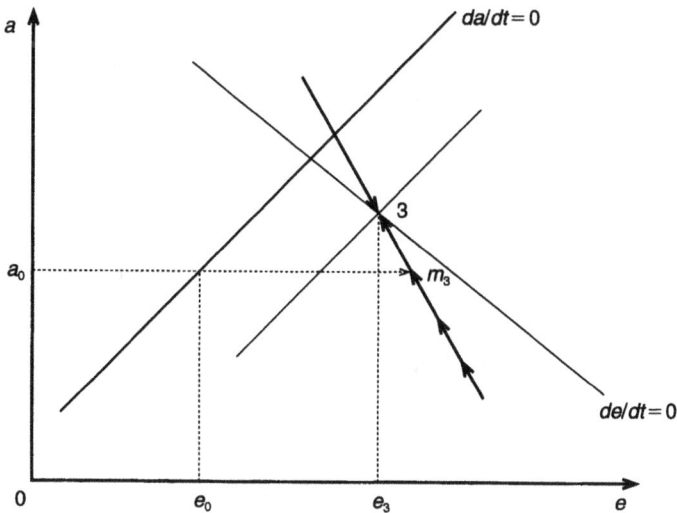

Figure 2.3 $\rho > \rho^*$ and $\alpha > \alpha^*$.

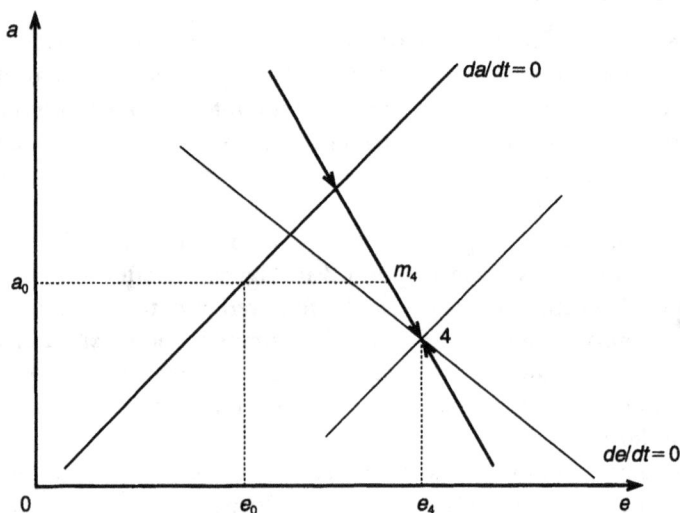

Figure 2.4 $\rho < \rho^*$ and $\alpha^* > \alpha$.

It could be argued that, because enlargement of the EU was endorsed by the Treaty of Nice, and because investors are, in general, risk averse, capital substitutability as well as mobility between the EU and the outside world would both be high. The reason for this is that investors would prefer to purchase assets issued by a large stable organization, both politically and economically. Then, Figures 2.3 and 2.4 exhaust all plausible possibilities. However, to complete this present investigation, the exchange rate variability under low capital mobility is examined ($\alpha < \alpha^*$).

As pointed out in the last section (p. 29), the slope of the $de/dt = 0$ locus is positive for $\alpha < \alpha^*$. Since the $da/dt = 0$ locus is also positively sloped, two possibilities must be discussed separately: slope($de/dt = 0$) > (<)slope($da/dt = 0$). The case of slope($de/dt = 0$) > slope($da/dt = 0$) is depicted in Figure 2.5, from which it is confirmed again that the equilibrium is still unstable, and only saddle point stable. It can be shown that, after an expansionary monetary shock, the exchange rate undershoots (overshoots) the new equilibrium value for high (low) asset substitutability. This conclusion is opposite to the case involving high capital mobility examined earlier (p. 31).

Another possible case of slope($de/dt = 0$) < slope($da/dt = 0$) is presented in Figure 2.6. The dynamic system means that the determinant of the coefficient matrix of equation 2.12 is positive in this case. Then according to the classification of patterns of trajectories (for example, Takayama 1994), the trajectories turn out to be "centers."[8] If the positive

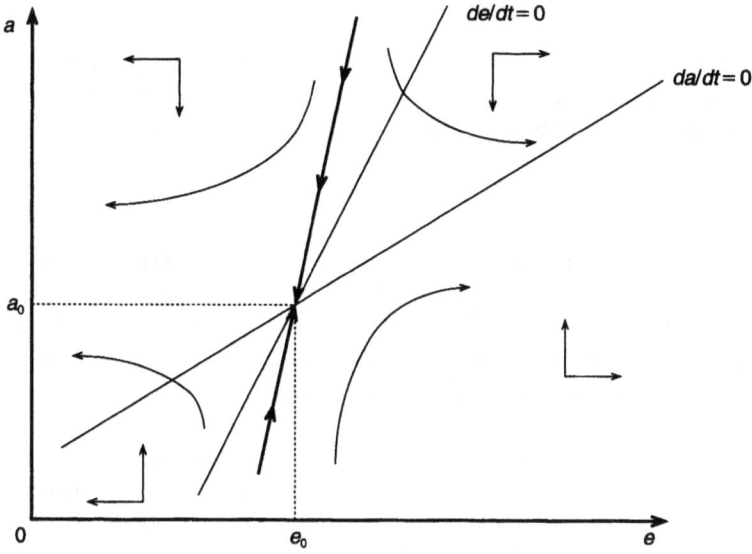

Figure 2.5 $\alpha < \alpha^*$, but slope$_{(de/dt=0)}$ > slope$_{(da/dt=0)}$.

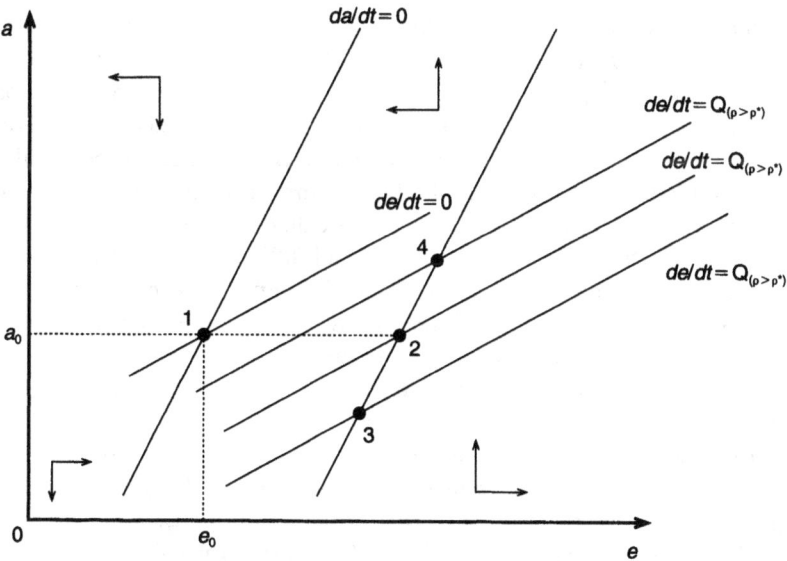

Figure 2.6 $\alpha < \alpha^*$, but slope$_{(de/dt=0)}$ < slope$_{(da/dt=0)}$.

determinant is smaller than a quarter of the trace (i.e. the discriminant of the characteristic equation is positive), the trajectories are converging spirals for the positive trace, but diverging spirals for the negative trace.

Policy implications

As the EU expands in the future, as stipulated by the Treaty of Nice, a small open economy, whose relationship with the EU countries becomes closer, is likely to be vulnerable through larger volatility of exchange rate against the euro. It is not clear how many countries among the EU members will eventually adopt the euro. However, one thing is clear: After the process of integration is completed, the euro will be the unified currency among member countries. As most of the developed non-member countries outside the EU will have even closer economic relationships with the EU countries, both ρ (the degree of asset substitutability) and α (the degree of capital mobility) are expected to be higher than before.[9] Thus, as examined earlier (pp. 31–32), Figure 2.3 will most likely be applicable for small, non-member countries.

As the figure makes clear, the exchange rate will be more volatile than before, as the possibility of overshooting suggests. The higher volatility will discourage international trade, and this undermines the gains from trade for such a small open economy. One of the theoretically possible countermeasures is to bring down the degree of asset substitutability through some discretionary policy such as transaction taxes. By so doing, a small country will find that it is in the situation represented in Figure 2.4. Thus, the unfavorable effect of higher volatility of exchange rate can be avoided.

Another countermeasure could be a temporary suspension of international capital transactions whenever it is called for. This policy has been adopted historically whenever a country had difficulty with the fluctuation in the exchange rate, with rapid flows of reserve currencies, or with a significant imbalance in the balance of payments. The policy is supposed to help such a country prevent even worse side-effects to their economy. This situation may be summarized in Figure 2.5, where the exchange rate volatility is lower under higher asset substitutability.

Figure 2.6 suggests that such a discouraging policy for making capital mobility lower may not be a favorable policy when the wealth effect is large enough to reverse the slope of the $de/dt = 0$ locus, which is flatter than the $da/dt = 0$ locus. Although it is far more implausible to assume a large wealth effect, volatile exchange rate fluctuation will persist, once this situation emerges.

Conclusions

This chapter sets forth a brief review of economic issues surrounding economic integration from the outsiders' (non-members') perspective. Outside economies, especially small open economies, would suffer serious harmful effects, both statically and dynamically, from the formation of an integrated regional economy. Focusing on the volatility of the exchange rate between a small country's national currency and the currency used in the integrated region such as the euro of the EU, several potentially harmful effects were pointed out; these include the so-called uncertainty hypothesis, the pass-through effects and pricing-to-market behavior.

It was also statistically vindicated that the introduction and the existence of the euro did not "contribute to greater exchange rate stability." Recognizing this evidence, we presented a model to investigate the effects of capital substitution and mobility. Both degrees of substitution and mobility are expected to be higher than before, as the EU's expansion was endorsed by the Treaty of Nice. It was demonstrated that, because of higher degrees of mobility and substitution, exchange rate volatility for outside economies is higher, as predicted by exchange rate overshooting of its long-run equilibrium value.

It was also demonstrated that such a high degree of exchange rate volatility can be avoided, if the degree of capital substitution can be lowered through, for example, a discretionary economic policy. Alternatively, to avoid higher volatility, temporary suspension of capital transactions could be adopted to make the degree of capital mobility lower.

Notes

1 Lawrence (1996) and Frankel (1997) contain a wide range of the literature regarding the development of the theories of economic integration. Baldwin and Venables (1995) survey the literature with emphasis on imperfect competition, while Corden (1984) focuses on the customs union theories under perfect competition.
2 It should be stressed that the standard deviation, or the variance, of the exchange rate is not a sufficient statistic to summarize the volatility of the exchange rate. See Engel and Hakkio (1996).
3 The exchange rates between the national currencies was in place until 2002 when the national currencies were due to be totally abandoned for those countries who adopted the euro.
4 Those exceptions include Delbecque (1989) and Gazioglu (1996).
5 Five different measures (including the two discussed here) and their relationships are examined in Wong (1997).
6 For empirical validity of the overshooting model, see, for example, Pappel

(1988). He obtained evidence of overshooting for Germany, but undershooting for Japan.

7   Thus, $(1/\beta)$ measures the semi-elasticity of the demand for money with respect to the interest rate.

8   If trajectories are centers, the degree of capital mobility is:

$$\alpha = [\sigma\beta + \epsilon(\omega_1 + \omega_2)] / [\rho\epsilon(1 - \omega_1 - \omega_2) - (1 + \rho\beta)]$$

9   Driskill and McCaferty (1980) found in their model of a small, open economy under flexible exchange rates that increases in the degree of capital mobility increase (decrease) that portion of exchange rate variability attributable to monetary (real) shocks. According to an explicit welfare analysis of capital market integration by Osler (1991), it was demonstrated that "a shift to integrated capital markets might, but need not, cause a Pareto improvement in welfare" (p. 104).

References

Akiba, Hiroya (1990) "International Trade Liberalization and Exchange Rate Variability," in H.W. Singer *et al.* (eds) *Trade Liberalization 1990s.* New Delhi: Indus Publishing Co.

Akiba, Hiroya (1997) "Forward Exchange Rate and the Interest Rate within a Production Economy," *Journal of Economic Integration*, 12: 227–41.

Arize, Augustine C. (1997) "Conditional Exchange-Rate Volatility and the Volume of Foreign Trade: Evidence from Seven Industrialized Countries," *Southern Economic Journal*, 64(1): 235–54.

Baldwin, R. and A.J. Venables (1995) "Regional Economic Integration," in G.M. Grossman and K. Rogoff (eds) *Handbook of International Economics*, Vol. 3. Amsterdam: North-Holland.

Coakley, Jerry, Farida Kulasi and Ron Smith (1998) "The Feldstein–Horioka Puzzle and Capital Mobility: A Review," *International Journal of Finance and Economics*, 3: 169–88.

Corden, W.M. (1984) "The Normative Theory of International Trade," in R.W. Jones and P.B. Kenen (eds) *Handbook of International Economics*, Vol. 1. Amsterdam: North-Holland.

Delbecque, Bernard (1989) "Exchange-Rate Dynamics in a Model with Imperfect Capital Mobility and Asset Substitutability," *European Economic Review*, 33: 1161–73.

Dornbusch, Rudiger (1976) "Expectations and Exchange Rate Dynamics," *Journal of Political Economy*, 84(6): 1161–76.

Driskill, Robert and Stephen McCafferty (1980) "Exchange-Rate Variability, Real and Monetary Shocks, and the Degree of Capital Mobility under Rational Expectations," *Quarterly Journal of Economics*, 95(3): 577–86.

Engel, Charles and Craig S. Hakkio (1996) "The Distribution of Exchange Rates in the EMS," *International Journal of Finance and Economics*, 1: 55–67.

Ethier, Wilfred J. (1998) "Regionalism in a Multilateral World," *Journal of Political Economy*, 106(6): 1214–45.

Feenstra, Robert C. and Jon D. Kendall (1997) "Pass-Through of Exchange Rates and Purchasing Power Parity," *Journal of International Economics*, 43: 237–61.

Feldstein, M. and C. Horioka (1980) "Domestic Saving and International Capital Flows," *Economic Journal*, 90: 314–29.

Frankel, J.A. (1997) *Regional Trading Blocs in the World Trading System*. Washington: Institute for International Economics.

Gazioglu, Saziye (1996) "Influences of Demand Shocks on Exchange Rate Volatility: Imperfect Capital Mobility and Substitutability," *The Manchester School*, 64(1): 79–95.

Hooper, Peter and Jaime Marquez (1995) "Exchange Rate, Prices, and External Adjustment in the United States and Japan," in Peter B. Kenen (ed.) *Understanding Interdependence*. Princeton, New Jersey: Princeton University Press.

Huisman, Ronald, Kees Koedijk, Clemens Koal and Francois Nissen (1998) "Extreme Support for Uncovered Interest Parity," *Journal of International Money and Finance*, 17: 218–28.

Isard, Peter (1995) *Exchange Rate Economics*. Cambridge: Cambridge University Press.

Keynes, John Maynard (1923) *A Tract on Monetary Reform*. London: Macmillan.

Kojima, Kiyoshi (1999) "Economics of Regional Integration," *The International Economy*, 5: 11–37 (Japanese with English summary).

Kowalczyk, Carsten (2000) "Welfare and Integration," *International Economic Review*, 41(2): 483–94.

Kumakura, Masanaga (2000) "Exchange Rates and Dynamics of Traded Goods Prices: Does Exchange Rate Uncertainty Matter?" Delivered at the NBER University Research Conference on Changes in Real Exchange Rates: Causes and Consequences.

Lawrence, R.Z. (1996) *Regionalism, Multilateralism, and Deeper Integration*. Washington: The Brookings Institution.

Levich, Richard M. (1985) "Empirical Studies of Exchange Rates: Price Behavior, Rate Determination and Market Efficiency," in Ronald W. Jones and Peter B. Kenen (eds) *Handbook of International Economics*, Vol. 2. Amsterdam: North-Holland.

Levin, Jay H. (1994) "On Sluggish Output Adjustment and Exchange Rate Dynamics," *Journal of International Money and Finance*, 13: 447–58.

Levin, Jay H. (1999) "Exchange Rate Undershooting," *International Journal of Finance and Economics*, 4: 325–33.

Lipsey, R.G. (1960) "The Theory of Customs Unions: A General Survey," *Economic Journal*, 70: 496–513.

Marston, Richard C. (1990) "Pricing to Market in Japanese Manufacturing," *Journal of International Economics*, 29: 217–36.

McKenzie, Michael D. (1999) "The Impact of Exchange Rate Volatility on International Trade Flows," *Journal of Economic Surveys*, 13(1): 71–106.

Mundell, Robert A. (1963) "Capital Mobility and Stabilization Policy under Fixed and Flexible Exchange Rates," *Canadian Journal of Economics and Political Sciences*, 29(4): 475–85.

Osler, Carol L. (1991) "Explaining the Absence of International Factor–Price Convergence," *Journal of International Money and Finance*, 10: 89–107.

Papell, David H. (1988) "Expectations and Exchange Rate Dynamics after a Decade of Floating," *Journal of International Economics*, 25: 303–17.

Sanchez, David A., Richard C. Allen Jr. and Walter T. Kyner (1988) *Differential Equations*, 2nd edn. Reading, Massachusetts: Addison-Wesley Publishing Co.

Takayama, Akira (1994) *Analytical Methods in Economics.* New York: Harvester Wheatsheaf.

Viner, Jacob (1950) *The Customs Union Issue.* New York: Carnegie Endowment for International Peace.

Wong, Clement Yuk Pang (1997) "Black Market Exchange Rates and Capital Mobility in Asian Economies," *Contemporary Economic Policy*, 15: 21–36.

Part II

Issues of institutional reform

3 Institutional reform and European governance

Political reflections on the Treaty of Nice

Koji Fukuda

Introduction

The Treaty of Nice was signed on 26 February 2001, and came into force on 1 February 2003.[1] The purpose of this treaty is the institutional reform of the EU and it deals with the so-called Amsterdam 'left-overs'. The task is becoming all the more urgent now that the fifth enlargement of the EU, involving the countries of Central and Eastern Europe, is underway. The Treaty of Nice was originally conceived at an Intergovernmental Conference (IGC) held in 2000 and this led to the Nice European Council being held between 7–11 December of that year. It resulted in the Nice Treaty, an agreement which revised the founding treaties. The Nice summit was the longest session in the history of European integration.

On the day after the Nice summit finished, a certain European newspaper said that the Nice Treaty was 'the worst treaty'[2] ever signed in European history. Some newspapers also reported that the Nice Treaty had been a failure.[3] However, are these evaluations appropriate? In order to verify the validity of these statements, it is necessary to clarify the following issues. To begin with, what standpoints could be adopted in the evaluation of this treaty (e.g. pro- or anti-European)? How much time should academics and interested parties devote to this evaluation? How should the features of this reform be viewed in the historical context of the EU? Furthermore, we should consider to what extent the overall structure of European governance has been transformed by the Treaty of Nice.

In order to answer these questions, this chapter focuses on the European governance,[4] examining some problems involving institutional reform, based on the reality of European integration, and its trends of contemporary political theory. Although a large number of studies have been made into European integration theories,[5] little is known about the 'new institutionalism' theories on European governance. It is important to understand how this research relates to the theoretical concerns surrounding the approach of multi-level governance. The purpose of this study is to examine the importance of these features: first, what might be the impact of the Nice Treaty's institutional reform on European governance? Second, what reforms are actually specified in the treaty and what difference will they make? Third, what should be done to enhance democratic legitimacy in the EU? Finally, we should like to explore further possible reforms of European governance.

Institutional perspectives and European governance

It might be said that one purpose of European integration is to compensate for the malfunctioning economies and political systems of individual Member States. With European integration, a new stage of political integration in connection with globalization and a realization of market integration and monetary union began. Institutional reform of the EU was necessary because of changes in the international environment due to globalization and institutional changes caused by the challenges of enlargement. The change in jurisdiction between the EC and the Member States arose through a broad interpretation of Article 235 EEC in the 1970s.[6] Subsequently, the transfer of authority to the EC from the Member States was brought about by the Single European Act and the Maastricht Treaty. Consequently, the citizens of the various Member States have found themselves moving towards integration with feelings ranging from deep unease to the utmost confidence.[7]

What kind of theoretical perspectives are applicable to the legal constitution as revised in Nice? The subject has been widely researched since the 1990s and, according to Peters,[8] the political theory of a 'new institutionalism' may be arranged into six areas, namely:

1   normative institutionalism,
2   rational choice institutionalism,
3   historical institutionalism,
4   empirical institutionalism,
5   international institutionalism;
6   societal/sociological institutionalism.[9]

Similarly, treaty reform, the theme of this chapter, can be viewed from four main perspectives.

First, the liberal intergovernmentalist approach, which has proved effective in the analysis of negotiations on 'major decisions in history'[10] or 'history making'[11] involving the EU Member States, such as the Intergovernmental Conference (IGC) 2000. This approach is represented by

Moravcsik, and derives from rational choice institutionalism. This approach focuses on the dynamism of European integration and is primarily a result of negotiations between the Member State governments.

The liberal intergovernmentalists argue that national governments define a set of state interests and are the most important actors for IGCs in the EU. From the 'intergovernmentalist' perspective, the Member State governments are the only important actors at the European level, and the EU remains a forum for bargaining. This approach holds that only the Member State governments have autonomy and can design the institutional system of the EU.[12] However, there are several limitations to this approach.

When we look carefully at the mechanism of the EU itself, we recognize that the EU is beginning to have the autonomy of an actual organization. The EU makes the rules and regulations, or can control the national governments in many sectors. Moreover, border-crossing profit or non-profit groups, autonomous unions, NGOs, and so on, are also beginning to have an influence on institutional systems designed by the EU.

Second is the 'historical institutionalism approach' as represented by Paul Pierson. This approach is characterized by the 'path dependence' of a policy. From this perspective, Pierson focused on 'the autonomous actions of European organizations, the restricted time-horizons of decision-makers, the large potential for unintended consequences, the likelihood of changes in COG preferences over time' and 'the resistance of supranational actors', 'Institutional barriers to reform', as well as the 'Sunk costs and rising price of exit'.[13]

Third, there is the 'social constructivism approach'[14] which belongs to the genealogy of sociological institutionalist or societal approach. It is based on the everyday language of social reality, which is already considered to exist in society. The constructivists argue that the role of language in discourse becomes crucial, and language is operative in every aspect of the EU.[14] The constructivist approach takes the position that where an actor and the structure are equivalent ontologically the European integration process is carried forward, by both interaction and structuralization, and a new regime is created.

Fourth, the governance approach[15] derives from three different perspectives: societal/sociological institutionalism, international institutionalism, and the 'regime theory'. The concept of governance is a convenient tool for referring to 'the formation and stewardship of the formal and informal rules that regulate the public realm, the arena in which state as well as civil society actors interact to make decisions.'[16] However, the concept of governance is not as clearly defined as that of globalization.

The concept of governance and institutional reform of the EU

Various ways of interpreting the treaty were identified by Several critics and, as a result, the concept of 'governance' has come to be well-known through extensive media coverage in recent years. The concept of governance offers the key to an understanding of European integration. The word 'governance' is used as a synonym of French 'gouvernement' (the art and method of rule) of the thirteenth century. It became English in the form of 'governance' in the fourteenth century (1338).[17] The origin of the word is the same as that of 'government', derived from the Latin *guberno* meaning 'political guide' or 'steering'.[18] It was introduced by Kratochwil and Ruggie to the field of politics and international relations theory in 1986. At the beginning of the 1990s, Rosenau *et al.* introduced the concept of 'the governance without the government'[19] into the field of the international relations theory.

In EU integration studies, the 'multi-level governance' approach[20] was introduced by Gary Marks in 1993, taken up by Maruks Jachtenfuchs and Beate Kohler-Koch (1995)[21] and further developed in a work by Hooghe and Marks (1996).[22] In the first instance, the concept of governance was introduced by Marks in order to analyse the EU structural policy. This concept was then expanded until it effectively became an analysis of the whole policy process in the EU. The governance approaches focus on the day-to-day process of policy cooperation within and between networks of multi-level governments and many private actors.

The 'network governance' approach of Beate Kohler-Koch and Rainer Eising (1999) is another well-known theory. They argue that 'network governance' has two special features.

First, it is not a mere academic analysis concept, but is also a useful political tool. Second, it acts as an effective method of discovering the role of the state, the rules of behaviour, the patterns of interaction and the level of political action in the EU. They categorized governance into four separate types:

1   statism,
2   corporatism,
3   pluralism, and
4   network governance (see Table 3.1).[23]

Furthermore, the approach influenced the report: *Our Global Neighborhood*[24] written by the UN Commission on Global Governance. Since the mid-1990s, the concept of 'global governance' has been used frequently in the fields of politics and international relations.

Table 3.1 A typology of mode of governance/approaches to European integration

			Organizing principle of political relations	
Constitutive Logic of the Polity		Common good	Majority rule Statism	Consociation Non-state Actors Corporatism
	Single Multiple	Individual interests	Intergovernmental Multilevel governance Pluralism	Supranational Network governance

Source: adapted from Kohler-Koch and Eising (1999: 23) and Imig, Doug and Tarrow, Sidney, *Contentious Europeans*, Rowman & Littlefield Publishers. INC (2001: 12).

Global governance is supported not only by nation states, but also international organizations, non-governmental organizations, as well as the private sector; and these networks work. What, then, is 'governance'? Philippe C. Schmitter defines it thus:

> Governance is a method/mechanism for dealing with a broad range of problems/conflicts in which actors regularly arrive at mutually satisfactory and binding decisions by negotiating and deliberating with each other and cooperating in the implementation of these decisions.
>
> Its core rests on horizontal forms of interaction between actors who have conflicting objectives, but who are yet sufficiently interdependent so that both would lose if no solution were found.[25]

Governance has been defined as 'the relatively standardized processes and institutions by which purposeful outcomes are produced in any political system'.[26] In what ways might the future of European integration be influenced by the globalization of systems or structures which affect Europe? It should be emphasized that the concept of governance can be used to highlight the unique nature of the EU system as a polity.

Romano Prodi, President of the European Commission paid particular attention to this concept.[27] A task force of twelve was set up to study 'European governance' under the Prodi European Commission. Based on studies by this task-force, the European Commission published *European Governance: A White Paper*[28] in July 2001 when Belgium took over the Presidency. Subsequently, the European Commission presented the *Report from the Commission on European Governance* (COM (2002) 705 final) in December 2002. It was based on suggestions drawn from reactions to the White Paper.

From the viewpoint of strengthening democratic legitimacy, it is vital to carry out a concrete system design, not only on a theoretical level, but also on a business level. In this reform, an awareness of the issues surounding how to involve the citizenry in European governance has vividly emerged.

The purpose and background of EU institutional reforms

Historical background of the institutional reforms: problems of the mechanisms in the Treaty of Amsterdam and necessity for reform

The governance structure of the EC was designed by the Treaty of Rome at the time of its foundation. Before going on to an in-depth analysis of the institutional reforms resulting from the Nice Treaty, it may be useful to briefly set out the institutional systems under the EC Treaty.

The Council of the EU which plays a central role in the decision-making process of the EU is made up of ministers from each member government. The ministers on the Council represent the interests of their respective countries. The Council is the EU's legislative body, sharing the important functions of accepting, modifying or rejecting votes on the European Commission's proposals together with the European Parliament.

The European Parliament is the only democratically elected international institution in the world, and represents the viewpoints of the people of Europe. It functions as the directly elected democratic expression of the political will of the people of the EU. It is the Community institution which represents all 379 million citizens of the EU. The European Parliament shares legislative power with the Council, and provides democratic control of the European Commission.[29]

The European Commission has both political and administrative roles within the EU. The twenty Commissioners are delegated by their countries, but they do not represent their countries. Instead, they represent the EU's interests. Their collective responsibility is a source of strain in the college, which is unelected, but plays the most political role in the Commission. The entire college, under the Jacques Santer Commission, was provoked into collective resignation in 1999 by charges of corruption and scandal concerning personnel management (nepotism) and mal-administration.[30]

As Scharpf pointed out in 1988, focusing on the level of the European Union alone is insufficient, since European integration has also called into question democratic legitimacy at the level of the nation-state.[31] From the 1970s to the beginning of the 1980s, despite the stagnation in integration, the processes of jurisdiction between the community and the Member State were derived from a broad interpretation of Article 235 EEC.

In June 1985, the Commission issued a report, *Completing the Internal Market. The White Paper*,[32] known as 'the Cockfield Report', detailed 'supply-side' economic policies for completing the internal market. In supply-side policies, government spending and social welfare are not emphasized.

The 1992 Programme made 286 specific proposals to achieve the objective of a true single internal market. This led directly to the first revision of the EEC Treaty: the Single European Act, which further encouraged the power transfer from Member States towards a community. It was signed in February 1986 and came into force on 1 July 1987. The Council gained new powers and a smoother decision-making process. The Single European Act was successful, so far as it increased the importance of EU institutions such as the Commission, the Council and the European Council.

In November 1989, the Berlin Wall fell and the German Democratic Republic opened its borders. In December 1991, the European Council negotiated the treaty on European Union in Maastricht (the Treaty of Maastricht). The Treaty was signed in February 1992, and came into effect in November 1993. This treaty is based on three 'pillars'. The first is the Community pillar (composed of the ECSC, the EAEC and the EC) which has a supranational character. The second is the Common Foreign and Security Policy (CFSP). The third pillar deals with justice and home affairs (JHA).

The second and third pillars are based on intergovernmental cooperation among Member States of the EU. The Maastricht Treaty created the Intergovernmental Conference (IGC) to examine the objectives of the treaty and has the power to revise them if it is found to be necessary,

An important feature of the Maastricht Treaty is the introduction of the 'principle of subsidiarity' (Article G, TEU, Article 3b, TEC). This principle means that the EU should take action on certain matters only if these matters cannot be dealt with in a satisfactory way by the Member States themselves.[33] It also ensures that decisions should be taken by those public authorities which stand as close to the citizen as possible. It is a principle which resists unnecessarily remote or centralized decision-making. Thus, the EU should only take action which can be more effectively carried out at a European level or when the Member States themselves cannot address the issue effectively.[34] This principle is based on a memorandum signed by the European Parliament, the European Commission and the Member States.

In 1996, IGC was held and resulted in the Treaty of Amsterdam, which revised the founding treaties. The purpose of the Treaty of Amsterdam[35] is to strengthen and simplify the formal bases of the EU.

The Treaty of Amsterdam clarified the 'principle of subsidiarity' which was laid down by the Maastricht Treaty. Subsequently, European decision-makers sought a way to integrate the governance of the bottom-up process with a top-down decision-making system and allow the participation of meso (middle) level governments. This treaty enhanced the social aspects of government and established the right of any citizen to have access to numerous European Parliament, Commission and Council documents.

The Treaty of Amsterdam also emphasized closer cooperation with prospective Member States and 'flexibility' (Article 43–5, TEU Provisions on closer cooperation). Flexibility of arrangements was essential to accelerate cooperation on political, security, defence and social issues with applicant states in Central and Eastern Europe.

The aims of IGC 2000

In December 1999, under the responsibility of the Finnish Presidency, the Helsinki European Council organized the IGC 2000. The Finnish Presidency suggested that this IGC should deal with institutional reform (the size and composition of the European Commission, re-weighting of votes and qualified majority voting (QMV) in the Council), as outlined in the European Council of Cologne, 3–4 June 1999. However, the interests of some member nations had been opposed to each other at the IGC which drafted the provisions on the Treaty of Amsterdam. As a result, the IGC 2000 focused on the issue of institutional reform which was the most important pending question, but a compromise was not reached.

IGC 2000 began on 14 February under the Portuguese Presidency. During the first half of the IGC, agreement was largely reached on the issue of QMV, but the Member States were unable to compromise on many other issues. In the negotiations under the French Presidency in the latter half of 2000, IGC 2000 found solutions for many institutional problems which would otherwise have caused significant problems in the move towards enlargement.[36]

Institutional reform necessary for enlargement envisaged in the Treaty of Nice

The contents of the Agreement of Institutional Reform

Reform of the EU through the Treaty of Nice runs parallel with the transformation of the international environment through globalization. The success or failure of the fifth enlargement will largely depend on the quality of this reform package. At this time, a strategy for EU enlargement was proposed, entitled *Agenda 2000*.[37] Enlargement to twenty-seven states was envisaged in October 1997, but it was later decided to reduce this target to twenty-five in December 2002 (by only adding ten new members, as opposed to twelve). Even this revised figure would be a radical system reform with an increase in new Member States provided for in the fiscal-reform programme. Increases in the number of Member States slow down the decision-making processes of the EU further and risk making it more inefficient.

However, if the EU is going to pursue efficiency of decision-making, the European Commission's power must be strengthened and, as Community Bureaucracy becomes stronger, concerns about the 'democratic deficit' also become stronger. In presenting *Agenda 2000*, the President called for a new IGC to be held as soon as possible in 2000. This IGC went on to address the institutional problems raised by the next enlargement, on which subject heads of government had not been able to find agreement in the Treaty of Amsterdam.

Agreement was reached on the following five points:

1   the size and composition of the European Commission,
2   the vote distribution (re-weighting) of QMV in the Council,
3   the scope of the QMV in the Council,
4   'the enhanced cooperation',
5   the re-distribution of seats in the European Parliament.

Essentially, the heads of government had to ask themselves what kind of reforms would be required by EU enlargement to include the countries of Central and East Europe.

The size and composition of the European Commission

At present, the President and other members of the Commission are appointed by common accord of the governments of the Member States (Article 214, TEC) in accordance with the Treaty of Amsterdam. However, under the terms of the Treaty of Nice, the President of the Commission will be nominated by the qualified majority of 'the Council meeting in composition of Heads of State or Government' (Article 217, TEC).

After agreeing on the Presidential candidate, the EU Council (of Ministers) adopts a list of Commissioner candidates (created according to proposals from each member nation) by a specific majority (Article 214, TEC).

New members, who are appointed by QMV in the Council, fill vacancies caused by the resignation, dismissal or death of a Commissioner.

We shall next compare and examine the present Treaty of Amsterdam and the Treaty of Nice on five points. First, we shall look at the problems involving the composition of the European Commission and the reform of its organization. The twenty-member Commission (that is, Germany, France, Britain, Italy and Spain, who are represented by two commissioners, and the ten remaining Member States with one commissioner each) will continue until the end of 2004.

However, under the Treaty of Nice, the new Commission will be made up of one member per Member State from 1 January 2005, although the number may be changed by the Council, acting unanimously (Protocol on the enlargement of the European Union, Article 4, 1).

It was planned that when EU membership reached twenty-seven states, the maximum number of Commissioners would be fixed by the Council. This number would have to be agreed unanimously and be less than the number of Member States. Almost all Member States believed that having more than twenty-seven members would not be good in terms of efficiency. Therefore, each new member country would have to agree to be represented according to an 'equal rotation system' on application. (Protocol on the enlargement of the European Union, Article 4.2).

The Council unanimously takes action on the total number of Commissioners, the determination of the order of rotation of each Member State and the methods of implementing policy that would follow the signing of the treaty of accession of the twenty-seventh Member State of the EU (Protocol on the enlargement of the European Union, Article 4.2.3). This Article was an attempt to allay fears that new member nations or small countries might not be able to send a commissioner in the future. To safeguard the principle of 'sovereign equality (equality of states)', Member States have agreed to the rule that every nation, whether large or small, sends only one member.

Next, we consider the status of the President of the European Commission and the problems involving the 'collegiality' of the European Commission. As the role of the President of the European Commission was not defined in the Treaty of Amsterdam clearly, for the Treaty of Nice it was decided to define and increase the President's powers.[38] The 'collegiality' of the European Commission is derived from its dependence on the President's individual authority. He decides on the allocation of portfolios and may reassign responsibilities. Some important political problems may arise and these can be analysed further by considering the selection method of the commission in three separate phases.

Phase one: The appointment procedure for the President of the European Commission

In the first phase of the appointment procedure of the President, 'the Council, constituted by the head of the state or the government head of a Member State', recommend a Presidential candidate, the Council of Ministers recommend other Commissioners. When the Council reaches common agreement on a Presidential candidate, and the President revises the list of candidates, it may be adopted by QMV in the Council.

The forum which nominates the President of the Commission was changed to the EU Council, constituted by head of the state or the government head of a Member State under the Nice Treaty. This differs from the usual EU Council, as specified by The Treaty of Nice: 'The Council shall consist of a representative of each Member State at ministerial level and authorized to commit the government of that Member State' (Article 203, TEC). This Article was an attempt to allay fears that new member nations or small countries might not be able to send a commissioner in the future.

The method of determining the Commission's Presidential candidate was changed by the Nice Treaty from a unanimous vote system to the QMV system in the EU Council. This revision is the institutional mechanism for avoiding difficulties with Presidential selection which could be predicted to occur when the EU enlarged to twenty-seven member states, and it will apply from 1 January 2005.

Phases two and three: the appointment procedure of the other Commissioners and the European Parliament's democratic control of Commissioners

In the second phase, the Presidential candidate chosen by the Council receives the recognition of the European Parliament as a whole, which gives the new President increased democratic legitimacy.

Let us now turn to the actual responsibilities of each Member State once the next President has been nominated, a revision which has only recently been substantially confirmed. The President is required to mould the Commission into one team through strong political leadership. The appropriate assignment is allocated to the right person, and he or she is given the authority to manage their assignment effectively.

In the third phase, the European Parliament assesses and recognizes the new Commission as a whole, and exercises prior democratic control over the Commissioners. Although each Commissioner receives conditional support from the Council, it is important that the President maintains the right to force individual commissioners to resign (in exceptional circumstances). This reform is intended to avoid a repeat of the mass resignation of the Santer Commission, when it was impossible to force individual Commissioners to resign. The Nice Treaty reforms can be interpreted as strengthening the status of the European Commission itself.[39]

Weighting of votes in the EC Council: vote distribution among Member States

The Nice Treaty provides for a change in the weighting of votes from 1 January 2005 and the revision of the EU Council is as follows. The appointment procedure for the director, and the vice-director of the EU Council's Secretariat, was revised from a unanimity vote system to a QMV system. The QMV system is the procedure by which the weighted distribution of votes awarded to each Member State is decided. A draft is then approved through the support of a fixed proportion of the vote (about 71 per cent).

The problems caused by incorporating both vote distribution and QMV in the decision-making process are important pending questions for the EU.

Should a new treaty prescribe that the majority in any vote be defined as containing a large number of Member States or not? This was precisely the question asked by several small and medium-sized states.

When vote-weighting is redistributed, should existing Member States be allowed to maintain their power and influence? The other question worthy of examination at this point is: how can the vote distribution awarded to smaller new members avoid the problem of appearing too small, while still remaining representative?

The Revision of the Nice Treaty brought about the enlargement to twenty-seven Member States, and the compromises between Member States were finally reached. The EU enlargement protocol changed the vote weighting of the fifteen Member States as illustrated in Table 3.2.

The Nice European Council was faced with the following dilemmas. As medium-sized and small countries requested, should a new treaty prescribe that the majority in any vote should always contain many Member States or not? What is the appropriate scale for preventing a small number in QMV? When the vote-weighting is redistributed, should the strength of existing Member States be maintained?

Let us now consider the division of votes in the EU Council in the EU-15, or the EU-16–26 and the EU-27 Member State scenarios.

Table 3.2 The EU-15 (after 1 January 2005)

Member State	Council- weighted votes (%)	EP seats	ECOSOC	Committee of regions	Commis- sion	Population (millions) (%)
Germany	29 (12.2)	99	24	24	1	82,04 (21.9)
UK	29 (12.2)	72	24	24	1	59,25 (15.8)
France	29 (12.2)	72	24	24	1	58,97 (15.7)
Italy	29 (12.2)	72	24	24	1	57,61 (15.3)
Spain	27 (11.4)	50	21	21	1	39,39 (10.5)
The Netherlands	13 (5.5)	25	12	12	1	15,76 (4.2)
Greece	12 (5.1)	22	12	12	1	10,53 (2.1)
Belgium	12 (5.1)	22	12	12	1	10,21 (2.7)
Portugal	12 (5.1)	22	12	12	1	9,98 (2.7)
Sweden	10 (4.2)	18	12	12	1	8,85 (2.4)
Austria	10 (4.2)	17	12	12	1	8,08 (2.2)
Denmark	7 (3)	13	9	9	1	5,31 (1.4)
Finland	7 (3)	13	9	9	1	5,16 (1.4)
Ireland	7 (3)	12	9	9	1	3,74 (1)
Luxembourg	4 (1.7)	6	6	6	1	0,43 (0.1)
Total	237 (100)	430	344	344	15	375,29 (100)
Qualified majority	169 (71.3)					(62)
Blocking minority	69 (29.7)					(38)

Source: Protocol on the enlargement of the European Union, Article 3, 4,1.4.2, OJ C 80/51,60/52.10.3.2001.

The EU-15, EU-16–26 and EU-27 (after 1 January 2005)

Should the votes of the candidate countries soon to be affiliated be added to those of the existing fifteen Member States? In which case, how should the votes be distributed to take into account the differing populations of the new Member States?

Should the smaller new members be allotted an over-representative number of votes in order to avoid the problem of their number of votes appearing excessively small? Where is a balance to be found?

The number of votes required for a majority under QMV will rise from 169 out of 237 (EU-15) to 255 out of 345 (EU-27). By 2005, when only a handful of candidate countries will have completed affiliation, the 'Declaration – the qualified majority threshold and the number of votes for a blocking minority in an enlarged Union' will have the force of law. From that time on, the vote-weighting will change whenever a new Member State joins.

There are three conditions that must be fulfilled under the QMV system in the Council, when the number of Member States reaches 27.

Scenarios involving more than EU-15 *(after 1 January 2005)*

1   169 out of 237 votes (71.3 per cent: EU-15); 256 out of 345 votes (73.9
     per cent: EU-27).
     Some countries with smaller populations and therefore very small
     numbers of votes would like to see this changed to a straight percent-
     age figure of 73.9 per cent to allow them slightly greater representa-
     tion.
2   A majority of Member States in favour.
     The Council will have to decide whether this will take the form of a
     simple majority or a two-thirds majority.
3   62 per cent of the overall population of the EU in support. Ninety-one
     votes will therefore be required for a blocking minority of the poten-
     tial twenty-seven member States.

If the EU grows as large as twenty-seven Member States, the EU Council
will then adopt a European Commission proposal whereby at least 62 per
cent of the EU population, a simple majority of Member States and more
than 258 (73.9 per cent) votes in support will be necessary for QMV.

The increased scope of QMV in the EU Council

Enlargement presents problems for the applicability of QMV. Although
there are several policy areas with flexible time limits or exception provision, in the future they will be absorbed into a majority system (as
opposed to the present unanimity system) divided into forty separate
policy and institutional areas. As part of the general shift in decision-
making in the Council from unanimity to majority voting, QMV will be
applied to about 90 per cent of all decision-making.

     Previously, vote distribution was basically decided according to the
population of Member States, under the Council's QMV system. This was
good news for states with large populations such as Germany but bad news
for the least populous states such as Luxembourg.

     However, the new QMV procedure with its three distinct conditions
should provide a system of checks and balances which will help the
smaller states to increase their representation and, at the same time, allow
the larger states to maintain their authority.

     Furthermore, it will also have the advantage of speeding up decision-
making because there will be much less chance of minority blocking and
no resorting to the use of votes.

     The QMV system is used to decide the appointment of the President
and the Commissioners of the European Commission, as well as Commun-

Table 3.3 The EU-27 (after 1 January 2005)

Member State	Council-weighted votes (%)	EP seats	ECOSOC	Committee of regions	Commis-sion	Population (millions) (%)
Germany	29	99	24	24	1	82,04 (17.1)
U.K.	29	72	24	24	1	57,61 (12.0)
France	29	72	24	24	1	59,25 (12.3)
Italy	29	72	24	24	1	58,97 (12.3)
Spain	27	50	21	21	1	39,39 (8.2)
Poland	27	50	21	21	1	38,67 (8.0)
Romania	14	33	15	15	1	22,49 (4.7)
The Netherlands	13	25	12	12	1	15,76 (3.3)
Greece	12	22	12	12	1	9,98 (2.1)
Czech Republic	12	20	12	12	1	10,29 (2.1)
Belgium	12	22	12	12	1	10,02 (2.1)
Hungary	12	20	12	12	1	10,09 (2.1)
Portugal	12	22	12	12	1	9,98 (2.1)
Sweden	10	18	12	12	1	8,85 (1.8)
Bulgaria	10	17	12	12	1	8,23 (1.7)
Austria	10	17	12	12	1	8,08 (1.7)
Slovakia	7	13	9	9	1	5,98 (1.1)
Denmark	7	13	9	9	1	5,31 (1.1)
Finland	7	13	9	9	1	5,16 (1.1)
Ireland	7	12	9	9	1	3,74 (0.8)
Lithuania	7	12	9	9	1	3,70 (0.8)
Latvia	4	8	7	7	1	2,44 (0.5)
Slovenia	4	7	7	7	1	1,98 (0.4)
Estonia	4	6	7	7	1	1,45 (0.3)
Cyprus	4	6	6	6	1	0,75 (0.2)
Luxembourg	4	6	6	6	1	0,43 (0.1)
Malta	3	5	5	5	1	0,38 (0.1)
Total	345	732	344	344	27	481,179 (100)
Qualified majority	255 (73.9)					(62)
Blocking minority	91 (26)					(38)

Source: Declarations adopted by the Conference, Declaration 20–21, OJC80/77, 10.3.2001, pp. 81–4. europa.eu.int/comm./enlargement *Agence Europe* 23/12/2000, 21/12/2000.

ity Policies on refugees, services, trade, intellectual property rights, structural funds and the environment. However, in the fields of social policy and the taxation system, the application of a unanimity system will still be maintained. The QMV system in the Council might be separated from the co-decision procedure with the European Parliament.

Governance of the European Union after Nice

*Democracy and governance in the EU: spatial/time governance in
European policy process*

Although many EU policies affect society and the working life of a citizen
directly, EU citizens are powerless to gain access to the policy processes of
the EU. The EU has propelled European integration efficiently, with
many of its institutions outside of the control of average citizens. However,
this elite-oriented decision-making process has proved a highly effective
method of instigating and carrying out policy.

Nevertheless, success with internal market integration and economic
growth has supplied the EU with some legitimacy. However, 'democratic
deficit' in the EU was regarded as an important problem which the Treaty
of Nice had to address.

The necessity for 'participating democracy', as opposed to 'representative democracy', became even more apparent during the world economic
depression of the 1990s, when large corporations were able to exert
undue influence in European governmental decision-making, through
the use of pressure groups.

According to Arend Lijphart, democracy can be classified into two
types: 'majoritarian democracy' (the Westminister Model) and 'consensus
democracy' (the Nagata-cho Model in Japanese Government).[40] His analysis suggested that the majoritarian democracy in the UK is effective if the
constituent is fundamentally a homogeneous target. Under majoritarian
democracy, if a minority group always remains a minority and therefore
remains weak, it could be said that the legitimacy of the system is spoiled.
Consensus democracy seems to apply to the continental countries in
Europe, and is more suitable for plural societies. Since composition units
are heterogeneous in this example, veto power can be granted to minority
groups.

Once consensus democracy is adopted, agreement must be thought of
as very important, otherwise the system will collapse. So, after the Luxembourg compromise, the unanimity system was adopted, which meant that
whenever a certain Member State had 'a vital interest', the use of veto was
acceptable in the Council's decision-making processes. However, under
the 'weighting of votes' system introduced by the Nice Treaty, if 73.4 per
cent of votes are obtained at the Council, the draft can be approved. In
other words, the number of votes required to form a blocking minority in
the EU-27 will be a maximum of 26 per cent of the total.

To give an example, if the diversity and heterogeneity in the system are
increased by EU enlargement, then it could be said that the institutionalization of 'deliberate democracy'[41] which repeats a prudent debate among

the governments of various levels, becomes indispensable, like the 'principle of subsidiarity'. However, if each country is allowed to continue its power of veto, in connection with an increase of new Member States, the time and cost of decision-making may increase sharply, and there is the possibility that the EU may lapse into malfunction. In this way, the Nice Treaty reforms reduced the scope of the unanimity system, and the new conditions for the weighting of votes system relax.

Furthermore, it was necessary to relax the easing of application conditions for the practical use of opt-out (inapplicability), otherwise known as 'enhanced cooperation'. Germany, the Belgian government and the Green Party in the European Parliament insisted that it should abolish unanimity and build a federal system. However, the UK showed unwillingness to cooperate in the field of social security, and preferred the continuation of the veto.

Although the trend away from unanimity towards QMV does not seriously affect issues such as the harmonization of a social security system, the UK still exercised its opt-out and refused to join the Social Charter[42] of the EU.

The UK also strongly resisted expanding QMV to the taxation system because its corporation tax rate was lower than in the continental countries, and postponed making a decision to opt in or out for another five years. It was the opinion of the UK representative that France also wanted to continue the veto in relation to agricultural policy, and had resisted to the last in the fields of service trade and intellectual property rights.

Germany and France, who experienced large influxes of refugees and had high immigration rates, reacted negatively to using QMV for decision-making relating to the refugee problem. Germany attached the condition of being able to unanimously decide on moving to QMV and, in the end, agreement was reached. France and other countries with strong agricultural economies are anxious about the possibility that the current agricultural subsidies will be cut, due to the necessity for a large allocation of resources to be set aside for the new applicant states' agricultural needs. The present Member States that receive generous community development funds, such as Italy and Spain, are also apprehensive that financial support from the EU will be reduced due to enlargement. On the one hand, Germany expects that EU enlargement could lead to an expansion in the domestic industrial product market, but on the other hand, Germany was anxious about the following problems which might occur as a result of increases in immigration and rises in the number of asylum seekers:

- the effect on the labour market,
- increases in social security costs,
- the possibility of rising crime levels.

The Netherlands, Denmark and other northern European countries were anxious about the East European countries where environmental policy has been conspicuously delayed.

The fifth expansion and institutional reform of the EU: 'enhanced cooperation' provided by the Treaty of Nice

Increasing the number of Member States, 'quantitative expansion' will inevitably lead to problems of quality in proportion to the increased quantity. In regard to this, areas such as public identity and possible conflicts of loyalty (where citizens of EU countries may be uncertain how much allegiance to show to the EU and how much to show to their own Member State) need to be considered. Important differences exist between the present Member States and the newly affiliated countries, especially culturally, socially, and politico-economically. A large economic gap may lead to a 'qualitative change' in European integration. That is, the enlargement of the EU raises problems involving the gap of wealth and poverty in areas within the Union.

Consequently, the solidarity of integration will lose pace, or it may become difficult for all Member States to become integrated at the same speed.

Thus, institutional reform after the Nice Treaty will surely increase the need for a policy to correct these disparities, and an institutional effort by the EU to help to fix the existing structural problems of Central and Eastern European countries, but the problem of 'differences' is by no means unique within the EU. The preamble of the Treaty of Rome, in 1957, comes full circle with 'the differences existing between the various regions and the backwardness of the less favoured regions'. In order to implement a policy which promotes a consistent employment policy within the Union, including the movement of the labour force, the European Social Fund and the European Development Fund were established.

This problem of a 'gap' between established and new EU members has been in evidence at every EU enlargement: the United Kingdom, Denmark and Ireland in 1973, Greece in 1981 and Spain and Portugal in 1985. The need for a policy to correct these 'regional gaps' became an important issue for the EC. In the Single European Act in 1986, the concept of 'cohesion' which attempts to resolve complaints and aims at economical union appeared.

As far as the most recent set of applications (the fourth expansion which affiliated Austria, Finland and Sweden in 1995) is concerned, the Treaty of Amsterdam states: 'the Community shall aim at reducing disparities between the levels of development of the various regions.' Article 158, TEC, was provided for in the treaty as there had been a consistent weakness of resolve surrounding these issues. The Treaty of Nice hardly alters this situation at all. The only alteration is in Article 159 (TEC), where the third paragraph is replaced by 'in accordance with the procedure referred to in Article 251 and after consulting the Economic and Social Committee and the Committee of the Regions' from 'a unanimity system' of the Council.

However, in fact, as an intergovernmentalist has pointed out, Council members fight over distribution of subsidies between the Member States, and they regard a structural policy as the area where each Member State protects the economic interests of its own country. Although the profits guidance side of a structural policy cannot be denied, it is also an error that can only be corrected by the expectation and economic interests of Member States and local governments.

In order to advance European integration in the long run, it is necessary to correct the structure where such a gap between areas exists. 'Closer cooperation', introduced by the Treaty of Amsterdam, is a very important instrument towards this end. 'Enhanced cooperation' provided by the Nice Treaty, can be seen to have similar aims.[43] The mechanism for 'closer cooperation' is 'to enable certain Member States to work together, in the interests of the Union, when not all of the Member States wanted to or could do so at that point, on the understanding that they would be free to join the group at a later date', under the Amsterdam Treaty.[44] However, severe conditions were imposed on the actual application of this mechanism.

The conditions of the 1995 application were eased in the Nice Treaty. 'Multi-speed' European integration was advanced by easing the Conditions of 'enhanced cooperation'. This means that the EU institutionalized not only 'spatial' governance but the governance of 'time' in the European integration process. The Treaty of Nice eases the path of affiliation by stating that integration can take place if eight nations agree, thus abolishing the veto power of any nations who disagree.

Transformation of European governance

In which ways should European integration change in relation to the globalization of the systems and structures affecting Europe? Economic globalization has led to many problems which cannot be managed or solved within the nation-state. The EU was conceived as a means to cope with such problems and has been developed in accordance with this concept. As far as 'the depths' are concerned, global political and economical structure which surround Europe enhance the European integration processes. Institutional reforms of the EU are positioned as tools for controlling globalization and political enlargement of the EU.

The idea which regards the EU as a complicated governance system, was originally treated as abstract political theory by EU researchers at first. However, at present, the European Commission itself is moving towards an understanding of the EU as a kind of governance system. Based on this, the European Commission proposed the institutional reforms presented in *European Governance: A White Paper*.

European integration developed policies centring on deregulation, aiming at the construction of an internal market towards the end of the 1980s. While this was the strategy of neoliberal globalization, it was also the process for 're-regulation' at the EU level. The application of the 'mutual recognition' principle for the regulations of each country, and the abolition of non-tariff barriers in economic activities, demanded that EU social and regional policies should be attended to. These policies work towards balancing and correcting the intensified competition produced by an internal market.

There was an acquisition of political power by social democratic political parties towards the end of the 1990s. This was in sympathy with the so-called 'Third Way' of the Blair government in the UK, and the 'new centrist' German government of Gerhard Schröder. The EU has followed the lead of these countries and developed a new integrated policy style for supply-side policies. The European Commission also tried to implement 'an active supply-side policy', and aimed to strengthen competition in the international market. It is a new interventionist principle, differing from monetarism and Keynesian principles, which aims at 'harmony with a macro economic policy and an active employment policy'[45] and has the same policy directivity as a 'European social model'.

Blair's 'Third Way' route was strongly influenced by the thought of the sociologist Anthony Giddens. The Third Way views the following as important: pluralism, equality, the protection of the weak, the freedom to be independent, that rights are accompanied by responsibilities, democratic authority and philosophical conservatism. There is a close resemblance between the supply-side policies of the European Commission and the route these social democratic political parties have followed. What do these revisions mean in practice?

The countries of the EU have differing political and administrative systems (typically involving multi-level government) embodying distinctive cultures and diverse sets of values. Harmonization of countries with such different outlooks is one of the most pressing problems facing the EU at present. This diversity increases further with each EU enlargement so the

EU should be aiming at correcting the gap between 'areas', followed by a correction of the gap between 'states'. Therefore, an analytic object should preside over the conflict of common interest and individual interest through subnational actors. How can the EU, or a Member State's government, coordinate and adjust the individual interest of actors covering these two (or more) levels?

Conventionally, in European integration theories, there is a confrontation between 'supranationalist' and 'intergovernmentalist' approaches, or between 'federalist' and 'confederalist' approaches. However, this confrontational thinking has been overcome and European governance, which was once considered as 'a mixed system' is now more likely to be viewed as constituting a single 'European Regime' or 'Euro-polity'.

The primary feature of European governance is that it functions as if the governance mechanism of the EU's many institutions and Member States' organizations are closely connected, not only in policy formation processes but also in the implementation processes, as if it were one regime. With regard to the policy process of the EU, coordination and cooperation with the EU international administration and Member State's administration have worked successfully for many years. The EU has become much more than a mere functional institutional framework, and has transformed itself into 'the thing more than regime of successful intergovernmental cooperation', tending towards an advanced 'Euro-polity'. Such a multi-level governance theory has also distanced itself from the theoretical confrontation between neo-functionalism and 'liberal governmentalism', as well as 'the constructivism' or the 'social constructionism' approach. That is, the governance approach does not assume the existence of a certain central authority; rather, the 'partnership' between Member States and EU institutions must be strengthened by more cooperative relations between these two actors in collusion with the actual citizenries of the EU nations themselves.

The actors which participate in governance are not found exclusively in governmental agencies, but are also present in private enterprises, NGOs, private sector organizations, or even individuals. The action norm of private actors differ from the rule defined by a Member State. To enable institutionalization, the EU has now allowed external, private sector actors to take part in the planning processes of European public policy processes by shifting to a system of rule from the community level.

'Multi-level governance' does not only mean the multi-layering of administration, but also the reconstruction of an administration system according to a certain common purpose. The plural nature of actors, and the policy processes pushed forward by non-hierarchical participation, are thought to be important network governance.

These customs, such as principles concerning relations between Member States and the EU, along with treaties, rules and regulations, directives, decisions, opinions and advice, do not simply function as rules but, more importantly, act as cultural norms based essentially on respect for the common good.

The European governance White Paper produced by the European Commission points out that it is regulations, procedures and customs, together, that affect the enforcement methods of policies at the EU level. By encouraging cooperation between the public sector, the private sector and private citizens, 'democratic deficit' is compensated for in the political processes of the EU and the legitimacy of EU governance can therefore be considered as being significantly enhanced.

The EU today derives its legitimacy from 'involvement' of the public, as an EU White Paper on the subject of governance pointed out: the foundation of this 'involvement' is 'participation'.

In short, it is necessary to institutionally unite the EU administration system and a Member Nation's administration system, and to transfigure European governance into a strong participatory democratic system, in which actors at various levels take part in EU policy-making with a strong sense of cooperation. This cooperation crosses the border of the public and private sectors, simultaneously and pluralistically, and at the multi-layer policy formation or implementation stages.

The political theory and statements which were based on abstraction from reality, will allow the EU to design and build a new system, and act as an example in the reality of the political world of the governance approach to European integration.

Conclusion: how to strengthen the legitimacy of European governance

On 15 December 2001, the Heads of State and Government of the EU approved the Laeken Declaration,[46] named after the Belgian chateau where the summit took place. The declaration set the agenda for discussions to be conducted by an advisory convention of parliamentarians and government representatives in March 2002. The Convention on the Future of Europe will make proposals for an overhaul of the treaties on European Union and the adoption of a possible European constitution. The Nice European Council concluded on a hopeful note with the national leaders expressing messages of mutual compromise.

The following were all reformed by the Treaty of Nice:

1   the size and composition of the European Commission,
2   the weighting of QMV in the Council,
3   the extension of QMV,
4   the move to co-decision,
5   'enhanced cooperation'.

European Union leaders have set out on the path of European integration, opening an intensive debate on reform of European Governance after Nice. On the question of how to advance integration, and interlocked with the idea of 'enhanced cooperation', the timing and pace of future integrations will be at the discretion of the Commission rather than the individual Member States.

Although this might appear to be relatively unimportant, it is important because it will have an influence on national sovereignty in the long run, and provide the dynamism that promotes European integration by speeding up decision-making using QMV in the Council.

The European Union has taken many measures to keep the public informed. While information needs to be targeted to special groups and easily understood by them, it is also true that the general public need to become more open-minded and eager for information, and willing to make the necessary effort.

In the governance website (http://europa.eu.int/comm/governance/index.htm) on the Nice Treaty set up by the European Commission, active arguments on the European-citizen level on 'the future of Europe' were developed before 31 March 2002. The European Council in Laeken decided that intensive examination using a specialist team should be carried out from 28 February 2002. The purpose of this reform is not only to improve the European governance for EU enlargement, but also to eradicate the criticism that European integration is controlled by an elite, and to clarify the justification for the EU's existence.

The EU can only claim to have real significance if it is oriented towards a 'citizen's Europe', and transparency is therefore crucial. The term 'transparency' can be interpreted as 'open access to information'; there are not many organizations or governments as open as the European institutions.

The EU believes that greater transparency and openness will close the gap between the European institutions and ordinary citizens. For example, the European Commission has taken a number of steps to improve the public's access to its documents. Its approach is based on the belief that the citizen's access to documents should only be constrained by the need to protect certain public and private interests.

As a further example, the Council is also making strong efforts to make more of its work accessible to the citizens, and votes on legislative matters, interpretations are now automatically made public. The public has also been given some rights of access to Council Documents and some Council discussions that are transmitted audio-visually.

The following methods are a prescription for strengthening European governance.

1   It is necessary to raise the transparency and accountability of European governance, and the enhancing management system for 'multi-level network governance'. *European Governance: A White Paper*, has given five principles of good governance: (i) openness, (ii) participation, (iii) accountability, (iv) effectiveness and (v) coherence. 'The application of these five principles reinforces those of proportionality and subsidiarity.' These principles must be respected by the European institutions and the Member State's governments.

2   The EU must continue to strengthen the cooperation between the European Parliament and the national parliaments, as well as administrative interaction through the Agencies or the Committees governance[47] ('Commitology') in the EU.

3   In order to secure the safety of the citizenry, to develop a horizontal cooperative relationship between the public and private sector, including the NGOs.

It is important that European citizens feel that they control and manage the EU system themselves. The European Commission must work hard to make their citizens participate consciously in European policy processes through 'e-government' and/or 'e-governance'. However, the 'e-Europe' may not be sufficient by itself to build a bridge to the European citizen. It will be imperative to devote time to the debate about the relationship between the information society and European democratic governance, if European Union is going to become the powerful, relevant and popular body that twenty-first century Europe will need.

Notes

1   http://europa.eu.int/comm/nice_treaty/index_en.htm, European Commission, 7GEN.REP.EU 2001, point 1, 4, pp. 7–8.
2   Taylor, Simon, (2000) *European Voice*, 14–20, December, 16, 46, 2.
3   For example, see Jean-Louis Bourlanges (2000) *Le Monde*, 13 December. (2001) *Le Monde* 8 May.
4   The European Commission (2001) 'White Paper on European Governance', COM (2001) 482 final, 25 July.
5   For example, see Ben Rosamond (2000) *Theories of European Integration*, St.

Martin's Press. See Hellen Wallace (2000) 'The Institutional Setting', in Wallace and Wallace, *Decision-Making in the European Union*, fourth edn, Oxford University Press, pp. 71–7, 524–5.

6 Weiler, Joseph, H. H. (1991) 'The transformation of Europe', *The Yale Law Journal*, 100, 8, 2403–83.

7 Hoskyns, C. and Newman, M. (eds) (2000) *Democratizing the European Union*. Manchester: Manchester University Press.

8 Peters, B. Guy (1999) *Institutional Theory in Political Science*. The 'New Institutionalism', London: Routledge.

9 Ibid., pp. 19–20.

10 Moravcsik, Andrew (1993) 'Preferences and Power in the European Community: A Liberal Intergovernmental Approach', *Journal of Common Market Studies*, 31, 4, 437–524.

11 Peterson, John (1995) 'Decision-Making in the European Union: Towards a Framework for Analysis', *Journal of European Public Policy*, 2/1, 69–93.

12 Karlheing, N. and Wiener, A. (2000) *European Integration after Amsterdam, Institutional Dynamics and Prospects for Democracy*, Oxford University Press, pp. 244–45; Smith, Steve, (2001)'International theory and European Integration', in M. Kelstrup and M. Williams (eds) (2001) *International Relations Theory and Politics of European Integration*, Routledge, p. 45.

13 See Pierson, Paul (1998) 'The Path to European Integration: A Historical–Institutionalist Analysis, ' in Sandholtz, W. and Sweet, A. S. (eds) *European Integration and Supranational Governance*, Oxford University Press, p. 33.

14 See Thomas Christiansen, Knud Erik Jørgensen and Antie Wiener (eds) (2001) *The Social Construction of Europe*, Sage, pp. 1–19.

15 See Maruks Jachtenfuchs (2001) 'The Governance Approach to European Integration', *Journal of Common Market Studies*, 39, 2, 245–64; Marks, G., *et. al.*, (1996) *Governance in the European Union*, Sage.

16 UNU (United Nations University) (2001) *UNU Annual Report 2001*, p. 15.

17 Robert, Anne-Cecile (2001) 'QUE VIVE L'EUROPE: L'union maux à mots', *Le Monde Diplomatique*, 9, 8–9.

18 Ibid.

19 Rosenau, James N. (1992) 'Governance, Order and Change in World, Politics', in James N. Rosenau and E. O. Czempiel (eds), *Governance without Government*, Cambridge University Press.

20 Marks, Gary (1993) 'Structual Policy and Multilevel Governance in the EC,' in Alan Cafruny and Glenda Rosenthal (eds), *The State of the European Community*, 2, Boulder, CO: Lynne Rienner, 391–410.

21 Maruks Jachtenfuchs and Beate Kohler-Koch (eds) (1995) *Europäische Integration*, Opladen: Leake & Budrich.

22 See Gary Marks *et al.* (1996) 'European Integration from the 1990s: State-Centric vs. Multi-level Governance', *Journal of Common Market Studies*, 34, 3.

23 Kohler-Koch, Beate and Eising, R. (eds) (1999) *The Transformation of Governance in the European Union*, London, Routledge.

24 Commission on Global Governance (1995) *Our Global Neighborhood: The Report of the Commission on Global Governance*, Oxford: Oxford University Press.

25 Schmitter, Philippe, C. (2001) *Jean Monnet Working Paper*, 14/01, p. 6.

26 Bromley, Simon (2001) *Governing the European Union*, Sage.

27 Prodi, Romano (2000) 'Speech to the European Parliament on the European

Council of Nice', European Parliament, Strasbourg, 12 December, Doc.Npo.Speech/00/499. Prodi, Romano (2000) *Europe As I See It*, Polity Press.
28 European Commission (2001) *European Governance: A White Paper*, COM (2001) 428, final, Brussels, 2S July. European Commission presented the following report:'Report from the Commission on European Governance', COM (2002) 705 final, in December.
29 See Koji Fukuda (1992) *The Administrative Structure and Policy Processes in the European Communities*, Tokyo: Seibundo Publishers, pp. 23–49.
30 Koji Fukuda (2000) 'On the Resignation of the European Commission and European Parliamentary Control', *The Waseda Journal of Political Science and Economics*, 341, January, 233–63.
31 Scharpf, Fritz W. (1988) 'The Joint Decision Trap: Lessens from German Federalism and European Integration', *Public Administration*, 66, 239–78.
32 European Commission (1995) 'Completing the Internal Market', White Paper from the Commission to the European Council.
33 See Karlheinz Neunreither (1993) 'Subsidiarity as a Guiding Principle for European Community Activities', *Government and Opposition*, 28, 2, 207–8.
34 Koji Fukuda (1997) 'Federalism and the Principle of Subsidiarity in the European Union (2)', *Political Science Review*, 45, 59–79.
35 See J. Monar and W. Wessels (eds) (2001) *The European Union after the Treaty of Amsterdam*. London: Continuum.
36 See *Agence Europe*, 23/12/2000, 21/12/2000.
37 European Commission (1997) *Agenda 2000*, Supplement to Bulletin of the EU.
38 European Commission (2001) *European Governance: A White Paper*, COM (2001) 428, op. cit. 23–8.
39 Koji Fukuda (2001) 'Reforming the European Commission', *Doshisha University World Wide Business Review*, 2, 2, 15–17.
40 Lijphart, Arend (1984) *Democracies: Patterns of Majoritarian and Consensus Government in Twenty-One Countries*, Yale University Press, 3–6, 21–36.
41 Føllesdall, Andres (2000) 'Subsidiarity and Democratic Deliberation', in E. O. Eriksen and J. E. Fossum (eds), *Democracy in the European Union*, Routledge, pp. 85–110.
42 The European Commission adopted the preliminary draft of Community Charter of Fundamental Social Rights in 1989.
43 Yataganas, Xenophon, A. (2001) 'The Treaty of Nice: The Sharing of Power and the International Balance in the European Union. A Continental Perspective', Harvard, Jean Monnet Paper 01/01, Harvard Law School, 3 March, 49.
44 According to Alexander Stubb, there are three forms of flexibility in the Treaty of Amsterdam. '(a) enabling clauses, (b) case-by-case flexibility, and (c) predefined flexibility'. Stubb, A. 'Dealing with Flexibility in the IGC', in E. Best, Gray, M. and Stubb, A. (2000) *Rethinking the European Union*, European Institute of Public Administration, p. 148.
45 European Commission (1993) 'Growth, Competitiveness, Employment', White Paper, COM (93) 700 final, December 1993.
46 See *Appendix: Presidency Conclusions*, European Council meeting in Laeken 14 and 15 December 2001.
47 See Cristiansen, T. and Kirchner, E. (2000) *Committee Governance in the European Union*, Manchester: Manchester University Press.

4 Drafting the Charter of Fundamental Rights

Towards a new phase of EU democracy

Noriko Yasue

Introduction

On 18 December 2000, leaders of the EU Member States signed the Charter of Fundamental Rights at Nice where the Intergovernmental Conference (IGC) was held for amending the basic treaty.

How had the EC/EU treated fundamental rights from the 1957 Rome Treaty to 1997 Amsterdam Treaty? The protection of fundamental rights had not been considered as an aim of the Community or within the scope of tasks provided by basic treaties. Fundamental rights were only concerned within the conditions of a single labour market and economic integration, such as non-discrimination among EC workers or between males and females. However, through the decisions of the European Court of Justice (ECJ), the protection was enlarged from 'labour' (as an element of the market) to 'person'. And from the early 1990s, the EU started discussions to draft its own 'Charter of Fundamental Rights'.

Why is it necessary for the EU to have the Charter of Fundamental Rights despite the existence of the European Convention for the Protection of Human Rights and Fundamental Freedoms (ECHR) and the constitutions of each Member State? There are several objectives of the Charter, as presented in the documents from the institutions and persons which took part in the drafting process: to make the rights visible for the citizens, to prepare for judicial and police cooperation, the strategy for the next enlargement and, finally, to confirm the legitimacy of the EU towards further political integration.

This chapter will also focus on the drafting process of the Charter. A special body called the 'Convention' was established by the Cologne European Council in June 1999, and a unique process, never tried before, was undertaken. The Convention covered the members of the European Parliament and national parliaments as well as the representatives of the governments. In addition, this process was opened up to the citizens, and the representatives of civil society obtained the opportunity to give their opinions officially.

What are the significance and political effects of the Charter? At present, the Charter has no legally binding power, but it does have political influence, which contributes to reinforce the legitimacy for further EU integration. The Charter can also be regarded as a 'Bill of Rights of the twenty-first century', because it includes rights targeted at new technologies, rights to receive 'good administration' and so on.

Finally, what is the impact of the Charter and its drafting process? The challenging nature of the Charter drafting process aroused interest in considering a new stage of democracy at the EU level. This chapter explores new phenomena on EU democracy deduced from the Charter and its drafting process.

The history of the protection of fundamental rights in the EC/EU

In this section, I provide an overview of how fundamental rights were treated in the EC/EU before the adoption of the Charter. When the European Economic Community was established by the Treaty of Rome in 1957, the protection of fundamental rights was not the aim of the Community. Only a few provisions concerning fundamental rights were found in the field of market integration, such as non-discrimination on the grounds of nationality or gender and the freedom to conduct business.

In 1977, three main institutions of the Community (the European Parliament, the Commission, the Council of Ministers) adopted the 'Joint Declaration of Human Rights',[1] which confirmed a respect for human rights in each institution. This declaration was endorsed by the European Council in 1978 and became the standard for the protection of human rights at Community level.

In 1974, three years before the Joint Declaration, the German Constitutional Court of Justice examined the question of the precedence over the German Constitution of EC derivative law. The Court held that it was unwilling to accord precedence of Community law over parts of the German Constitution dealing with fundamental rights in the absence of a codified catalogue of fundamental rights at the Community level (Solange I).[2] However, after the adoption of the Joint Declaration, a number of decisions by the ECJ have referred to fundamental rights, and jurisprudence has accumulated. In 1986, the German Constitutional Court appreciated a series of ECJ decisions in the Solange II case.[3] This position was basically maintained by the German court before the ratification of the Maastricht Treaty in 1992.

The Single European Act (SEA), which came into force in 1987, provided for fundamental rights in its preamble. It stated that Member States 'work together to promote democracy on the basis of the fundamental rights recognized in the constitutions and laws of the Member States, in the Convention for protection of Human Rights. . . .'

In December 1989, Member States adopted the 'EC Social Charter' (Charter of the Fundamental Social Rights of Workers), which had no binding power at that time. In the previous year, the European Council affirmed the importance of the social dimension related to the Single Market, and the Commission requested the Economic and Social Committee to make a study of the Social Charter. Their conclusions were presented at the Madrid European Council in February 1989, and the draft Social Charter was adopted in June. Among Member States, only the UK refused to join the Social Charter. But, in 1997, when Tony Blair of the Labour Party became Prime Minister, the UK opted to join the Charter.

At Strasbourg in December 1989, the Social Charter was finally adopted in the form of the Declaration of Nations. The Community has to pay respect to the Charter, although contents of each provision are to be stipulated by the derivative law of the Community. In the same year, the European Parliament adopted the resolution which asked for the drafting of the Charter of Fundamental Rights.[4]

The Maastricht Treaty, adopted in 1992, explicitly provided the concept of fundamental rights in the body of the treaties. Article F(2) required the Union to respect fundamental rights as one of the general principles of Community law:

> the Union shall respect fundamental rights, as guaranteed by the European Convention for the Protection of Human Rights and Fundamental Freedoms signed in Rome on 4 November 1950 and as they result from the constitutional traditions common to the Member States, as general principles of Community law.

The Maastricht Treaty also introduced 'EU citizenship'.[5] This is not the same concept as the fundamental rights, because EU citizenship is given to only the nationals of the Member States. Its significance, however, is in the fact that the political rights of the citizens are established at the EU level.

There have always been suggestions that the Community itself should join the framework of the ECHR. In 1994, the Council of Ministers officially sought the opinion of the ECJ as to whether the Community was judicially competent for the accession to ECHR. The judgment of the ECJ was passed in 1996.[6] The Court's view was that the Community had no competence to participate in the ECHR under the present treaty, and it would be necessary to amend the basic treaty before the accession to

ECHR. Amending the treaty was not a troublesome obstacle, but some judges of the ECJ were unwilling to submit judicial decisions before the tribunal of the ECHR, to be constituted by many members from outside the EU, including former communist countries.

In the Treaty of Amsterdam, adopted in 1997, the protection of fundamental rights is provided as one of the principles of European Union. Article 6(1) of the EU treaty declares that the EU is founded on the principles of liberty, democracy, respect for human rights and fundamental freedoms, and the rule of law, principles which are common to the Member States. Also, it stipulates, under Article 7, concrete measures against the violation of fundamental rights. If a Member State is in serious and persistent breach of Article 6(1), competences including voting rights will be suspended. Furthermore, Article 13 of the EC treaty states:

> the Council, acting unanimously on a proposal from the Commission and after consulting the European Parliament, may take appropriate action to combat discrimination based on sex, racial or ethnic origin, religion or belief, disability, age or sexual orientation.

These articles were not considered to be applicable to the present Member States. However, in the spring of 2000, when an extreme right-wing party took power in Austria, these articles came into focus.

In the Treaty of Nice, signed in February 2000, the fruit of the negotiations at IGC, Article 7 of the EU treaty was reinforced. The European Parliament has competence to give accordance to the decision of the Council of Ministers. Therefore, each institution of the EU now has a responsibility to take necessary measures against violations of fundamental rights by the Member States.

Thus, the EU gradually committed to the protection of fundamental rights, and the demand for the drafting of the EU Charter of Fundamental Rights became dominant. In 1996, the Commission set up three 'Committees des Sages' concerning fundamental rights. One of these Committees, the Special Committee for Fundamental Rights, proposed to draft the Charter.[7] The first annual report of human rights prepared by the European Council came out for the year 1998–9,[8] and formally declared that the EU would launch a human rights policy. Moreover, from 1998 to 2000, the Social Action Program that confirmed the importance of social rights promoted the adoption of the Charter of Fundamental Rights. The Parliament adopted several resolutions, in which they demanded the creation of their own Charter of Fundamental Rights. In addition, the EU Ombudsman and NGOs firmly insisted on creating the Charter.

The aims of the Charter

This chapter describes the reasons why it is necessary for the EU to draft its own Charter of Fundamental Rights, even though all Member States are in the ECHR and have their own constitution providing fundamental rights.

The objectives of the Charter can be found in the documents and papers written by the institutions and the persons involved in the drafting process.

First, it was necessary to put together diverse forms of sources of law that the EC/EU has utilized for the protection of fundamental rights. We can find numerous documents using such expressions as 'visible rights for the citizens' repeatedly.[9] Most of the rights listed in the Charter are stipulated or confirmed by the constitutions of Member States, derivative EU law, case law, several international conventions and so on. However, the ways of using these sources of law in the EC/EU treaties has been not only inconsistent but also confused.[10] For the citizens, it seems to be very obscure. The fundamental rights must be presented in a clear manner, even if the institutions of the EU can protect them without the Charter.

Second, the EU has to consider and prepare for the implementation of the judicial and home affairs policy. Through the Treaty of Amsterdam, the policies related to immigration and the movements of persons, as well as judicial and police cooperation, were reinforced. In these policy areas, it is easy to imagine that the EC/EU will have to make a commitment on human rights and privacy. These policies have also been criticized based on accusations that the democratic control of the European Parliament and judicial control of the ECJ are not sufficient, together with the common security and foreign policy. In particular, the Schengen Information System, introduced to prevent and investigate cross-border crimes based on the Schengen Convention, has been criticized by the ECHR on the grounds that it lacked adequate measures for the protection of personal data. With the Treaty of Amsterdam, the Schengen Convention was added to the basic treaty. Therefore, the EU institutions are increasingly obliged to protect fundamental rights, although the EU data protection directive is now in force.

Third, the Charter is expected to play a significant role in the next phase of enlargement. The EU is now negotiating with twelve candidate states, including ten mid-European and east European countries, and two Mediterranean countries. In this fifth enlargement, countries with a lot of unstable factors will be gaining EU membership. Before starting the negotiations, the EU required the candidate states to meet a series of conditions, namely the 'Copenhagen Criteria', including establishment of democratic political systems, observance of fundamental rights and protection of minority rights. As the EU demands the candidate states meet these criteria, the EU itself has to show clearly the standards under which its own institutions operate.

Finally, it is very important to confirm the political and spiritual legitimacy to go forward with political integration. In the Committee of Constitutional Affairs of the European Parliament,[11] discussion is now going on about the EU Constitution for further political integration. Although this argument did not become the main view of other EU institutions, some groups would like to put the Charter of Fundamental Rights in the first part of the EU Constitution. At the very least, the Charter is expected to be a symbol of legitimacy for further European integration.

The drafting process of the Charter

The Drafting body called the 'Convention'

The procedure adopted for the drafting process was unique and had significant meaning. Since 1990, several institutions, organizations and political parties have demanded that the EU create its own Charter of Fundamental Rights. When Germany became the presidential state of the European Council in 1999, Joschka Fischer, the German minister of Foreign Affairs, placed the EU Charter of Fundamental Rights as one of the most important issues in the Presidential Program titled *Europe's Path into the 21st Century*. The European Council, held in June 1999 at Cologne, finally decided to draft the Charter.[12] As explained above (p. 68), from the 1970s, the German Constitutional Court had paid much attention to the protection of fundamental rights in the EC/EU. Fischer proposed a unique measure for the drafting of the Charter.

In October 1999, the drafting body was established at Tampere, Finland.[13] Finland is the home country of Mr Soderman, the EU Ombudsman, who had enthusiastically attempted to promote the democratic nature of the Community and to realize citizen's rights based on the principle of transparency. The efforts of these two Member States, Germany and Finland, had a significant influence on propelling the drafting process.

In February 2000, the drafting body named itself the 'Convention' (until then, called 'Enceinte'). The Convention constituted a variety of members: fifteen members from the representatives of the heads of states or governments, one from the European Commission (Commissioner of Justice and Home Affairs), sixteen from the European Parliament and thirty from the national parliaments. The membership is noteworthy in that it was very unusual, even epoch-making, to accept members of national parliaments at the first stage of drafting formal documents in the EU.[14]

Among the members of the Convention, Roman Herzog, who had been the vice-president of Germany and also the judge of the German Constitutional Court, was elected as chairperson. Besides the formal members, two members from the ECJ and two from the Council of Europe (one from the ECHR) participated in the Convention as observers. And the EU Ombudsman, the Economic and Social Committee[15] and the Committee of Region[16] were required to express consulting opinions during the drafting process.

Furthermore, the Convention posted the draft Charter on the Internet and collected opinions from citizens for a limited period. Various types of NGOs in civil society gained the opportunity to officially announce their opinions on the draft charter.

The role of the national parliaments and EU democracy

Why did members of the national parliaments succeed in joining the drafting process? The answer can be found in the recent development of parliamentary cooperation in the EU.

During the 1990s, the national parliaments of the Member States had strongly demanded an opportunity to participate in the policy-making process and their activities had achieved some results in the Treaty of Amsterdam.[17]

The declaration, annexed to the Maastricht Treaty, was the first official document that proclaimed the importance of the role of the national parliaments in the EU. In deepening the economic and political integration in Europe, the national parliaments were anxious about losing the traditional competence of control over governments and weakening law-making power. The power attributed to the national parliaments on EU policy varies among the countries. In Germany, the UK and Denmark, parliaments have sufficient power to control their governments. However, other national parliaments have limited power, even if they also have a special committee for European issues.

In France, the constitutional amendment of 1992 for ratifying the Maastricht Treaty – délégations pour les Communautés Européennes (the Parliamentary Delegations of European Affairs) – increased their competence. The French government has gradually recognized that parliamentary discussions on European matters are sometimes helpful for protecting the national interest during bargaining at the Council of Ministers in the EU.

The most serious problem for the parliaments was the 'time limit'. The national parliaments could start their discussions only after learning that some important matters had been set on the agenda of the Council. It was too late for the national parliaments to exercise influence on the government, because the EU had already completed their decision process. Such cases frequently occurred, even before parliaments started discussions.

At the insistence of the national parliaments, the protocol annexed to the Treaty of Amsterdam confirmed that national parliaments should have time available for deliberation of the draft EC law. The EU also needed to have this provision in order to assure the rapid and smooth implementation of the EC laws in the Member States with the cooperation of national parliaments.

The Treaty of Amsterdam, in its annexed protocol, approved the 'Conférence des Organs Spécialisés dans Affaires Communautaires' (COSAC, Conference of European Affairs Committees) to present their opinions officially.[18] COSAC, consisted of ninety members from parliaments of Member States and six members from the European Parliament, was established in 1989. The need to promote cooperation between the two levels of parliaments has been insisted upon by the European Parliament from early in its history. However, recently, the national parliaments have been gradually taking the initiative for this collaboration. The two levels of parliaments act in cooperation in some ways, but at the same time they are rivals and compete for leadership in the development of EU democracy.

Before the Treaty of Amsterdam, COSAC had concluded and presented many statements, for example, on institutional reform, such as the form of 'final document'. Moreover, according to the protocol annexed to the Treaty of Amsterdam, COSAC can present opinions officially under the term 'contributions'. Article 4 of the Protocol on the role of national parliaments in the European Union stipulates that COSAC

> may make any contribution it deems appropriate for the attention of the institutions of the European Union, in particular on the basis of draft legal texts which representatives of governments of the Member States may decide by common accord to forward to it.

And Article 6 provides that COSAC may address to the EU institutions 'any contribution which it deems appropriate on the legislative activities of the Union, notably in relation to the application of the principle of subsidiarity, the area of freedom, security and justice as well as questions regarding fundamental rights.'

During the negotiation of the treaty amendment by the IGC, national parliaments were discussing simultaneously on the same issue as the IGC. From this experience, many governments learned that it was important to hear the voices of national parliaments, because, without their support, any treaty would not be ratified. However, national parliaments were not allowed to participate in the negotiation themselves.

In drafting the Charter of Fundamental Rights, members of the national parliaments formally participated with the members of the Parliament.

Therefore, cooperation between the two levels of parliaments was realized. Needless to say, active discussions arose in each national parliament.[19]

The involvement of civil society

It was epoch-making for the EU to positively involve civil society in the Charter drafting process. The Convention sought the views of NGOs and other representatives of civil society. They set up a Charter website and released copious documentation submitted to the body. Prior to autumn 2000, dozens of opinions were formally presented by various groups. Their opinions were available to all citizens on the Internet so that the principle of transparency was followed.

According to the EU Ombudsman, the principle of transparency includes the following concepts:[20]

a   the process by which decisions are made should be understandable,
b   the decisions themselves should be reasoned,
c   as far as possible, the information on which reasons are based should be available to the public, and
d   meetings by public bodies deciding on matters that will have direct impact on the citizens should be open and public, so that citizens can follow them and listen to the arguments.

Obviously, the Charter drafting process was a test case for realizing the transparency principle. Mobilization of the civil society in drafting the legal text became common in the domain of the international environmental treaties after the Earth Summit in Rio, 1992. This, then, was the first time the EU utilized such a method in creating an official text, even though it has no binding power.

However, we must note that the process taken for drafting the Charter can only be accomplished under very limited conditions. The protection of fundamental rights was more of a question of philosophy and, as such, has few conflicts with the national interest. Therefore, it is not appropriate to conclude that the process taken for drafting the Charter is applicable to every policy domain in the EU.

On 2 October, 2000, the Convention unanimously adopted the draft Charter and presented it to the European Council. The European Council at Biaritz, France, approved the Charter and submitted it to the European Parliament and the Commission. The former approved it on 14 November, and the latter on 6 December. Finally, the Charter was proclaimed on 7 December.

The nature of the Charter of Fundamental Rights

Introducing all of the rights enumerated in the Charter is beyond the intention of this chapter; instead it aims to clarify the distinctive nature as well as the judicial and political effects of the Charter.

Characteristics of the Charter

The Charter does not necessarily confer new rights on citizens. Each right or freedom is taken from precursor texts, such as the EC/EU treaty, EC derivative laws, other charters, conventions or jurisprudence of the ECHR, and so on. The Charter brought together the results of all the efforts previously made for protecting fundamental rights.

Certainly, there is some criticism that the Charter appears to be a 'show case' of rights.[21] However, as already examined above (pp. 71–72), one of the main reasons to draft the Charter is to make these rights visible to citizens. Above all, rights deriving from the jurisprudence of the ECJ and the ECHR had been less visible to citizens.

There are certain rights that raise new issues of fundamental rights, for example, the right relating to biotechnology (prohibition of human cloning) and the protection of personal data. These provisions seek to respond to the challenges of new technologies in the twenty-first century.

The Charter is also innovative in including economic and social fundamental rights as well as the more traditional civil and political rights. In addition, it lays new ground in protecting and assuring cultural diversity as a fundamental right. This provision is very important when the EU considers the next enlargement to the mid-European and eastern European countries, most of which have ethnic minority problems.

Furthermore, the Charter introduces the concept of the 'right to good administration'[22] as a citizen's right and a principle of democracy. Article 41 stipulates that 'every person has the right to have his or her affairs handled impartially, fairly and within a reasonable time by the institutions and bodies of the Union.' Additionally, it provides for:

> the right of every person to be heard, before any individual measure which would affect him or her adversely is taken; the rights of every person to have access to his or her file, while respecting the legitimate interests of confidentiality and of professional and business secrecy; the obligation of the administration to give reason for its decisions.

These series of rights have been developed from the jurisprudence of the ECJ, and also by the EU Ombudsman, Jacob Soderman, who has actively committed to these matters in treating complaints from citizens.[23]

Their efforts and the proclamation of the Charter is supported by a new regulation for public access to information. In accordance with Article 255 of the Treaty of Amsterdam, the EC institutions adopted the regulation of public access in May 2001,[24] and it was in force by the end of the year. Although the Charter itself has no binding force, the aim of protecting fundamental rights vis-à-vis the EC/EU administration can be attained through this regulation.

The right to good administration is inserted in Chapter 5 of the Charter, entitled 'Citizenship'. In this chapter, the meaning of 'Citizenship' extends from the definition in the Treaty of Maastricht. In addition to the 'Maastricht Citizenship', the Charter includes the rights related to good administration and universally provides non-EU citizens with these rights. The Charter helps to avoid the criticism that only citizens who are nationals of the Member States can enjoy EU citizenship.[25] Therefore, 'Citizenship' is merged into the tone of universality laid down in the whole Charter.

Judicial and political effects

The Charter guarantees fundamental rights to every person, except some of the rights in Chapter 5 entitled 'Citizenship'. It provides protection against the acts and omissions of the EC/EU institutions and bodies as well as entities established in the framework of the Union, such as Europol. The EU institutions, bodies and Member States are obliged to follow the provisions of the Charter when implementing EU legislation. However, the Charter does not require Member States to amend their constitutions formally or in substance.

The Charter was adopted separately from the Treaty of Nice and its annexed protocols, and with no legally binding force. The argument that the Charter should have binding force was broadly shared among the drafting body, the Parliament, EU Ombudsman and some parts of the Commission. In the end, though, in the final decision of the European Council, they chose not to make it legally binding. However, the accumulation of jurisprudence based on the Charter would lead to judicial effect in substance. The Court will surely refer to the Charter as a guide for interpreting the general principles of Community law. Moreover, as mentioned above (p. 77), derivative Community laws – for example, the Regulation on the Access to Information – will virtually bring fundamental rights into force.

We should not underestimate the Charter due to its character as a declaratory instrument. It has significant effects, in that EU institutions will not be able to reject or ignore it, even though it has no binding force.

Most members of the drafting body expected the Charter to be inserted into the basic treaty in the near future. Their intent could be found in the working documents produced in the drafting process, and also in the final chapter of the Charter. Some articles of the final chapter are not necessary, if the Charter maintains only a declaratory status. For example, Article 52(2) stipulates that 'rights recognized by this Charter which are based on the Community Treaties or the Treaty on European Union shall be exercised under the conditions and within the limits defined by those Treaties.' We can easily discover from these articles the underlying expectation of the drafting body. They thoughtfully stipulated in order to prepare for the moment in the future when the Charter would be put into the basic treaty.[26]

What are the standpoints of the Member States? There exist, in fact, counter-forces, such as the UK government. On the other hand, there are more drastic groups who wish to create an EU Constitution, into which the EU governance system provided in the Basic Treaty and fundamental rights in the Charter would be integrated. We cannot predict the definitive statute of the Charter. This question will be discussed in the next IGC on the treaty amendment to be held in 2004.

Whether it will have judicial constraint power or not, the Charter has already accomplished its primary purpose; that is, to make fundamental rights obvious to the citizens. Moreover, the Charter has had significant political effects, because it gave the EC/EU the legitimacy towards further political integration and enlargement.

The relationship with the ECHR

Historically, the argument as to whether the EC can or should join the ECHR has long been the main issue when discussing the protection of fundamental rights. However, it is not the aim of this chapter to review the judicial discussions about the accession to the ECHR. This section intends to describe how the Charter deals with the ECHR, and what influence the Charter has on this historical question.

During the drafting process of the Charter, the Convention examined provisions of the ECHR and other protocols as well as jurisprudence of the European Court of Human Rights, and determined to put Article 52(3) in the Charter as follows:

> Insofar as this Charter contains rights which correspond to rights guaranteed by the Convention for the Protection of Human Rights and Fundamental Freedoms, the meaning and scope of those rights shall be the same as those laid down by the said Convention. This shall not prevent Union law providing more extensive protection.

By this provision, the relationship between the ECHR and the Charter is reinforced to some extent, and interpretation gaps are to be prevented. However, it remains uncertain as to whether the jurisprudence of the two courts will be compatible or not.

According to the documents of the drafting process of the Charter, the accession of the EC/EU to the ECHR is still possible, even after the EU adopted the Charter of Fundamental Rights. Mr Prodi, the President of the European Commission, also confirmed this view in his speech at the Assembly of the Council of Europe. The House of Lords of the UK, though welcoming the adoption of the Charter, strongly supports the EC's accession to the ECHR, because they are very cautious of the possibility of the ECJ actively deciding on matters of fundamental rights in the Member States. On the other hand, the ECJ does not seem to applaud the EC's accession to the ECHR. The Charter can also be an instrument on which the EU could act as self-reliant in the domain of fundamental rights. This question requires further debate.[27]

Concluding remarks: towards a new phase of EU democracy

The cooperation between national parliaments and the European Parliament institutionally improved and achieved considerable results in developing EU democracy over more than ten years. The relationship that has been established from this experience produced positive effects for the drafting process of the Charter. In fact, there remain numerous problems between the two levels of parliaments, because both seek to take leadership in the framework of the COSAC and there are some clashes of opinions on several political issues. However, parliamentary democracy in the EU basically functions as a two-layer system (or multi-level in the federal states) and the EU is quite likely to develop a multi-level democracy model in European policy-making.

The EU achieved the participation of the civil society in the drafting process of the Charter. According to the EU Ombudsman, the principle of transparency means not only allowing citizens public access to the documents, but also making the policy process open as widely as possible. In this way, the drafting process of the Charter was a challenge for developing a pluralistic democracy.

The Charter is successful in presenting a wider concept of 'citizenship' than the notion of 'EU citizenship' introduced by the Treaty of Maastricht. Since the Treaty of Maastricht, EU citizenship has been criticized by some groups of the civil society in that it was a very closed and privileged (or discriminatory) notion in relation to Third World nations. The notion of citizenship provided in the Charter ameliorates these criticisms and expands the rights allowed for Third World nations; for example, the rights to good administration. The universality of the Charter was put forward and with a clear image of openness.

A role of the Charter is to reinforce the confidence of the EU both internally and externally. For the internal dimension, the adoption of the Charter increases the possibility for the EU to pursue the policies of judicial and police cooperation, including criminal procedure and preventive measures. These policies are very sensitive to personal rights and privacy and, without the protection of the Charter, they can easily infringe on fundamental rights.

For the external dimension, the Charter has two effects. The first concerns the fifth enlargement of the EU. The next enlargement will certainly involve the minority problem and bring unstable factors with it. The Charter provides the EU with clear reasons to take preventive measures and necessary action to fight against violations of fundamental rights, in complementing articles of the basic treaty. The second effect concerns the relationship with developing countries. The Charter responds to the reproach of the countries to which the EU offers economic and development aid. The EU has imposed conditionality on these countries in the field of fundamental rights and democracy. The Charter assures the consistency between the internal standards and external conditions and increases the credibility of the EU.

Thus, the Charter is qualified as the symbol of legitimacy and a milestone of political integration, and its drafting process presents an innovative method of decision-making that will open a new phase of EU democracy.

Notes

1 *OJC* 103 of 27 April 1977; *OJC* 299 of 16 November 1977.
2 The Solange I Case [1974] 2 CMLR 540.
3 The Solange II Case [1987] 3 CMLR 225.
4 Resolution Adopting the Declaration of Fundamental Rights and Freedoms of 12 April 1989 (A2-3/89, *OJC* 120 of 16 May 1989); Resolution on the Community Charter of Fundamental Social Rights of 22 November 1989 (A3-69/89, *OJC* 323 of 27 December 1989).
5 Yasue, N. (1992) *The Birth of European Citizenship: Starting from Maastricht* (in Japanese). Tokyo: Maruzen.
6 Opinion 2/94 [1996] RCJI–1759.
7 Report of the Expert Group on Fundamental Rights, 'Affirming Fundamental Rights in the European Union: Time to Act', Brussels, February 1999; see also two other reports entitled, 'For a Europe of Civic and Social Rights', 1996, and 'Leading by Example: A Human Rights Agenda for the EU for Year 2000'.
8 Council of the European Union, EU Annual Report on Human Rights 1998–1999, Brussels, 1 October 1999.

9 Soderman, J. 'Hearing on the Draft Charter of Fundamental Rights of the European Union', Speech in Brussels, 2 February 2000; Vitorino, A., Speech at Congrés annuel 2000, Academy of European Law Trier, Tréves, 27 October 2000; House of Lords, European Union Committee Publications, European Union, Eighth Report, 1999–2000.

10 Report of the Expert Group on Fundamental Rights, op. cit., p. 8; House of Lords, op. cit.

11 Committee on Constitutional Affairs, Report on the Constitutionalisation on the Treaties (2000/2160INI).

12 European Council Conclusion, Cologne, 3–4 June 1999.

13 Tampere European Council Presidency Conclusions Annex; composition method of work and practical arrangements for the body to elaborate a draft EU Charter of Fundamental Rights.

14 Dutheil de la Rochére, J. (2000) La convention sur la charte des droits fondamentaux et le processus de construction européenne, in *RMC*, no. 447 April, pp. 223–7.

15 Resolution, CES 1005/2000, 20 September 2000.

16 Resolution, CdR 140/2000, 20 September 2000.

17 Yasue, N. (2001) 'The EU Integration and French Parliament – The Amsterdam Treaty and Article 88-4 of French Constitution', in A. Ishikawa (ed.) *The Actualities and Development of the EU Law* (in Japanese). Tokyo: Sinzansha.

18 Yasue, N. (2001) 'COSAC: National Parliaments and European Parliament, Seeking for the Double Democratic Legitimacy', *Worldwide Business Review* (in Japanese), 2, 2: 20–33.

19 For example, Hanel, H. 'Rapport d'information fait au nom de la délégation du Sénat pour l'Union Européenne sur l'élaboration d'une Charte des droits fondamentaux de l'Union Européenne', annexe au procés verbal de la séance du 7 juin 2000, Sénat, Session Ordinaire de 2000; Assemblée nationale, Colloque 'La Charte des Droits fondamentaux de l'Union Européenne', 26 April 2000.

20 Soderman, J. 'Transparency as a Fundamental Principle of the European Union', speech at Humboldt University, Berlin, 19 June 2001.

21 House of Lords, op. cit.

22 Commission of the European Communities, European Governance, A White Paper, Brussels, 25 July 2001, *COM* (2001) 428 final.

23 Soderman, J. (1998) 'The Citizenship, the Administration and Community Law,' XVIII FIDE Congres, 3–6 July.

24 Regulation (EC) No. 1049/2001 of the European Parliament, Council and Commission documents, *OJ* L145, 31/5/2001; Fukuda, K. (1995) *The Evolution of International Administration*, 2nd edn (in Japanese). Tokyo: Seibunndo.

25 Balibar, E. (1998) *Droit de cité: culture et politique en démocratie.* Paris: Editions de l'Aube.

26 House of Lords, op. cit.; Dutheil de la Rochére, J. (2000) 'La Charte des droits fondamentaux de l'Union Européenne: quelle valeur ajoutée, quel avenir,' *RMC*, no. 443, pp. 674–80.

27 Morange, J. (2001) 'La Charte des droits fondamentaux de l'Union Européenne,' *RFDadm*, 17(3) May–June; House of Lords, op. cit.

5 The Nice Treaty and the reformation of the EC judicial system

A contribution to the protection of rights of individuals in the Community?

Takao Suami[1]

Introduction

The judicial system of the European Union has played a vital role in the process of European integration. The importance of this role is incomparable to that of any other judicial system. Without incorporating such a system in the founding treaties that were concluded in the 1950s, European integration would never have reached its present advanced stage of unification. Yet, in spite of all treaty amendments from the latter half of the 1980s, the judicial system has remained intact up to the present time, except for the establishment of the Court of First Instance (the CFI) by the Single European Act.[2] This does not mean that problems do not exist in the current system. Indeed, the perception that the present structure of the system can no longer be maintained as it now stands has become the widely accepted opinion among academics as well as practitioners in the Community. After the Treaty of Amsterdam was concluded in 1997, discussions to reform the judicial system seemingly became more active,[3] leading to the Treaty of Nice signed in 2001 to tackle amendments to the EC Treaty for the first time. The purpose of this chapter is to examine the reforms resulting from the Nice Treaty from the viewpoint of the protection of individual rights, and through such a process offer ideas for evaluation in planning future changes to the judicial system.

The purpose of the Nice reform

As both Community courts, the European Court of Justice (ECJ) and the CFI, clearly acknowledge in their papers, the genesis of the present reform was chiefly motivated by serious anxiety over the steady increase in new cases brought before both courts, and concerns as to the effect on the proper functioning of the judicial system in the future.[4] Such concerns were well-founded since the increase in the volume of cases had already caused increasing delays in the conclusion of judicial procedures in the ECJ,[5] though the delay in processing cases was more evident in the context of preliminary rulings rather than direct actions.[6] Taking into account the already sluggish proceedings before national courts, the additional delay upon preliminary rulings was of serious concern because such lengthy proceedings tended to make national courts more reluctant to submit issues to the ECJ. Furthermore, additional factors, including the enlargement of the European Union, were expected to foster further increase of cases and that unacceptable delays in the delivery of judgments in the Community courts would result from there.[7]

Taking these considerations into account, it was quite natural that the Nice Treaty deliberations should include discussions on ways to maintain and improve the effectiveness of the judicial system. However, one of the primary purposes of any judicial system is to maintain safeguards for the protection of the rights of individuals. Particularly, in the Community, individuals are assigned the important role as guardians of the Community law through their exercise of individual rights derived from those laws.[8] Accordingly, judicial efficiency should not be understood as a final goal of the reform but, rather, should be regarded as an instrument to achieve another, higher purpose.[9] In other words, although lengthy proceedings should be avoided as a matter of course, hastily and rashly deliberated procedures are also undesirable for the judicial system. Any efficient yet just judicial system has to appropriately balance these two competing principles.

Safeguards for the rights of individuals

Before going on to an in-depth analysis of the reforms resulting from the Nice Treaty, it may be useful to briefly set out the judicial scheme under the EC Treaty as it applies to the safeguarding of individual rights guaranteed by the Community law.

A review of Community acts

One situation exists where the rights of individuals, including both natural and legal persons, are prejudiced by an action or inaction by any Community institution which is incompatible with Community law. The EC Treaty provides several avenues for direct action to remedy such a situation.

Direct action before the Community courts is the most direct way to give legal remedy to affected individuals. The typical example is an action for annulment under Article 230.[10] Under this Article, an individual can bring an action directly against a Community institution before the Community court. However, due to several drawbacks, direct actions under Article 230 can provide insufficient protection to the affected individuals. For example, an action for annulment cannot make a normative act be subject to judicial review because only a decision is contested by the individual under an action for annulment.[11] Even if the contested act falls into the category of a decision, the case law of the ECJ has imposed strict requirements on the standing of the individuals in case the decision is not addressed to the individual applicant.[12]

These drawbacks, however, are alleviated to some degree in actions brought before national courts. The task of executing Community law is largely entrusted to the Member States.[13] Most regulations and all directives need a certain amount of implementation at the level of the Member State. Therefore, under national law, an individual whose interests are affected by measures implemented at a national level can initiate proceedings before a national court by asserting the illegality of a Community act which was the basis of such a national measure. Such acts may then be reviewed by the ECJ upon submission from the national court under the preliminary ruling procedures of Article 234. Besides direct actions, such procedures play a role in giving individuals another avenue to gain access to a review by the ECJ.

Thus, the preliminary rulings complement the lacunae within the system for legal protection. As several judgments of the ECJ indicate, both direct actions and preliminary rulings are interrelated and aim at attaining the same objective, as far as legal protection to the individuals is concerned.[14]

Review of the Member States acts

Another example of when individuals need legal protection is where the rights of individuals are prejudiced by violation of Community law by a Member State. The EC Treaty provides a separate action responding to failure of a Member State to meet obligations under the Community law; that is, an action to deal with an infringement of Community Law by a Member State under Article 226. However, this action is neither directly aimed at protecting the rights of individuals nor fully effective in rectifying such unlawful situation.[15]

In this context, the role of the preliminary ruling procedure, as noted above, is a valuable avenue for individuals. Community law grants individuals various rights which they can invoke before national courts. The ECJ created these rights, such as direct effect and state liability, through teleological interpretation of Community law, and has been consistently developing them from the early stages of the Community.[16] Relying on these rights, an individual can challenge a national measure, before a national court, as being incompatible with Community law. The challenged national measure can then be reviewed by the ECJ upon submission from the national court.[17] Similar to the review of Community acts as previously mentioned, the preliminary ruling procedure actually functions as a forum where individuals may challenge national legislation as being incompatible with the Community law.[18]

In summary, both direct actions and preliminary rulings are indispensable instruments to provide legal protection to individuals in the Community. Therefore, in order to promote protection of the rights of individuals, each of these two avenues should be improved respectively. In addition, the appropriateness of sharing responsibility between the two should also be examined because, if one of the two is overloaded, the function of the entire system will inevitably be adversely affected.

Realizing speedy procedures

Legal protection to individuals and present delays in procedures

It is clear that the major objective of judicial reform in the Nice Treaty is to prevent the effectiveness of the judicial system from deteriorating and to improve it, if possible, to ensure speedy procedures in the Community courts. In any judicial system, the procedural duration for rendering judgments should be kept to a reasonable length of time. This principle has to be applicable to individuals and, in particular, the general public. In contrast to the other party, Member States or Community institutions, individuals simply do not have the financial resources needed to pursue time-consuming procedures, whether national or Community, to their ultimate end. Indeed, the duration of court procedures has more affect on individuals than Member States and Community institutions. Overall, the swiftness of court procedures greatly contributes to the legal protection of individuals. Therefore, the question of whether the reforms of the Nice Treaty will enable Community courts to render legal remedies more quickly than before should be examined.

By and large, there are two means to improve the effectiveness of a judicial system by shortening the duration of court proceedings. The first is to increase the capacity of the system itself. If more human and financial resources are devoted to the judiciary, it would not be so difficult to improve both qualitative and quantitative aspects of the system at the same time. However, due to its generally weak political position, the judiciary is routinely under-funded, with its budget constrained governmentally. Accordingly, it becomes even more imperative for any judicial system to efficiently allocate limited human and financial resources.

Capacity building

Creation of the judicial panel

It can be argued that the simplest way to strengthen the capacity of a judicial system to deal with cases properly and quickly is to create an additional court and to increase the number of judges.

One considerable innovation of the Nice Treaty is the increase in judicial capacity. Thus, a new judicial organ, the 'judicial panel' (*chambers juridictionnelles* in French) was created. The Nice Treaty provides that a judicial panel will be established by the Council and that certain jurisdiction will be transferred to such a panel from the CFI (new Articles 220 and 225a). The CFI will work as an appellate body to the panel (new Article 225). The creation of the judicial panel will fundamentally change the structure of Community courts from a two-tier to a three-tier system and contribute much to the capacity of the judicial system. However, since the Treaty provisions only lay down the framework of the panel,[19] the details of the panel have to be determined by a unanimous decision of the Council.

As there is considerable uncertainty about both the organization of the panel and the extent of its jurisdiction, it is too early to appreciate the impact of these innovations. However, it is clear that the panels offer a significant opportunity to strengthen the capacity of the Community judiciary to deal with cases.[20] It should be recognized that, in order to make the best use of such opportunities, a considerable degree of jurisdiction should be transferred to the panels.

The number of judges

The increase of the number of judges is also a simple method to solve the caseload problem of any judicial system. The establishment of the judicial panels will necessarily add more new judges to the present small Community bench, although the exact number will remain unknown until such time as the Council adopts its decision (new Article 225a). Besides this, any substantial development cannot be found in the Nice Treaty for the ECJ and the CFI in this respect.

An increase in the number of judges at the ECJ is a delicate issue. The EC Treaty now fixes the number of ECJ judges at fifteen (Article 221) but, instead of excluding the exact figure in the EC Treaty, the Nice Treaty introduces a new requirement that the number of judges must be the same as that of the Member States (new Article 221). On the one hand, the appointment of a judge from each Member State is essential to incorporate all legal traditions into Community law but, on the other hand, the allocation of more judges to the ECJ needs careful consideration.[21] The ECJ is given the character of both a constitutional court and a court of last instance, being assigned the task of keeping the coherence and uniformity of Community law. Taking those elements into account, the unlimited expansion of the ECJ, which leads to too many judges, may pose a serious problem to the operation of the ECJ. Therefore, the outcomes reached at Nice are considered to be acceptable.

In contrast to the ECJ, the increase in the number of CFI judges will not cause any serious problems for the judicial system.[22] The CFI already sits in chambers in principle,[23] and it is not necessary, with rare exceptions, to sit in plenary session. Furthermore, since the CFI decisions are subject to review by the ECJ, being responsible for ensuring the uniformity of Community law, differences among these chambers can be rectified through appeal. Nevertheless, the Nice Treaty failed to make any breakthrough on the number of CFI judges. The current provisions do not mention anything about the number of judges, but the Nice Treaty introduces a requirement that the CFI shall comprise at least one judge from each Member State (new Article 224). The exact number is then determined as fifteen in the Statute attached to the Nice Treaty (Article 48 of the new Statute). It is unfortunate that this figure is the same as the present number of judges. Furthermore, the substance of procedure for future increase is relaxed by the Nice Treaty. The composition of the CFI is currently determined by the Council with unanimity (Article 225, para. 2). Under the Nice Treaty, an amendment to the Statute is necessary to increase the number, but can be made by a unanimous decision of the Council without the need to amend the Treaty itself (new Article 245). This means that the Council's power to determine the number will not actually change after the Nice Treaty comes into effect. The increase in the number of CFI judges has always been a subject of discussion and the need to increase them has already been widely recognized.[24] As long as the size of the ECJ cannot expand too much, it can be argued that more human resources should be devoted to both the CFI and the judicial panels. The Council is required to make its best effort to realize the increase immediately.

Allocation of resources

Proper relation among the Community courts

It has become clear that the Nice Treaty will not bring about a quick expansion of the capacity of the Community judiciary. As a result, serious consideration has to be given to the second avenue of achieving efficient use of limited resources.

As noted above (p. 86), there will, in fact, be three types of Community courts under the Nice Treaty. To make the judicial system (which is made up of those three courts) more efficient, first, a fair and proper hierarchical balance will have to be maintained among them. Should one of three courts shoulder more burden than the others, it would be difficult to make the system function well; an excessively burdened court tends to work as a kind of bottleneck in the whole system and obstruct the efficient handling of cases. Second, efficient use of human resources will also have to be pursued in each court. In order to escape the lengthening of procedures somewhere in the system, it is important for the capacity of any particular court to match the volume of cases brought before it.

Allocation of jurisdiction

DIRECT ACTIONS

To begin with, it should be recognized that the provision in regard to the allocation of jurisdiction between the Community courts, the ECJ and the CFI is amended by the Nice Treaty. Unlike the present treaty, a new Article 225 directly guarantees the CFI jurisdiction for a certain class of direct action.[25] However, as far as the individuals are concerned, this does not mean that the substance of the CFI's jurisdiction will expand by the implementation of the Nice Treaty. This is because all direct actions brought by individual and legal persons are currently dealt with by the CFI already. Since 1994, the CFI has had the jurisdiction to hear all cases brought by individuals.[26]

Before the initiation of the IGC leading to the Nice Treaty, it had been generally accepted that all jurisdiction for direct actions, not only those brought by individuals but also those brought by Community institutions or the Member States, should be transferred to the CFI.[27] However, the new Statute still places actions brought by any parties other than individuals within the jurisdiction of the ECJ (Article 51 of the Statute). Furthermore, it should be noted that there is an area where the jurisdiction of the CFI in regard to direct actions will be diminished by the Nice

Treaty.[28] When taking the upgrading of the CFI to an independent and autonomous court by the Nice Treaty (new Articles 220 and 225) into account, it may seem that these restrictions on the jurisdiction of the CFI are not consistent with the court's new status. However, at the outset, the CFI was established as an administrative court with the task of protecting the interests of individuals against unlawful acts of Community institutions.[29] If we focus on this characteristic, it will not be difficult to understand that the restrictions are compatible with the original nature of the CFI.

To sum up, irrespective of the treaty amendments, as far as direct actions are concerned, the current balance between the ECJ and the CFI, including the judicial panels, are unchanged by the Nice Treaty.[30] Unless the new Statute is amended so that the CFI can expand its jurisdiction to actions brought by any parties other than individuals, it will not receive any new types of cases after the implementation of the Nice Treaty.[31]

PRELIMINARY RULINGS

Despite the treaty's treatment of direct actions, there is an innovation included in the Nice Treaty. To date, preliminary rulings have been exclusively handled by the ECJ (Articles 225 and 234). However, the Nice Treaty will enable the CFI to give preliminary rulings in specific cases (new Article 225, para. 3). The treaty provisions do not define which area of jurisdiction will be transferred to the CFI, and the exact sphere of specific areas shall be determined in the Statute (new Article 225, para. 3). As it does not mention anything about it, however, the new Statute has to be amended in the future with a view to making a preliminary ruling by the CFI possible.

It is clear that the transfer of jurisdiction to the CFI on preliminary rulings will necessarily add a new burden on the court. How much burden depends on which specific areas are selected for the transfer.[32]

The ECJ has already suffered from a steady increase of references from national courts in the past. As a result, the duration of proceedings for preliminary rulings in particular has been consistently lengthening.[33] Compared with the ECJ, it seems that the CFI is functioning better since, according to available statistics, it has not yet become troubled with lengthy procedures.[34] Taking these situations into account, it can be argued that jurisdiction for numerous areas should be transferred to the CFI. Otherwise, the purpose of the transfer, which is to reduce the caseload of the ECJ, will not be accomplished. However, because of an increasing caseload, it seems prudent not to conclude that the present CFI will be able to bear additional burden deriving from the new task of preliminary rulings and to solve future problems deriving from the enlargement of the EU. Hence, the transfer of the new jurisdiction to the CFI has to be accompanied by another measure to reduce any burden borne by it. Without such a measure, it is difficult to avoid the risk that the new jurisdiction will increase the duration of proceedings before the CFI. In this context, the creation of the judicial panels can contribute a great deal to maintaining the effectiveness of the CFI.

JUDICIAL PANELS

The expansion of the CFI's jurisdiction needs to be compensated by the transfer of some of its present jurisdiction to the judicial panels.

Once the establishment of the judicial panels is determined, substantial jurisdiction has to be granted to them in order to reduce the workload of the CFI. According to the declaration attached to the Nice Treaty, it is expected that the judicial panel will be first established to deal with staff cases, which means disputes between the Community and its workforce.[35] As the number of staff cases has been about 30 per cent of all cases brought before the CFI in recent years, the transfer of jurisdiction over staff cases will contribute considerably to a reduction of the CFI workload.[36] Jurisdiction over cases concerning Community intellectual property rights is also a subject of discussion.[37]

When deciding on specific areas entrusted to the panels, we should be careful of the overall balance of burden among the three courts. In particular, the transfer of jurisdiction from the ECJ to the CFI must be outweighed by the transfer of jurisdiction from the CFI to the judicial panels because, in addition to its original areas of jurisdiction, the CFI will have to deal with appeals against decisions of the panels.

APPELLATE PROCEDURES

It is expected that both the ECJ and the CFI will work as appellate courts under the Nice Treaty. When considering the overall balance among the three courts, we also have to take rules on appeal procedures into consideration. This is because, even if certain jurisdiction is transferred to a lower court, the amount of burden will not change much, assuming that appeals are brought against decisions of a lower court in numerous cases.

There are two situations in which decisions by the CFI are subject to review by the ECJ. Even under the present treaty, the ECJ is working as an appellate body on points of law against decisions by the CFI (Article 225, para. 1). In addition, the transfer of jurisdiction for preliminary rulings to the CFI is accompanied by a mechanism which enables the ECJ to review the rulings by the CFI for the purpose of ensuring the uniform application of Community law (new Article 225, para. 3). However, the possibility of review by the ECJ is considerably limited. This is because, in principle, rulings by the CFI have to be final and that no right of appeal against ruling by the CFI is admitted.[38] Review by the ECJ of CFI rulings is exceptionally admitted to protect the unity and coherence of Community law.[39] There are two means to gain a review by the ECJ.[40] The first is by the CFI referring the case to the ECJ at its own discretion. The second is by the ECJ reviewing rulings by the CFI on its own initiative. This can be done if there is a serious risk to the unity or consistency of Community law (Article 62 of the new Statute).[41] Taking these points into account, it can be concluded that such a review will probably not be a large burden on the ECJ. Finally, in appellate proceedings, deliberation at the ECJ is expected to be made as short as possible in order to avoid prolonging the whole procedure including a national court procedure.[42]

With the establishment of the panel, the CFI will also become an appellate body for decisions of judicial panels (new Article 225, para. 2). In contrast to appeals to the ECJ on decisions of the CFI, reasons for appeal are not strictly limited to legal questions. Provided that the decision establishing the panel allows it, the CFI will review factual issues as well as legal issues (new Article 225a). Therefore, the possibility that review of factual issues may be a burden to the CFI cannot be denied, since the review of factual issues and examination of evidence requires considerable time. The decision of the CFI is further subject to exceptional review by the ECJ where there is a risk to the uniformity of Community law (new Article 225, para. 2). To initiate such a review, the ECJ decides whether it will review the CFI decision at the proposal by the First Advocate-General (Article 62 of the new Statute). Since a party to the case does not have a right of appeal to the ECJ,[43] this review will not be a significant burden to the ECJ.

Reform to the ECJ

Despite the transfer of jurisdiction on preliminary rulings to the CFI, the ECJ will, as before, maintain a significant responsibility for giving rulings under the Nice Treaty. In addition, the Nice Treaty will give additional assignments to the ECJ. First, the treaty adds a new jurisdiction as an appellate court for preliminary rulings by the CFI, although it is not clear how much burden this will impose. Second, the Nice Treaty indicates the possibility that the ECJ's jurisdiction will be expanded to include disputes between private parties concerning the application of intellectual property legislation (new Article 229a).[44] These new assignments may disturb the smooth operation of the ECJ.

In order to respond to these changes, under the Nice Treaty there are several improvements on the ECJ's internal organization and administration to speed up its procedures.

First, the Nice Treaty shows a very positive attitude towards the use of chambers. Unlike the CFI, it is a current principle that the ECJ sits in plenary session (Article 221),[45] although the number of cases decided by chambers, in fact, has outweighed that of cases by plenary session in recent times.[46] The Nice Treaty makes alterations in this principle of plenary session for the ECJ. Under the Nice Treaty, a full court where all judges are present will only be held in exceptional cases. There are three types of benches created in the ECJ: a small chamber consisting of three or five judges; the Grand Chamber consisting of eleven judges; and a full court consisting of all judges (Article 16 of the new Statute). The situations in which it is mandatory to hold a Grand Chamber or full court are considerably limited (Article 16 of the new Statute),[47] and other cases not falling under such situations will be automatically entrusted to a small chamber. The more active use of chambers will, in fact, do much to increase the capacity of the system as a whole. As long as the number of judges cannot increase beyond the number of the Member States, more frequent use of chambers remains the sole means to improve the efficiency of the ECJ. Therefore, the choice of the Nice Treaty is understandable.

Second, the Advocate General has to submit its opinions in all cases before the ECJ under the present Article 222, while opinions of the Advocate General are not required for all cases under the Nice Treaty (new Article 222).[48] The new Statute provides that where the case raises no new point of law, the ECJ may decide that it shall be determined without an opinion of the Advocate General (Article 20 of the new Statute). The new rule will better enable the Advocate General to avoid wasting the office's limited resources and to concentrate on important issues.

Access of individuals to justice

Quality of legal protection

While there are several improvements on the effectiveness of the Community judiciary in the Nice Treaty, it must be recognized that swift justice does not always satisfy the requirements necessary for proper justice. For example, if swift justice becomes degraded into hurried or scantily deliberated justice, individuals will not receive sufficient legal protection, much in the same way as where justice is delayed. In addition to rendering judgments within an acceptable duration, courts should give individuals appropriate and qualitative legal remedies. Therefore, it is time to switch our attention from the duration of proceedings to the quality of legal protection given to individuals.

In this context, we have to pay more attention to points which remain unchanged by the Nice Treaty. Such examination will indicate what are the subjects to be resolved by any subsequent reform.

Direct action: the standing of individuals

The first point to be considered is the limited standing of individuals in direct actions. Individual standing in direct actions has caused heated debate, in particular for actions for annulment (Article 230) and actions for failure to act (Article 235). The necessity for expanding the standing of individuals who were not an addressee of a decision has been discussed for a long time.[49] Even among the Member States, France showed its support to the proposal that the standing for individuals should be expanded.[50] However, this essential issue was not dealt with by the Nice Treaty. This can be partly explained by the fact that the major objective of the reform was to reduce the delay in the delivery of judgments through a reduction of the caseload of the Community courts.[51] Such an objective seemed incompatible with the relaxation of the standing requirements for individuals, since expanding grounds for standing would cause an increase in the caseload.[52]

However, the expansion of standing cannot be ignored as a means of improving the legal protection afforded to individuals.[53] Without access to courts, individuals would never receive any legal protection.

In opposition to such an assertion, it may be argued that, even if individuals are not allowed to bring actions before the Community courts, they will still be left the opportunity to challenge the illegality of Community acts before national courts. However, the preliminary ruling procedure cannot serve as a total substitute for direct action as a means to protect individual rights. This procedure is founded on a very delicate balance between the ECJ and national courts. In many respects, the procedure rests on the active and voluntary cooperation of national courts. For example, first, the initiative to refer a question to the ECJ is left totally in the hands of the national courts. If a national court decides not to refer a question to the ECJ, there will be no means to force the court to change its decision.[54] Second, since the task of the ECJ is limited to the interpretation of Community law, there is no guarantee that the national court, which is responsible for applying the Community law to the facts of the case concerned, will follow the real intention of the ECJ, even though the preliminary ruling is binding on the national court.[55] As these characteristics indicate, the ECJ does not have the power to fully control the conduct of the national courts. Hence, it is essential to expand the scope of standing for individuals in direct actions with a view to allowing individuals sufficient access to legal remedy.[56]

Preliminary rulings

The necessity to shorten the procedural duration of decision-making

The second point concerns the structure of the preliminary ruling procedure. It was agreed at Nice that part of the jurisdiction of the ECJ would be transferred to the CFI, but the structure of the procedure nevertheless remained unaffected by the Nice Treaty.

As far as the preliminary ruling procedure is concerned, there is a consensus that the major issue is how to shorten the procedural duration of decision-making for such rulings. When making a comparison between direct actions and preliminary rulings, it is difficult to find a substantial difference in the duration of proceedings at the ECJ. However, in the case of preliminary rulings, it should not be forgotten that, in addition to the duration for the ruling, there is the additional time it takes to obtain a judgment in the national court before an individual may attain an ultimate legal remedy. According to recent statistics (ECJ, Statistics of judicial activity of the Court of Justice 2001, http://curia.eu.int), it took an average of 22.7 months to obtain a ruling in 2001. From the viewpoint of the protection of individual rights, it may be contended that such a duration is almost intolerable. Unless adequate interim relief is provided under national law, the rights of individuals will be irrecoverably damaged by such a lengthy procedural duration. Therefore, even before the opening of the IGC, it comes as no surprise that a consensus has developed that something needs to be done to rectify this situation.

Alternatives discussed before the IGC

Before the IGC, there were several ideas proposed which would fundamentally change the present structure of the preliminary ruling procedure. All of these ideas were intended to reduce the workload of the ECJ by decreasing the number of referring cases. The proposed options are summarized below.[57]

The first option would be to restrict the level of national courts which would be allowed to request a preliminary ruling from the ECJ. There are two alternatives within this idea. One alternative is to limit the referring court of any Member State to its Supreme Court, whereas the second alternative is to deprive courts of first instance the power to refer cases.[58]

The second option sought to alleviate a national court of the last instance from its obligation to refer a case to the ECJ.[59] Under current ECJ case law, this obligation is exempted only in exceptional cases.[60] This option actually intends to broaden the scope of such exceptions.

The third option proposed the introduction of a filtering system.[61] Under this option, the ECJ would have wide discretion in deciding which questions from national courts should be answered by itself under certain selection criteria, such as case novelty, complexity or importance.[62] Such a change stands in contrast to the ECJ's present legal obligation to respond to questions referred by national courts with few exceptions.

The fourth option proposed that certain jurisdiction over preliminary rulings should be transferred to other courts. There are also two alternatives under such an option. One alternative would be to transfer certain jurisdiction to the CFI.[63] The possibility that the CFI would give preliminary rulings is clearly excluded under the present treaty (Article 225, para. 1). Under this alternative, however, jurisdiction over preliminary rulings would be shared by both the ECJ and the CFI. The second alternative is that, in addition to the present Community courts, new judicial bodies, responsible for dealing with the references from national courts, would be created in each Member State.[64] This alternative remains undeveloped as, for example, it is unclear whether or not those bodies would have the status of a Community court or national court. Lastly, the option has been proposed whereby measures would be created to encourage national courts to apply Community law more actively under its own responsibility.[65] For example, for this purpose, the appointment of the Community legal adviser or Advocate General was discussed.[66]

To sum up, the first three options generally concentrate on decreasing the number of references from national courts. For example, in the first option, since more than a majority of references come from lower national courts,[67] such limitation on referring courts in the Member State would considerably reduce the number of references. In contrast, the next two options intend to increase the capacity of the Community court system to handle references by dispersing the workload of the ECJ to other courts. This strategy is very simple, but can be effective. The last option does not conflict with the other options, and should be viewed more as a measure to supplement them. Although there are a few drawbacks to each of these options, it seems that all of them would contribute to the decrease of the ECJ's workload.

The conclusion of the Nice Treaty

The Nice Treaty finally adopted the option of transferring certain limited jurisdiction over preliminary rulings to the CFI. If various elements surrounding the judicial system are suitably considered, many will reach the same conclusion and, in this sense, the conclusion of the Nice Treaty is easily understandable.

First, the first three options – limitation on referring courts, relaxation of obligation to refer and the filtering system – originate from the same basic perception that it is inevitable to alter the present framework of the preliminary ruling procedure in order to solve the problem in question. However, each such option results in some damage to the cooperative relationship between the ECJ and national courts, as well as the uniform application of Community law throughout all Member States. To begin with, as the Community courts and most legal literature clearly acknowledge, the essence of the preliminary ruling procedure is cooperation between these two judicial organs.[68] Although it preserves a supreme power to give official interpretation of Community law, the ECJ is not considered as a court higher than the national courts in the context of courts of appeals in a national judicial system. This close relationship between the ECJ and national courts is based on a mutual reliance between them that, whenever any national court makes a reference to the ECJ, its decisions will in principle assist the referring national court to properly apply Community law.[69] However, the first option undercuts such cooperation and widens the distance between the ECJ and lower national courts by depriving some of them of the right to refer cases,[70] whereas the third option tends to restrict the right of national courts to receive assistance from the ECJ. In all cases, it seems that both of these options are incompatible with the spirit underlying the present scheme of the preliminary ruling procedure.

Furthermore, the changes in the present system proposed in the first and second options may have the adverse effect of jeopardizing the uniform application of Community law.[71] In order to ensure the uniform application of Community law, it is necessary for the ECJ to decide on all important issues on Community law brought before national courts through the preliminary ruling procedures. However, the reduction of references under these options may result in lost opportunities for the ECJ to review important questions affecting Community law. The changes brought about by these options will also prejudice individual rights. As the Community courts pointed out, the limitation of access by national courts to the ECJ, by depriving them the right of reference, may lead to individuals being deprived of effective judicial protection, as well as prejudicing the uniform application of Community law.[72]

It is reasonable, therefore, that the Nice Treaty adopted a conclusion which would not change the structure of the present procedure under Article 234. The Commission showed its adherence to keeping the present relation between the ECJ and national courts.[73] Furthermore, it seems that most legal literature took a view that every national court should have the right to make a reference to the ECJ.[74] By being determined to maintain the present structure, the only feasible solution was to increase the judicial capacity to render rulings. Both of the two alternatives in the fourth option are sure to contribute to such an increase of judicial capacity. However, the creation of new judicial bodies requires more drastic changes to the present system than the transfer of jurisdiction to the CFI. For example, in the early 1990s, it was proposed that four regional courts should be established as a Community court and that the ECJ should become a supreme court located above these courts,[75] but it seems that this proposal was not seriously considered by the Member States or Community institutions. Accordingly, the most feasible and least defective choice was to transfer jurisdiction to the CFI. In contrast to direct actions, there is strong opposition to such transfer of jurisdiction for preliminary rulings.[76] This opposition mainly derives from the fear that the division of jurisdiction for preliminary rulings will prejudice the uniform application of Community law. In the Nice Treaty, this concern is compensated for through the introduction of a mechanism whereby the ECJ may review a ruling by the CFI (new Article 225, para. 3). While we can no longer make a choice to allow the present burden to fall on the ECJ, it is inevitable that the CFI will assume certain tasks in the field of the preliminary ruling.[77]

Keeping the framework of cooperation: reflections on the relation between the EC and the Member States

In addition to the options discussed above, there was a proposal to replace the preliminary ruling procedures with a more hierarchical system in which the ECJ as the supreme court would be positioned above national courts in the Community.[78] Even in the Community courts' documents, the possibility of replacing the present system with a hierarchical appeal system was considered. In this system, national courts would be required to give judgment on Community law, and any party to the national proceedings could request the national court to forward its judgment to the ECJ for review on points of Community law.[79]

The Nice Treaty did not accept this proposal and adhered, instead, to maintaining the present relation between the Community courts and national courts. The relationship between these two courts can be regarded as a reflection of the relationship between the Community and the Member States. In the process of the treaty amendments during the late 1980s, some national sovereignty has been newly transferred to the Community. The establishment of the Economic and Monetary Union, with the introduction of a common currency, is a symbol of such a transfer. However, this limited transfer of national sovereignty has not caused any fundamental changes in the nature of the Community. With the limited transfer of sovereignty, the principle of subsidiarity was introduced as a general principle governing the exercise of competences assigned, respectively, to the Community and the Member States (Article 5), and has been working as a restraint on the exercise of Community competence.[80] The principle of subsidiarity assumes that both the Community and Member States are in a position to cooperate with each other to pursue the same objectives in situations where the Community does not have exclusive competence. In other words, the cooperative nature of relations between the Community and Member States has still been maintained, despite the past amendments to the EC Treaty or the development of case law,[81] and will not be changed even once the Nice Treaty comes into force. In this sense, it is reasonable that the present structure of Article 234 will be maintained under the Nice Treaty, too.

Assuming, however, that the present structure should be maintained, there is still some room to discuss concerning whether the current balance under Article 234 correctly reflects the relation between the EC and the Member States.[82] In this sense, we cannot exclude the possibility that the present procedure may be amended in the future.

Decentralization of the application of EC competition law and its impact on the preliminary ruling

While accepting the conclusion of the Nice Treaty, we need to be cognizant that a new threat to the present preliminary ruling procedure may result from the decentralized application of Community competition rules.

To date, the enforcement of EC competition law has largely been centralized in the Commission,[83] although it is legally possible for both national courts and national competition authorities to apply such competition law where there is a direct effect on Community law[84] or where the Council Regulation and national law,[85] respectively, is involved. The Commission has already taken steps to encourage and to undertake the national application of EC competition law itself.[86] Nevertheless, by and large, both national courts and authorities have not been very active in applying the law.[87] Therefore, the Commission recently adopted a more active policy to promote national application of the law and proposed radical amendments to procedural legislation in order to remove impediments to the development of national application.[88] If the situation develops in accordance with the Commission's expectations, these national authorities will create an intimate network with the Commission and perform the task of enforcing Articles 81 and 82 of the EC treaty over cases which would be more suitably dealt with by them. As a result, the number of decisions by these authorities will necessarily increase considerably. Meanwhile, should any party, either an addressee of the decision by a particular national authority or other parties having a direct and individual concern, be unable to accept that decision, such a party will likely bring an action against the decision before a national court under national law. In this case, the national court in charge will be necessarily forced to decide whether the contested decision is lawful in the light of EC competition law. While receiving necessary assistance from the ECJ under the preliminary ruling procedure, the national court will ultimately decide on the merits of the case on its own authority. Thus, in cases where the national authority applies EC competition law, it is expected that individuals will be able to obtain remedies against the wrongful conduct of the authority through proceedings in any national court.

It is conceivable, however, that, from the viewpoint of the rights of the individuals, judicial review by national courts of the decisions of national authorities will produce two problems, each of which will need to be solved.

The first problem concerns differences in legal remedies among the Member States. Needless to say, national proceedings are regulated by national laws. As national laws on remedies have not yet been harmonized, the substance of such remedies vary in each Member State of the Community. It follows that the extent of legal protection given to individuals will also vary from country to country, subject to some restrictions imposed by the case law of the ECJ.[89] It goes without saying that such variance among the Member States is undesirable for the uniform application of Community law. However, differences among national remedies is not a problem specific to the application of the EC competition law. As the enforcement of Community law is, in principle, entrusted to national competent authorities, with few exceptional areas, it is common in most aspects of Community law that the differences in national laws relating to remedies has produced different results in the context of the protection of the rights of individuals. In order to solve such problems, the ECJ actively intervened in national procedural autonomy in the first half of the 1990s, based on the theory of effectiveness of Community law, and handed down several innovative judgments, harmonizing national remedies.[90] After that, however, the ECJ has taken a less supportive attitude towards further development of the former active case law.[91] The question of how the ECJ will react to national procedural autonomy has not been entirely settled.[92] The decentralization of enforcement of EC competition law may stimulate controversy over this issue again.

The second problem concerns differences in legal remedies between the ECJ and national courts. Both the Community and Member States are expected to share responsibilities for the application of EC competition law under the Commission's new strategy. As a result, it follows that both the ECJ and national courts are going to apply the same law to similar facts of cases and to decide on the merits of such cases. It is worth noting that this phenomenon is quite specific to the application of the EC competition law. This is because, in the case of other Community laws, either the ECJ itself or the national courts are assigned the task of deciding on the merits of cases.[93] Accordingly, differences in views between the ECJ and national courts on the merits of similar non-competition cases cannot be made as clear as in competition cases. It is thereby conceivable that such differences may cause problems to arise affecting the rights of individuals. For example, assuming that a company which was engaged in restrictive agreements challenged a decision addressed to itself by a national competition authority in a national court, and obtained an unfavourable judgment therein, such a company would naturally desire to appeal against the judgment to the ECJ if the ECJ has previously given a more favourable judgment to another company in similar circumstances. As the preliminary ruling by the ECJ provides only an official interpretation and does not control a determination of a national court to the full extent, this procedure will be insufficient to rectify such situations. Indeed, such situations may create new pressures for additional change to the present system of preliminary rulings.[94]

Such a problematic situation seemingly derives, in essence, from the difference between the nature of the Community as a whole and that of competition policy. As previously discussed, the non-centralized nature of the EC has not previously changed. However, among the activities of the Community, competition policy is a special activity where the Commission has been granted extensive powers to enforce Community law.[95] The competition policy is a much more centralized area than other policies. As a result, there seems to be a mismatch between the nature of competition policy and that of the preliminary ruling procedures. In other words, the essence of the problem is that the rights of the individual in the centralized area are protected under procedures based on the premise of the non-centralized nature of other areas. It is impossible to assess the degree of the problems caused by this inconsistency. Provided that the existence of this problem becomes visible, however, the question of whether such inconsistency is permissible under the Community framework requires further examination.

Conclusion

It is true that the Nice Treaty has opened the door for judicial reform in the Community. However, it is too early to fully evaluate the results brought about by the treaty. Many important matters are still entrusted to future decisions of the Council. Likewise, there are still some important issues that the Nice Treaty did not touch on at all.

It is not necessary, however, to doubt the results brought about by the Nice Treaty too much. It is a typical process of the development in the history of the Community that certain matters which should have been amended but escaped necessary change would later become subjects of subsequent treaty amendments, and thereby eventually gain broader reformation in the new treaty. Hence, it is important to remember that reformation of the judicial system only recently began under the Nice Treaty.

The design of the judicial system in the Community is closely related to the essential relationship between the EC and the Member States. This is particularly true as it relates to the structure of the preliminary ruling procedure under Article 234. It is probable that further reform of the judicial system will be discussed again in the forthcoming inter-governmental conference scheduled to be convened in 2004.[96] Some elements, which may affect the nature of the Community to a greater or lesser extent, for example, the convening of a Convention before the IGC and the incorporation of the Charter of Fundamental Rights,[97] will likely be addressed in the next IGC.

Judicial reform has experienced a promising beginning and will hopefully continue further to ensure the protection of the rights of the individual as well as achieving other important objectives.

Notes

1 School of Law, Waseda University, Tokyo, Japan. The author is very grateful to Professor Koen Leanerts and Mr Ignace Maselis since discussions with both of them provided the genesis for this chapter.
2 Article 225 (ex Article 168) of the EC Treaty; Council Decision 88/591, OJ 1988, L 391/1 and OJ 1989, L 241/4.
3 Johnston (2001), Judicial Reform and the Treaty of Nice, 38CMLRev.499, 500–1, Kluwer Law International, Netherlands. Rasmussen, Remedying The Crumbling EC Judicial System, 37CMLRev.1071, 1078–9, Kluwer Law International, Netherlands.

4 The ECJ and the CFI (1999) The Future of The Judicial System of The European Union (Proposals and Reflections) 5–9.

5 Turner and Munoz (2000) 'Revising the Judicial Architecture of the European Union,' 19YEL1, 4–19, Oxford University Press, UK.

6 The duration of proceedings for preliminary rulings had been constantly lengthening until 1998 and had become almost double in the period between 1983 and 1998 (Id., at 15).

7 Rasmussen, supra note 2, at 1072–3.

8 G. Mancini (2000) *Democracy & Constitutionalism in the European Union* 201–2, Hart Publishing, UK.

9 The so-called Due Report recognizes that both the effectiveness and the protection of the citizens are the objectives of the reform (The Working Party, The Report by the Working Party on the future of the European Communities' Court system (January 2000), reproduced in A. Dashwood, and A. Johnston (eds) (2001) *The Future of the Judicial Systems of the European Union*, 160, Hart Publishing, UK.

10 In addition to both an action for annulment and an action for failure to act under Article 232, there are other types of direct actions. For instance, an individual can invoke the objection of illegality before the ECJ in order to avoid the application of unlawful Community acts under Article 241, even if he no longer relies on action under Article 230 (objection of illegality). An individual is also entitled to get compensation from the Community in the case of non-contractual liability before the ECJ under Articles 288 and 235 (an action for damages). Furthermore, disputes between the Community and its staffs are settled before the ECJ under Article 236 (staff cases).

11 Lenaerts, K. and D. Arts, *Procedural Law of the European Union* 158–63 (R. Bray ed. 1999), Sweet & Maxwell, UK.

12 The contested act is required to have a direct and individual relation to the applicant. However, it is difficult for such an individual applicant to satisfy such requirements (Id., at 163–81).

13 Shaw, J. (1993) *European Community Law*, 58–9 and 117.

14 Case 314/85 Foto-Frost v. Hauptzollamt Lübeck-Ost [1987]ECR4199, 4231, para. 16; Case T-219/95R; Danielsson and Others v. Commission [1995]ECR II-3051, para. 77; Case C-321/95P Stichting Greenpeace Council v. Commission [1997]ECR I-1651, para. 33.

15 Although the Member State is required to take the necessary measure to comply with the judgment (Article 228, para. 1), the judgment is not directly enforceable against the Member State. The only sanctions against the Member State not in compliance with the judgment are payment of a lump sum or a monetary penalty imposed through an additional decision by the ECJ.

16 Lenaerts K. and P. Van Nuffel, Constitutional Law of the European Union 526–9 and 580–4 (R. Bray ed. 1999), Sweet & Maxwell, UK.

17 The judgment of a national court which is based on the ruling by the ECJ is enforceable against the Member State in accordance with its national law. As a result, unlike a judgment of the ECJ under Article 226, the Member State is forced to comply with Community law. Accordingly, these rights have contributed much to realizing the supremacy of Community law.

18 G. Mancini, supra note 8, at 9.

19 Care should be taken about the status of the judicial panel. The panel is not considered as an independent court, not being comparable to either the ECJ or the CFI. The panel is attached to the CFI under the new Article 220. This means that, although the panel is expected to, in fact, enjoy power as a first

instance from the functional point of view, it is still a part of the CFI from a structural point of view.

20 It had become generally recognized before the opening of the IGC that a new judicial organ, whether it is set up within the CFI or as an independent organ outside the CFI, would be necessary to properly respond to the increase of the caseload (Albors-Llorens (1998) Changes in the Jurisdiction of the European Court of Justice under the Treaty of Amsterdam, 35CMLRev.1273. 1289), Kluwer Law International, Netherlands.

21 The ECJ and the CFI, supra note 4, at 18–19.

22 Id., at 19; Commission, Reform of the Community courts, Additional Commission contribution to the Intergovernmental Conference on institutional reform 6 (1 March 2000).

23 Council Decision, supra note 2, Art. 2(4); CFI Rules of Procedure, Art. 11(1). The CFI is able to render a decision even by a single judge pursuant to the decision in 1999 (OJ 1999, L 114/52).

24 Rasmussen, supra note 3, at 1974; It was pointed out that the consensus on the need to increase six judges was made before the conclusion of the Nice Treaty (Johnston, supra note 3, at 512–13 (2001)).

25 Articles 230, 232, 235, 236 and 238 of the EC Treaty.

26 Brown, L. and T. Kennedy, The Court of Justice of the European Communities 80 (5th edn, 2000); Council Decision 93/350, OJ 1993, L 144/21, Council Decision 94/149, OJ 1994, L 66/29, Sweet & Maxwell, UK.

27 Scorey, A New Model for the Communities' Judicial Architecture in the New Union, 21ELRev.224, 227 (1996), Sweet & Maxwell, UK. For example, the Commission is in favour of the idea that the CFI should be given general jurisdiction in all direct actions (Commission, supra note 21, at 4).

28 Although the present treaty allows the possibility for transferring all types of direct actions to the CFI (Article 225), the exact scope of its jurisdiction has to be determined by a unanimous decision of the Council (K. Lenaerts and D. Arts, supra note 11, at 14). To the contrary, under the new Article 225, there is no possibility that the CFI will deal with direct actions against the Member States brought under Articles 226 and 227.

29 K. Lenaerts and D. Arts, supra note 11, at 13.

30 Even under the Nice Treaty, the new Article 225 excludes jurisdiction of both those assigned to a judicial panel and those reserved for the ECJ in the Statute for the ECJ.

31 It is noteworthy that the declaration attached to the Nice Treaty requests the ECJ and the Commission to reconsider the division of jurisdiction between the ECJ and the CFI (Declaration on Article 225 of the treaty establishing the European Community).

32 One author proposes that cases concerning Community intellectual property rights should be included in the scope transferred (Johnston, supra note 3, at 508).

33 Turner and Munoz, supra note 5, at 11–16; The Working Party, supra note 9, at 156–7.

34 For example, the duration of proceedings before the CFI between 1997 and 1998 was fortunately not prolonged (Turner and Munoz, supra note 5, at 17–19).

35 Declaration on Article 225a of the treaty establishing the European Community.

36 For example, it is reported that in 1998 staff cases represented 34 per cent of all cases brought (Turner and Munoz, supra note 5, at 17). The task of the

judicial panel includes mediation between the parties. This is a reflection of the present practice. According to one survey, it is reported that staff cases account for 90 per cent of the court settlements concluded in the past (Schønberg, Coping with Judicial Over-Load: The Role of Mediation and Settlement in Community Court Litigation, 38CMLRev.333, 338 (2001), Kluwer Law International, Netherlands).

37 Declaration by Luxembourg, OJ 2001, C 80/1.

38 The ECJ and the CFI, Contribution by the Court of Justice and the Court of First Instance to the Intergovernmental Conference 4 (2000).

39 Id.; For example, under new Article 229a, the ECJ may be given jurisdiction to deal with disputes about the secondary legislation on Community industry property rights. In contrast, the CFI may be given jurisdiction on preliminary rulings for Community intellectual property rights under new Article 225, para. 3. Without review by the ECJ, it seems almost impossible to maintain the consistency of the Community law.

40 Johnston, supra note 3, at 508.

41 The Declarations expect further amendments to the Statute to be adopted just after the Nice Treaty came into force; Declaration on Article 225(2) and (3) of the treaty establishing the European Community, essential provision of the review procedure. Declaration on Article 225(2) and (3) of the treaty establishing the European Community.

42 In such a case, the ECJ should act in accordance with an emergency procedure (Declaration on Article 225(3) of the treaty establishing the European Community).

43 In the past, there was discussion about whether or not a right to bring a question before the ECJ should be given to parties to the dispute (Lenz, The Role and Mechanism of the Preliminary Ruling Procedure, 18 Fordham Int'l L.J.388, 394 (1994)).

44 Johnston, supra note 3, at 506–7.

45 The use of chambers is still an exception in the light of the EC Treaty. In order to use a chamber, the ECJ has the power to lay down criteria to select cases assigned to chambers (Article 9 of the Rules of Procedures of the ECJ).

46 K. Lenaerts and D. Arts, supra note 11, at 6.

47 A Grand Chamber shall be convened for a case, a party of which is a Member State or a Community institution, at their initiative and a full court shall be convened for cases specified in the Statute (Article 16 of the new Statute).

48 Johnston, supra note 3, at 515–16.

49 Turner and Munoz, supra note 5, at 47–8; Arnull, Private Applicants and the Action for Annulment since CODORNIU, 38CMLRev.7, 7–9 (2001), Kluwer Law International, Netherlands.

50 The French delegation, Memorandum on Reform of the Judicial System of the European Union, CONFER 4726/00, 23–4 (2000).

51 Johnston, supra note 3, at 506; Dashwood and Johnston, The Outcome at Nice: An Overview, in The Future of the Judicial System of the European Union 222 (A. Dashwood and A. Johnston eds (2001), Hart Publishing, UK).

52 It is pointed out that the fact that the courts are absorbed in reducing their workload exists under present case law as a rationale to restrict the scope of standing for individuals (Arnull, supra note 49, at 51).

53 Johnston, supra note 3, at 506; Dashwood and Johnston, supra note 51, at 222; Turner and Monoz, supra note 5, at 91–2.

54 Lenz, supra note 43, at 397.

55 G. Mancini, supra note 8, at 17–18.

56 Turner and Munos, supra note 5, at 42–5.

57 Id., at 63–8; The ECJ and the CFI, supra note 4, at 21–7; Commission, supra note 22, at 3–4.

58 The ECJ and the CFI, supra note 4, at 22.

59 Commission, supra note 22, at 4; The Working Party, supra note 9, at 165. Under the present Article 234, the national court against whose decision there is no judicial remedy has an obligation to refer a question before the ECJ.

60 K. Lenaerts and D. Arts, supra note 11, at 48–51; Case 283/81 CILFIT v. Ministry of Health, [1982]ECR3415, paras 13–16.

61 The ECJ and the CFI, supra note 4, at 23.

62 The Community courts are in favour of this idea (Id.), but the Working Party set up by the Commission does not support it because it is incompatible with the cooperation and dialogue between the ECJ and national courts (The Working Party, supra note 9, at 171); Rasmussen, supra note 3, at 1091–2.

63 The ECJ and the CFI, supra note 4, at 25–6; Commission, supra note 22, at 3; The Working Party, supra note 9, at 172.

64 The ECJ and the CFI, supra note 4, at 26–7.

65 Commission, supra note 22, at 3.

66 Turner and Monoz, supra note 5, at 67–8.

67 Lenz, supra note 43, at 409.

68 O'Keeffe, Is the Spirit of Article 177 under Attack?, Preliminary References and Admissibility, 23EL.Rev.509, 516 (1998), Sweet & Maxwell, UK. K. Lenaerts and D. Arts, supra note 11, at 18–19; The ECJ and the CFI, supra note 4, at 24–5. Case C-221/88 Busseni [1990]ECR I-495, para. 13.

69 For example, in cases where it is obvious that an issue on Community law submitted by the preliminary question has no relevance to the merits of the action before a national court, the ECJ will not be legally obliged to give a response to such a question (K. Lenaerts and D. Arts, supra note 11, at 39–40).

70 The Community courts are themselves not positive to the first idea (The ECJ and the CFI, supra note 4, at 22).

71 Turner and Munoz, supra note 5, at 63–4.

72 The ECJ and the CFI, supra note 4, at 22.

73 Commission, supra note 22, at 4; The Working Party, supra note 9, at 163–4 and 171.

74 Turner and Munoz, supra note 5, at 63. However, it should not be forgotten that there is a scholar who supports limiting the right of lower courts (Rasmussen, supra note 3, at 1104–7).

75 Jacqué and Weiler, On the Road to European Union – a New Judicial Architecture: an Agenda for the Intergovernmental Conference, 27CMLRev.185, 192–195 (1990), Kluwer Law International, Netherlands.

76 Rasmussen, supra note 3, at 1100–3; Furthermore, Professor Van Gerven is of the opinion that the preliminary rulings should remain within the exclusive jurisdiction of the Court of Justice (van Gerven, (1996)) The Role and Structure of the European Judiciary now and in future, 21ELRev.211, 215, Sweet & Maxwell, UK.

77 It is noteworthy that before the conclusion of the Amsterdam Treaty, it was proposed that certain preliminary ruling jurisdiction should be removed from the ECJ (Scorey, supra note 27, at 228).

78 M. Jarvis, The Application of EC Law by National Courts, The Free Movement of Goods, 452–3 (1998), Clarendon Press, UK; Rasmussen, supra note 3, at 1089.

79 The ECJ and the CFI, supra note 4, at 24–5.

80 K. Lenaerts and P. Van Nuffel, supra note 16, at 99–101.
81 Dashwood and Johnston, Synthesis of the Debate, in The Future of the Judicial System of the European Union 58–9 (A. Dashwood and A. Johnston eds (2001) Hart Publishing, UK).
82 Johnston, supra note 3, at 521.
83 V. Korah, An Introductory Guide to EC Competition Law and Practice 21–4 (6th edn, 1997), Hart Publishing, UK.
84 Case 127/73 BRT v. Sabam, [1974]ECR51, para. 16.
85 C. Bellamy and G. Child, European Community Law of Competition 824–5 (5th edn by P. Roth, 2001); Article 9 of Council Regulation No. 17 provides that national authorities are competent to apply Articles 81(1) and 82, as long as the Commission has not initiated its procedure (OJ 1962, 13/204 (English Special Edition 1959–62, at 87), Sweet & Maxwell, UK.
86 In the 1990s, the Commission adopted two notices in order to encourage national application; Commission Notice on Cooperation between National Courts and the Commission in Applying Articles 85 and 86 of the EC Treaty, OJ 1993, C 39/6; Commission Notice on Cooperation between National Competition Authorities and the Commission in Handling Cases Falling Within the Scope of Articles 85 or 82 of the EC Treaty, OJ 1997, C 313/3.
87 Commission, XXVIIIth Report on Competition Policy 1998, 329–62 (1999).
88 Commission, White Paper on Modernization of the Rules Implementing Articles 85 and 86 of the EC Treaty, Commission Programme No. 99/027 (28 April 1999); Proposal for a Council Regulation on the implementation of the rules on competition laid down in Articles 81 and 82 of the treaty and amending regulations (EEC) No. 1017/68, (EEC) No. 2988/74, (EEC) No. 4056/86 and (EEC) No. 3975/87, COM(2000) 582 final (27 September 2000); J. Rivas and M. Horspool (eds) (2000), *Modernisation and Decentralisation of EC Competition Law.*
89 D. Wyatt and A. Dashwood, European Community Law 79–80 (3rd edn, 1993), Sweet & Maxwell, UK. T. Hartley, *The Foundations of European Community*, 230–1 (3rd edn, 1994), Clarendon Press, UK.
90 Jacobs, (1997) Enforcing Community Rights and Obligations in National Courts: Striking The Balance (Chapter 3), in Remedies for Breach of EC Law 26–36 (J. Lonbay and A. Biondi eds), Wiley, UK.
91 Kilpatrick, Turning Remedies Around: A Sectoral Analysis of the Court of Justice (Chapter 5), in The European Court of Justice 144–7 (G. de Burca and J. Weiler eds. 2001), Oxford University Press, UK.
92 de Burca and Ryall, The ECJ and Judicial Review of National Administrative Procedure in the field of EIA (Chapter 8), in The Europeanisation of Administrative Law, Transforming national decision-making procedures 146–50 (K. Ladeur ed., 2002); Case C-126/97 Eco Swiss China Time Ltd v. Benetton International NV [1999]ECR I-3055, Dartmouth/Ashgate, UK and USA..
93 Under the preliminary ruling procedure, both the ECJ and national courts are dealing with the same case. However, it goes without saying that the ECJ is only able to interpret Community law and not to decide the merits of the case.
94 The Community institutions are assigned the task of enforcing Community law in the field of trade law, such as the imposition of anti-dumping duties. However, Community acts are not subject to judicial review by national courts.
95 J. Shaw, supra note 13, at 59.
96 Declaration on the future of the Union.
97 Laeken Declaration on the Future of the European Union, Annex I to Presidency Conclusions European Council meeting in Laeken (14 and 15 December 2001).

Part III

The Nice Treaty and Europe's future

6 Emergence of a new sphere of social policy by the European Union

Searching for innovative systems of social governance in the context of globalisation

Tomoko Hikuma

Introduction

European integration has been developing steadily since the end of the Second World War and has gained pace since the establishment of the European Union through the signing of the Treaty of Maastricht in February 1992. In the early years of European integration, the policies and activities of the EU were regarded as economic-centred and little attention was paid to social dimensions. As many researchers, such as Swaan and Hantrais have pointed out, social policy tinted with a certain political ideology is of significant concern in the internal affairs of nation states in modern European history.[1] For this reason, it is generally recognised that the governments of Member States of the EU are reluctant to transfer social policy jurisdiction rights to organisations at the transnational level.

However, as the process of European integration moved forward, more attention began to be paid to social policy at the EU level. Preliminary steps were taken to redress the lack of attention to social policy issues in the 1970s, and further measures were taken from the middle of the 1980s into the 1990s. As Leibfried and Pirson assert:

> the process of European integration has eroded both the sovereignty and autonomy of Member States in the realm of European social policy. National welfare states remain the primary institutions of European social policy, but they do so in the context of an increasingly constraining multi-tiered polity.[2]

Within this context, the present chapter will focus on the existence, extent and context of the new sphere of social policy created by the EU.

Following this introduction, the next part of the chapter presents a historical analysis of the development of EU social policy concerning the Member States and their citizens up until the Amsterdam Treaty of 1997. Following that, some of the leading European integration theories relating to EU social policy will be examined. This offers a key to understanding the position of the EU and EU social policy. Then, in parallel with these theories, the chapter goes on to consider three concrete examples demonstrating transnational features of EU social policy. Based on this background, it will be argued that a new sphere of social policy, with an innovative legal and institutional framework, can be perceived. Also, the idea of social governance by the EU, which has recently emerged in parallel with European integration theories, will be considered. Next, the development and characteristics of EU social policy towards countries outside of the EU will be explained as an important part of the new sphere. Then, recent trends in EU social policy after the Amsterdam and Nice Treaties will be summarised. The dominant view is to see the new social sphere as having become a component of social governance in network/multi-layered polity and this view may offer new perspectives on social and civil rights. Finally, as a conclusion, the issues surrounding the necessity of the social sphere of the EU and the possibilities it offers in the era of globalisation will be considered. Considerable parts of this chapter will deal with EU social policy before the Nice Treaty, as it is important to have a historical framework within which the characteristics, achievement and potential of this treaty can be analysed and evaluated.

Before going into the main body of the chapter, three premises will be confirmed. The first premise is concerned with the scope of EU social policy. There are various definitions of European social policy. A minimalist interpretation would focus on income distribution or individual welfare entitlements, whereas a more detailed interpretation would focus on issues such as the formal labour market, income transfer systems and social security policies, or any policies modifying market outcomes including industrial relations policies, education, vocational training and family policies, immigration, regional inequalities, and declining sectors.[3] This chapter will discuss social policy at the EU level in a broad sense, but it will not review individual policies in detail. A related point is that European social policy tends to be directed and applied to three categories; namely, to Member States and citizens, to candidate countries, and to the outside of 'Europe' in terms of international cooperation. This chapter is especially concerned with the first and the last categories. The second premise is concerned with the term, 'the EU'. According to the Treaty of Nice, the EU consists of the so-called 'three pillars', which are the European Communities (the Community dimension, comprising the arrangements set out in the EC (European Community), ECSC (European Coal and Steel Community) and Euratom (European Atomic Energy Community)); the CFSP (the Common Foreign and Security Policy); and the PJCC (Police and Judicial Cooperation in Criminal Matters). It is usually accepted that only the first pillar, 'the EC', is able to have supranational characteristics and the other two pillars are intergovernmental ones. Therefore, the term 'the EU' in this chapter is used to indicate this first pillar, particularly 'the European Community'. Also, all the historical names of the EU (the ECSC, EEC and EC) will be referred to by the generic term of 'the EU'. The third premise is concerned with the principle of subsidiarity. Although this principle will not be discussed in detail in this chapter, it should be borne in mind that it forms the basis of EU social policy. This ensures that the EU does not take action unless it is more effective than action taken at national, regional or local level (TEU Article 3b).

A new sphere of social policy by the EU towards citizens of the EU?

Brief history and events of EU social policy until the end of the 1990s

EU social policy in the foundation era

First of all, how was social policy at the EU level regarded in the very early stages of European integration? The Schuman Declaration of May 1950, which proposed the establishment of the ECSC, stated that: 'the pooled basic production by the ECSC will be offered to the world as a whole without distinction or exception, with the aim of contributing to raising living standards and promoting peaceful achievement.' Furthermore, Article 2 of the Treaty of Rome, signed in 1957, specified that:

> the Community shall have as its task, by establishing a common market and an economic and monetary union and by implementing common policies or activities, to promote throughout the Community a harmonious, balanced and sustainable development of economic activities, a high level of employment and of social protection ... the raising of the standard of living and quality of life, and economic and social cohesion and solidarity among Member States.

It is often said that social policy is a relatively new area for the EU. Nevertheless, as demonstrated here, the Schuman Declaration and the Treaty of Rome do include some crucial components concerning social policy in its wider sense, though the degree and concrete methods of implementation were left open to discussion. In addition, it should be noted that, through this treaty, Member States voluntarily committed themselves to entrusting a part of their national sovereignty to the EU and EU law. The Treaty enabled the establishment of legal frameworks, including the enactment of secondary legislation of social policy, and facilitated actions and programmes therein. Moreover, a new institutional framework based on certain roles and actions of the Council of the EU, Commission, Parliament and Court of Justice in order to form and implement policies within the EU was created. All these measures were innovative attempts to develop new systems which did not exist in any international organisations or treaties among nations at that time. However, this does not, of course, indicate that legal and institutional grounds for a common policy on social issues were clearly specified.

As Falkner stated:

> the social chapter of the 1957 EEC treaty (EECT) lacked explicit competence for EC-level intervention. The dominant philosophy was that welfare would be provided by the economic growth stemming from the economics of a liberalised market and not from the regulatory and distributive capacity of public policy. To the extent that social provisions were included at all, they concerned the cost aspect of social policy and constituted small concessions for the more interventionist camp.[4]

Still, as Kleinman and Piachaud clearly argue, it is hard to say that European social policy did not exist in the early history of the EU, when one takes into account policies for equal opportunity for men and women, and sections on agricultural policy for unemployed or poverty-stricken farmers.[5]

EU social policy up to Maastricht – the appearance of workers' rights at the EU level

What were the main trends and incidents of social policy at the EU level from the 1970s to the signing of the Maastricht Treaty in the early 1990s? In the 1970s, attention started to be paid more broadly to European social policy and calls were made for the introduction of such policy, particularly because of the increasing differences in levels of economic growth within the EU and the social situation at that time. The abstract new concept of a 'People's Europe' appeared at the beginning of the 1980s and more definite actions in the field of social policy were discussed. Policies and provisions advocated included areas such as equal opportunities and rights between men and women and free movement of persons. In addition, action programmes based on the European Social Fund were undertaken (e.g. Council Directives 75/117/EEC, 76/207/EEC, 68/360/EEC, 73/148/EEC, and Council Regulation (EEC) No. 1612/68).

In contrast to these developments, however, opinions concerning concrete suggestions related to other social policy areas in the Council of the EU were widely divergent, and this led to deadlocks, particularly in the 1980s. One of the fundamental reasons for this was the limitation of the institutional framework that required proposals and laws concerning EU social policy to be adopted unanimously by all the Member States. For example, many draft directives on the harmonisation of labour conditions, such as those concerning atypical work, working time and the European Works Council, were abandoned because of opposition by a single Member State. In order to break through this deadlock, the leaders of the Member States declared a new aim of creating the 'European Union' from the European Community (EC) in 1983. The resulting Single European Act of 1987 emphasised not only economic cooperation but also political cooperation among the EU countries, as well as social cohesion and reinforcement of social policy within EU policy. Notably, qualified majority voting, which required a certain number of votes from Member States in order to adopt issues in the Council, was introduced for the first time in this Single European Act, in the area of social policy in respect of safety at work. Also, there was finally recognition of development in the systematic consideration of working time issues, with intentional inclusion of work safety procedures, at the EU level. Furthermore, a provision promoting social dialogue between European social partners was introduced for the first time.

Following on from these developments, the Social Charter (the Community Charter on the Fundamental Social Rights of Workers) was introduced in 1989. Although the Charter is not legally binding, it is a guidepost of EU social policy. The Charter was agreed by all twelve member countries except the UK, reflecting the Commission's interest in the social dimension and in response to requests from organisations such as trade unions. As is well known, the Charter covers the social policy field broadly and divides it into twelve aspects, including social protection, vocational training, and policies for the elderly, children and people with disabilities. It also calls on the Member States to respect the contents of the Charter and on the Commission to promote suggestions in this regard.

In the Maastricht Treaty of 1992, in spite of the difficulties of deciding basic rules regarding social policy at the IGC (Intergovernmental Conference), the Social Protocol and Agreement was adapted by the same eleven countries and finally annexed to primary legislation. Though most pro-posals concerning individual social policies were not agreed on in the Council even in the 1990s, this annexed agreement greatly expanded the range of social policy that could be decided by qualified majority. In addition, it should be noted that the Agreement formally specified the new position and role of social partners in the legislation procedure in EU social policy (Article 2–4). In short, these legal and institutional reforms led to major developments in social policy, especially related to 'workers' rights and protection' at the EU level. Moreover, a new idea of 'European Citizenship' was introduced in the treaty, and some rights and duties of EU citizens were noted for the first time, partly aimed at responding to a 'deficit of democracy' in the EU and to criticism of the lack of citizenship and general rules of equality among the people of the EU (Article 8 and 8e).

EU social policy from Maastricht to Amsterdam – the appearance of civil rights at the EU level

What happened to EU social policy after Maastricht up to the Amsterdam Treaty? The Amsterdam Treaty, which was agreed in 1997 and came into force in 1999, has at least four novel points in terms of social policy. First of all, the Social Protocol and Agreement annexed to the Maastricht Treaty was finally incorporated into the treaty, taking advantage of a change in the British government. Two legal bases of social policy were linked together, incorporating the universal application of the decision-making process especially in the Council, and this has given impetus to further development of EU social policy. Second, the new Article 13 concerning non-discrimination and taking appropriate action for it, was adapted unanimously by the Council in order to combat any discrimination based on sex, racial or ethnic origin, religion or belief, disability, age and sexual orientation. This provision was followed by a report in 1996 submitted by the Comite de Sages, a committee set up in 1995 to officially discuss social policy issues. The report criticised the social provisions of the EU for being scattered and limited to workers. Third, it was stated for the first time that the EU and the Member States should bear in mind the fundamental social rights, including those set out in the European Social Charter in 1961 by the Council of Europe and in the EU Social Charter in 1989 (Article 136). Fourth, in order to achieve the objectives of Article 136 related to social provisions, it was stated that the Commission shall encourage cooperation between the Member States and facilitate the coordination of their actions in all social policy fields particularly relating to employment, labour law and working conditions, basic and advanced vocational training, social security, prevention of occupational accidents and diseases, occupational hygiene, and the rights of association and collective bargaining between employers and workers (Article 140).

Following the Amsterdam Treaty, two new directives on establishing a general framework for equal treatment in employment and occupation, and on implementing the principle of equal treatment of persons irrespective of racial or ethnic origin, were adopted in the Council in 2000 (Council Directives 2000/78/EC, 2000/43/EC). It may well be said that, during this period, EU legal action for equal treatment of men and women in the labour market was gradually extended over two or three decades to equal treatment regardless of racial or ethnic origin, religion or belief, disability, age and sexual orientation. Moreover, EU social policy, which for so long mainly related to the economic and employment fields, has started to deal with social policy for citizens as well as dialogue with NGOs beyond 'work and workers', though the effectiveness of EU social policy in this field is still unknown.

As a whole, over its brief history, the targets of EU social policy have widened and deepened in parallel with the development of an innovative legal and institutional framework and concurrent new methods of decision-making. This expansion of scope is epitomised by the appearance of workers' rights at the EU level in the era of the Maastricht Treaty and of civil rights at the EU level in the era of the Amsterdam Treaty, both for internal citizens. It could be said that there has been a reduction in objections to the formation and implementation of policies at transnational level, even if social policy by the EU is regarded as being under the control of Member States and governments.

EU social policy and European integration theories

How can this social policy by the EU be characterised and interpreted? First of all, three theories of European integration that have recently been under active discussion in relation to EU social policy will be considered: 'intergovernmentalism' derived from neo-liberal institutionalism; 'neo-functionalism', which is one of the traditional European integration theories; and 'historical institutionalism', which is part of new institutionalism.

According to liberal intergovernmentalism, which has been in the mainstream of European integration theory for a long time, the main actor within the EU is the national government of the Member State, and the EU exists in limited form as a place of intergovernmental negotiations where influence and autonomy for individual countries is gained.[6] In brief, in this theory, the EU and social policy at the EU level are explained as a means for governments to keep a balanced and efficient method of common decision-making between the governments of the Member

States, including the introduction of qualified majority voting in the Single European Act.

In contrast, neofunctionalism, developed as a theory by Haas, criticised this typical comprehension that the nation state is the only or dominant actor and asserts a different theory in respect to European integration.[7] Neo-functionalism attracted the attention of researchers until the beginning of the 1970s and then lost support partly because of the slow development of European integration. However, neo-functionalist theories started to be reconsidered in response to deepening and widening integration in the 1980s and the early 1990s. Recent neo-functionalists emphasise four main theories: functional spillover, the formation of coalitions/cultivated spillover, elite socialising/bureaucratisation/depoliticisation, and the formation of transnational interest groups. Using these theories, the neo-functionalists conclude that the EU has supranational aspects beyond state and national sovereignty. However, some researchers, particularly in the area of labour relations, have until quite recently expressed severe criticism of the values and validity of neo-functionalist theories, especially in the social policy field. For example, Streeck and Schmitter pointed out that this field lacks dynamism, because European companies and employers' groups are not willing to be concerned with the regulations of the labour market.[8] They also stated that cooperation within the EU should be understood as intergovernmental rather than essentially supranational, and that the application of neo-functionalist theories to the area of social and labour policies should be deferred.

Despite these criticisms, Jansen's recent work has supported the neofunctionalist approach.[9] He examined the Single European Act, the Social Protocol and Agreement of the Maastricht Treaty in order to measure the development of cooperation and joint decisions among the Member States in the area of social and labour policies using Lindberg and Scheingold's five-point scale to measure the degree and influence of political integration (1970, 1971). He concluded that the Single European Act as a whole is at integration point 1 or 2, which indicates that all policy decisions are made by national process or only at the beginning of a Community decision-making process. This is because the Member States imposed various limits on political integration in the social policy field and avoided creating more comprehensive cooperation systems. The Social Protocol and Agreement are assessed as being at point 3, which indicates that policy decisions are taken on both national and supranational levels, but that national activity predominates. This result is due to some improvements in joint decision-making systems and on the extension in the role of the EU in the area of qualified majority voting, social partners' participation and a new collective bargaining system at the supranational level. As a consequence of this analysis, Jansen concluded that the integration theories developed by neo-functionalists are applicable. He mentioned that 'functional spillover' accords well with the adoption of common rules of free movement of labour and working conditions, and 'cultivated spillover' is in accord with the information and consultation of workers, the integration of persons excluded from the labour market and social dumping. Additionally, he has proposed new forms of spillover called institutional/legalistic spillover, derived from concrete policy implementation through the process of the extended qualified majority after the introduction of the treaty. In addition, the theories of coalition-building, elite socialising and international interest organisations are accounted for by the positive role of the Commission in promoting action programmes in order to realise the Social Charter, by cooperation with the European Parliament, and by the formal participation of some organisations such as the UNICE (Union of Industrial and Employers' Confederations of Europe), CEEP (European Centre of Enterprises with Public Participation) and ETUC (European Trade Union Confederation), working together with some international interest groups in the process of decision-making at the supranational level. To sum up, Jansen emphasised that the devolvement of authority to the EU level in the area of social and labour policy has certainly increased during the past ten to fifteen years as political integration beyond the states has progressed.

Pirson also analysed characteristics of the European integration using social policy as an example, from the standpoint of historical-institutionalism.[10] This standpoint focuses on social processes as historical phenomena, and includes rational choice analyses that consider issues of institutional evolution and path-dependence to be crucial. He concluded that certain transnational features are observed in the field of EU social policy, although some limits over EU control are exerted by Member State governments. According to his opinion, the transnational aspects emerge based on two sets of claims, which are 'gaps' between the institutional and policy preference of Member State governments and the actual functioning of institutions and policies, and the difficulties in closing emerged gaps reliably. The gaps are created by four factors: partial autonomy of EU organisations, restricted time-horizons of political decision-makers, unanticipated consequences and shifts in Chiefs of Government policy preferences. Concrete EU social policies on issues of gender equality, the expansion of health and safety regulations and the enactment of Social Protocol and Agreement in the Maastricht Treaty are applied to explain the gaps and growing significance of European policy.

Summarising the arguments of theories related to European integration and EU social policy, it can be said that, recently, a certain degree of consensus on the existence of transnational features of EU social policy or so-called 'supranationality' in the EU and EU social policy can be observed.

Some examples related to the transnational features of EU social policy

To what extent are these explanations of the transnational features of EU social policy development and European integration theories applicable? Does this transnational feature really have effectiveness beyond the control of the sovereignty of nation states or is it designed as a means of following the volition of individual Member States? This next section considers three different areas as examples, which seem to relate to and indicate the existence of the transnational features of EU social policy: the role of the ECJ and its judgement; extension of the area of qualified majority voting; and new roles by various actors.

Role of the ECJ and its judgement

The Court of Justice has the responsibility to ensure that Community law is appropriately interpreted and applied, and the ECJ is officially regarded as the supreme guardian of Community legality. The ECJ has wide jurisdiction to examine various types of actions, such as proceedings for failure to fulfil an obligation, proceedings for annulment and proceedings for failure to act and appeals. The ECJ also, has another important role, aimed at preliminary rulings preventing different interpretations of the Community law by the Member States and ensuring the effective application of the law. As Steiner states, the ECJ daringly created the jurisdiction and Community law through its judgements by bridging the gaps between EU treaties, which basically just regulate a framework of provisions, responding to the stagnation of Community legislation in the 1970s and the early 1980s.[11] Many cases related to social policy fields have been heard in the ECJ, and the accumulated work of the EJC has come to be a significant source of EU law at present. Under such conditions, it is apparent that not all the judgements at national level follow the original intentions of any one Member State.

Four cases are provided here as examples. First are two cases brought by the Commission on the failure of the French and Italian governments to fulfil their obligations to prohibit night work, based on Article 5 of Council Directive 76/207/EEC on the implementation of the principle of equal treatment for men and women as regards access to employment, vocational training and promotion, and working conditions. In spite of objections from the two national governments, the ECJ declared in 1997 that the French and Italian republics should not have retained the national law prohibiting night work by women (Case: C–197/96, C–207/96). The third case deals with a preliminary ruling from the Court of Appeal in the UK referred to the ECJ concerning early payment of an occupational pension after retirement, based on the second paragraph of Article 119 of the treaty on equal pay for men and women. This was originally appealed before an industrial tribunal and then the Employment Appeal Tribunal in the UK by Mr Barber against the Guardian Royal Exchange Assurance Group, where he worked. After his claim was dismissed in both tribunals, the case was taken to the Court of Appeal. In spite of the judgements of the tribunals at the national level, the ECJ stated in 1990 that Article 119 of the treaty applies directly to pensions of that type and to all forms of discrimination identified with equal work for equal pay, and that the respective national court must safeguard the rights which it confers on individuals. This judgement of the ECJ has significantly influenced pension systems in the Member States (Case: C–262/88). The fourth case also concerns a preliminary ruling from the Supreme Court of the Netherlands to the ECJ in order to clarify the interpretation of Articles 2 and 3 of Council Directive 76/207/EEC, particularly concerning refusal to enter into a contract of employment with a pregnant candidate, who was considered to be suitable for the job, because of the possible adverse consequences of employing a pregnant woman. This case was appealed by Ms Dekker to a District Court and then a Regional Court of Appeal in the Netherlands against Stichting Vormingscentrum voor Jong Volwassenen (VJV), demanding VJV pay her damages for possible financial loss. Though the appeal was dismissed in both courts, the ECJ judged in 1990 that the employer was in direct contravention of the Articles, but that Member States have freedom to choose between the various solutions appropriate for achieving the purpose of the Directive (Case: C–177/88).

As we have seen, the ECJ has a leading role in the area of social law in EU countries and it can be said that the validity of EU social policy beyond the sovereignty of Member States has frequently been observed through its activities.

Extension of the area of qualified majority voting

Legislative decision-making at the EU level is determined through a process of interaction between many institutions in the EU, particularly by the 'institutional triangle' formed by the Council of the EU, the Commission and the Parliament. Drafts of proposals are basically drawn up by the Commission and finally come into effect after adoption by the Council. The Council is composed of ministers of the Member States and was originally set up for the purpose of controlling supranational features of the High Authority in the EU. In the adoption of proposal drafts in the Council, there are three voting methods: unanimous, majority and qualified majority. As stated earlier in this chapter, unanimous decision, which means that a proposal is rejected even if a single county objects, was required in the field of social policy. However, qualified majority voting was introduced in the areas of health and safety at work by the Single European Act and the scope of this voting method has been further extended since then. In the Social Protocol and Agreement annexed to the Maastricht Treaty, the qualified majority was extended to working conditions, the information for and consultation of workers, equal opportunities and treatment of men and women with regard to the labour market, the integration of workers excluded from the labour market, and initiatives designed to combat social exclusion.

This introduction of qualified majority voting made it possible for proposals on social policy at the EU level to be adopted, even if certain governments do not agree. Moreover, all the Member States, including the states objecting to the new policy, have to obey the decision and have to implement it. The extension of areas for qualified majority voting also gave new impetus in EU social policy to form and implement new secondary legislation such as directives on the European Work Council and the Protection of Young People at work (Council Directives 94/45/EC, 94/33/EC). In this way, qualified majority voting has promoted the effectiveness of social policy at the EU level and this effectiveness is increasing as the voting system extends.

New roles for various actors

There have been increases in the impact of the official and unofficial roles of different actors, who often have different views to national governments, on the development of the EU. First, not only the autonomy of the Commission but also the effectiveness of the European Parliament, in terms of legislative power, has developed since the middle of the 1980s. The members of the Parliament have been elected by direct universal suffrage since 1979 and this is regarded as the expression of the democratic will of the citizens. However, in the beginning, the consultation procedure was applied to Parliament only in terms of decision-making, which just meant that the Council had to consult with the Parliament and take its views into account. By the Single European Act, a new cooperation procedure was introduced and this makes it possible for the Parliament to amend proposals in the areas of non-discrimination, the Social Fund, vocational training, economic and social cohesion, health and safety of workers and so on (Article 252). Later, the codecision procedure, in which Parliament and the Council share legislative power, came into force in the Amsterdam Treaty (Article 251). These changes in procedure have given a new status to Parliament as one of the main legislative bodies and the importance of its role in the EU has been increasing.

The ETUC, CEEP and UNICE, which are crucial actors in the field of social policy, have started to gain formal positions in the EU. As mentioned earlier, social dialogue has developed since the Single European Act (Article 139) and then the Maastricht Treaty formally required the Commission to consult with social partners before submitting proposals on social policy at the EU level. Also, when the social partners form contractual relationships, including agreements in the process of consultation with the Commission, these can be proposed to the Council. There have been two EU directives in the area of social policy agreed by the ETUC, UNICE, CEEP through this new process: Directives on Parental Leave in 1996 (Council Directive 96/34/EC) and Part-time Work in 1997 (Council Directive 97/81/EC). Furthermore, with the promotion of civil dialogue at the EU level, NGOs have also started to join the official processes of EU policy-making as actors representing opinions on certain issues since the Amsterdam Treaty. This will be treated in more detail below.

Considering these developments, it can be said that the new roles of a range of different actors, who have different views and powers from the governments of Member States, have been officially created and recognised at the EU level. In addition, the actors and their formal activities have been contributing more and more to the formation of EU social policy.

An emerging new sphere of social governance in the EU

The brief history of EU social policy shows that certain concepts and limited policies have existed since the early period of European integration. Social policy in the EU has gradually developed over time, together with legal and institutional development. Although there is some controversy, recent European integration theories assert this social policy at the EU level has certain autonomy vis-à-vis national governments. Some examples taken from the role of the ECJ and its judgement, the extension of the scope for qualified majority voting, and new roles by various actors also indicate that the transnational features of EU social policy is surely recognised. In other words, this social policy has a certain discretion and potentialities that previous social policies and welfare states did not offer.

Reviewing all of these, the powers of nation states in terms of social policy have been partly shifting to or rather, have come to be shared with, the EU. Of course, this dimension is originally derived from the political agreements of Member States. The outcomes of this process have become more apparent through the 1990s and it can be said a new sphere of social policy has been created by the EU. Moreover, Fukuda has recently pointed out that these European integration theories have led to the idea of the governance approach to European integration and a theory of multi-level governance at the end of 1990s and the beginning of the twenty-first century.[12] This multi-level governance has a certain distance from the theoretical confrontation between intergovernmentalism and neofunctionalism, and from both constructivism and social construction-ism, which support the dominant position of either the government of Member States or supranational organisations. Though there is no clear definition of governance as a term, governance is conceived as a compre-hensive theoretical framework that comprises various established political theories. A common understanding of the concept of governance has been emerging recently, focusing more on the formation of orders and systems at the global level through agreements of free will between inter-related actors at various levels, in order to realise common interests and values. Fukuda also mentions that the Commission itself has recently started to express a view that the EU is a part of this governance system. Additionally, Falkner stated, with regard to the formal contribution of various actors within the EU, that there has also been a change within the governance in the EU itself from a hierarchical towards a network style.[13]

In short, a newly emerging sphere of social policy implemented on the basis of an innovative legal and institutional EU framework constitutes a part of social governance. This sphere consists of a combination of regional, national and supranational aspects, and of various actors at those levels, so that it may provide social and civil rights for the people from dif-ferent perspectives.

A new sphere of social policy by the EU targeting people outside the EU?

In addition to the issues already discussed, in terms of a new sphere of social policy and newly emerging social governance, it is worth paying attention to the social policies of the EU towards countries outside of Europe, particularly in the 1990s. It goes without saying that EU policy directed at candidate countries has been developed, and this is further discussed in Chapter 7. Here, the EU's social policy towards other countries, especially policies aimed at developing countries, will be in focus, since it involves different approaches from those of EU internal social policy. It seems that this offers important implications for the discussion of the future of social policy and social governance by the EU.

EU social policy towards countries outside the EU could be seen at first as the development of a cooperation policy in external relations. To be precise, this began in the 1960s for the ex-colonies with the Yaounde Conventions based on Article 131 and 136 of the Rome Treaty, and then the Lome Conventions since 1975, which expanded the policy targets to non-ex-colonies, namely to the ACP (African, Caribbean and Pacific states). These Conventions and their policies led to the signing of the Cotonou Agreement in 2000 aiming at cooperation for 'reducing and eventually eradicating poverty consistent with the objectives of sustainable development and the gradual integration of the ACP countries into the world economy'.

Furthermore, it seems that new concepts and approaches, different from the EU's internal ones, have been considered with respect to external social policy. This has gradually converged with and been reflected in policy formation in the 1990s. One of the crucial concepts is the necessity to create basic rules or legal frameworks for ensuring fundamental social/labour rights, which are inextricably linked to basic human rights, at the international or global level. This includes not only the citizens of the EU but also all people outside of the EU, considering the position of the EU in the era of globalisation. Another notable aspect of these social policies are that they are often discussed in conjunction with trade policy.

The basic ideas underpinning these developments are shown in the Commission's *A White Paper on European Social Policy in 1994*. In this paper, it is stated that:

1   the European social model is not impervious to outside influence from other parts of the world;
2   the Commission intends to strengthen links with international organisations such as the OECD, ILO, the Council of Europe and the UN;
3   discussion is now necessary on the social rules needed to complement trade. The Union recognises that other regions may need to compete on the basis of lower labour costs, but it is not in the interests of international cooperation that the exploitation of workers should become an instrument of international competition. A multilateral, progressive and multi-faceted approach to social rules is therefore proposed, which is founded on partnership and positive incentives for social progress in developing countries;

4   the Commission considers that the future WTO must tackle the subject without delay, so that respect for basic social rights, combating unfair trade conditions, and environmental and social issues will have to be discussed in this context (COM(94)333). Notably, some of these approaches have already been realised and legislated for by the EU.

The first concrete approach to these concepts is the development of a framework of special incentive arrangements with legal binding for the purpose of promoting sustainable development and ensuring core labour standards. This was attempted by the EU as two Council Regulations applying a four-year scheme of generalized tariff preferences (1995–8) in respect of certain industrial products originating in developing countries (Council Regulation (EC) No. 3281/94) and on applying multi-annual schemes of generalised tariff preferences from 1 July 1996 to 30 June 1999 in respect of certain agricultural products originating in developing countries (Council Regulation (EC) No. 1256/96). Article 9 of both regulations provides that these regulations may at any time be temporarily withdrawn in whole or in part in circumstances including the practice of any form of forced labour as defined in the Geneva Conventions of 25 September 1926 and 7 September 1956 and ILO Conventions No. 29 and 105, and export of goods made by prison labour. In addition, Article 7 provides that this incentive of Article 9 would be expanded to freedom of association and protection of the rights to organise and the application of the principles of the right to organise and to bargain collectively (ILO Conventions No. 87, 98), and a minimum age for admission to employment (ILO Convention 138). The agreement of the EU is obtained by the decision of the Council based on a qualified majority after a one-year investigation of the facts by the Commission (Article 10–12). Indeed, the ICFTU (International Confederation of the Free Trade Union) and ETUC made accusations of forced labour in Myanmar and child labour in Pakistan to the Commission in October 1995. Then, as a first case, this Regulation was imposed in 1997, forcing Myanmar to be temporarily withdrawn from the Community scheme of generalised tariff preferences because of its use of forced labour (Council Regulation (EC) No. 522/97). In 1998 a new Council Regulation for extending the previous two regulations was also adopted (Council Regulation (EC) No. 1154/98).

Considering these social policies by the EU, it may be said that innovative ways of social governance based on a new sphere of EU social policy beyond the state have been emerging on the international as well as the regional level. This social policy of external relations for the EU is likely to be the subject of increasing attention in the near future, as are other innovative methods, such as those implemented by the ILO and by the

NALLAC (North American Agreement on Labor Corporation) in the NAFTA (North American Free Trade Agreement)

EU social policy after 2000 – towards the establishment of fundamental social and civil rights, and a new way for social governance at the EU level

EU internal social policy from Nice through Lisbon to Laeken

After the Amsterdam Treaty, the Nice Treaty was signed in February 2000. In this section, EU internal social policy up to the present will be described. The major concern of the Nice Treaty was institutional reform in preparation for the enlargement of the EU. However, some amendments were made in terms of social policy and this implies that decisions in these areas might be taken in the future. First, a new paragraph 2 was added to Article 13 on non-discrimination. This paragraph provides for the Council to adopt Community incentive measures, excluding harmonisation of laws and regulations of the Member States, to support action taken by the Member States in order to combat discrimination based on sex, racial and ethnic origin, religion or belief, disability, age and sexual orientation. Second, the scope of codecision procedures in Article 137 is expanded to include the combating of social exclusion and the modernisation of social protection systems without prejudice to social security and social protection of workers. Also, it is newly stated in Article 137 that the Council shall act unanimously to apply the codecision procedure in the areas of protection of workers where their employment contract is terminated, as well as representation and collective defence of the interests of workers and employers, and conditions of employment for third-country nationals legally residing in Community territory. Third, the establishment of a Social Protection Committee with advisory status to promote cooperation on social protection policies between Member States and with the Commission is provided for in Article 144.

The Lisbon Council was held in March 2000 after the signing of the Treaty of Nice. It is noted that the Lisbon presidency conclusion starts with a section on employment, economic reform and social cohesion. This attempted at focusing widely on the promotion of EU social policy with a new strategic goal for the next decade in order to create a competitive and dynamic knowledge-based economy in the world, capable of sustainable growth with more and better jobs and greater social cohesion. Three methods were proposed for achieving this goal:

1   the information society, R&D and structural reform;

2   modernising the European social model and building an active welfare state, investing in people and combating social exclusion;
3   sustaining a healthy economy.

(Bulletin EU 3–2000)

Szyszczak (2001) noted that:

> during the Lisbon Summit of March 2000 a number of factors came together to ignite a new ten-year strategy for economic reform of the European Union. A new process, labelled the 'open method of co-ordination', has harnessed what were seen as separate, competing and, seemingly, irreconcilable issues of employment policy, labour law, social protection and economic policy into a new paradigm. Within this paradigm, strategies have emerged to create new forms and modes of governance which are being used alongside the conventional techniques of economic integration using harmonization, co-ordination and convergence mechanisms.

Szyszczak outlines three distinctive governance techniques: economic governance, regulatory governance and self-organised networking governance. This self-organised networking governance is a new form of governance and 'the distinctive features of the implementation of the new approach to social policy lie not only in new forms of law but also new processes which contribute to the development of a poly-centric approach of European integration.[14]

At the Nice European Council in December 2000, one crucial topic was the Charter of Fundamental Rights of the EU, drafted as a result of cooperation between many different institutions, bodies and groups. This Charter is based on the Universal Declaration of Human Rights of 1948, the European Convention of Human Rights of 1950, the European Social Charter of 1961 and the EU Social Charter of 1989. This chapter does not discuss the Charter further but it should be noted that it makes fundamental rights applicable at the EU level although it is not legally binding and discussions are ongoing. It is also important to mention that the modernisation of the European social model and the emphasis on the promotion of quality in all areas of social policy were discussed and agreed in the European Council based on the European Social Agenda in 2000. One of its main goals is to increase competitiveness and to achieve full employment based on the ideas of employability, entrepreneurship, adaptability and equal opportunity. For this, the necessity of policies for quality of training, quality of work, quality of industrial relations and quality of social policy are stressed whilst respecting the diversity of

Member States on this topic. Moreover, the presidency conclusions paper of the Nice European Council intentionally stated that the draft of Company Law, which had been a long pending question since 1959, had finally been agreed at Nice (Bulletin EU 12–2000). Following this, the Council Directive on supplementing the Statute for a European Company with regard to the Involvement of Employees was adopted in October 2001 (Council Directive 2001/86/EC).

After this, the European Council meeting in Laeken was held in December 2001, with the aims of promoting full employment and fleshing out the European social model in response to the Lisbon conclusion. During this meeting the main focus was on the four following topics of discussion: first, the Council approved the fact that the social partners are willing not only to further develop social dialogue but also to develop and improve coordination of tripartite consultation. It was agreed that a social affairs summit of this kind would be held before every European Council. Second, the agreement of the Parliament and the Council on the Directive on informing and consulting workers and on the protection of workers in the event of the insolvency of their employer were welcomed in order to prevent and resolve social conflicts. Third, the necessity for a first report on social inclusion and establishment of a set of common indicators eradicating poverty and promoting social inclusion was posited. Fourth, there were demands for the adequacy of pensions and the stability and modernisation of pension and healthcare systems (Bulletin EU 12–2001). Furthermore, 'the Lisbon Strategy' was released by the Commission in January 2002 to propose social policy at the EU level for the coming decade (COM(2002)14 final).

To sum up, the trend of extending EU social policy to civil rights and civil dialogue during the era of the Amsterdam Treaty continued through to the Nice Treaty. Through reforms of the institutional framework, codecision procedures have gradually expanded and various actors have started to become officially involved in EU social policy. This tendency for a wider range of actors is also shown in the drafting process of the Charter of Fundamental Rights of the EU. Also, at the European Council meeting in Laeken in 2001, social protection at the EU level started to be focused on more firmly and concretely than before. Overall, in terms of concrete social regulations, it appears that the EU has adopted a policy of setting 'core' or 'minimum' standards of social and civil rights rather than attempting to approximate, harmonise or converge every aspect of social and civil law of all Member States.

EU external social policy from Nice through Lisbon to Laeken

In terms of the EU's external social policy after Amsterdam, an approach based on stimulating international cooperation with multilateral institutions, such as ILO, WTO, OECD, UN, WHO, Council of Europe and NGOs, in order to underpin strategic social policy implementation for developing international codes of conduct and for ensuring core social/labour standards have been observed. In this context, the EU has announced the rejection of any methods involving the use of sanctions as a response to the infringement of the core standards. The EU, also supports ways of increasing multilateral technical assistance, of making better use of SIA (Sustainability Impact Assessments: a method assessing the influence of trade on sustainable development), and of promoting private and voluntary schemes of social labelling. This approach is comprehensively explained in a new Communication by the Commission entitled 'Promoting core labour standards and improving social governance in the context of globalisation' released in July 2001 (COM(2001)416 final). Furthermore, the EU has recently decided to make further concrete plans for 'corporate social responsibility' in response to the European Council meetings in Lisbon and Nice. This initiative is described in a new green paper called 'Promoting a European Framework for Corporate Social Responsibility' presented by the Commission in July 2001 (COM(2001) 366 final).

In thinking about future EU external social policy, the presidency conclusions of the Laeken European Council in December 2001 described two main views. First, the European Council welcomed the outcome of the Ministerial Conference in Doha, which launched a new round of global trade negotiations based on an approach balanced equally between liberalisation and regulation. It was emphasised that the EU should promote the social and environmental dimension of that round of negotiations. Second, it was stated that unified Europe needs to shoulder its responsibilities in the governance of globalisation when confronted with a globalised, but highly fragmented, world. 'In short, a power wanting to change the course of the world affairs in such a way as to benefit not just the rich countries but also the poorest. A power seeking to set globalisation within a moral framework, in other words to anchor it in solidarity and sustainable development' (Bulletin EU 12–2001).

Considering external social policy at the present, it is clear that the EU is searching for innovative systems of realising practical and effective international core social and labour standards, as well as efficient methods of cooperation with external countries. In these circumstances, it is significant that not only the creation and implementation of official international standards, but also the private use of these standards, has recently been brought into question. The development of relevant criteria of use seems to be controversial, but essential.

A new sphere of social policy and a challenge for social governance by the EU

In this chapter, the existence of a new social sphere in the EU and the content of this sphere have been discussed in conjunction with some European integration theories and examples related to the characteristics of EU social policy. Consequently, it is argued that the challenge for the EU has been to create a new sphere of social policy in certain areas, especially in setting up and protecting minimum social and civil rights which are sometimes beyond the control of the modern nation state. However, this does not deny the importance of the roles of states and other actors at the national and local level. On the contrary, these actors have increasing importance in the face of the newly emerging networking governance in the shared social sphere. Furthermore, the social policy of the EU is clearly observable not only internally but also externally, as described in this chapter. These internal and external directions in the social sphere are both supported by EU institutional and legal frameworks, but the two directions often have different approaches and double standards in terms of the realisation of social and civil rights.

The fundamental question which remains is why the EU has continued to expand its social policy formation, in spite of considerable objections to and criticisms of the related political integration. According to Room, the European Commission was interested in at least four interrelated matters in terms of EU social policy at the end of the 1980s.[15] First is the Europeanisation of industrial rights that have already been won by workers in individual countries at the national level. This is beneficial both for industrial democracy and for avoiding unemployment, as rights can be introduced in Member States where social protection and labour regulations are lax. Second is the harmonisation of various areas, such as vocational qualifications, training systems and social security in order to promote or realise the idea of free movement of labour. Third is the coordination of social security systems including educational and care systems for the movement of dependents of workers. It can be said that these three matters are related to controversial and unresolved issues concerning social dumping. Fourth is the response to the inevitable social costs accompanying the Single Market and to the redistribution of the fruits produced by the Market based on ideas of solidarity and social cohesion. The fruits themselves are allocated neither spontaneously nor equally to disadvantaged areas and groups within the EU. Through such social action, the EU and EU policies also gain support from EU citizens.

Moreover, the limitation or so-called 'crisis' of western welfare states in the 'borderless world' and the necessity to find innovative ways of overcoming it may be pointed out. Rhodes mentioned that welfare states were truly in crisis in the 1990s:

> Arguably the new strains appearing in welfare were due precisely to a contradiction between capital accumulation and profit making and the need to legitimize that process via social spending. Moreover, there was now an international dimension to this contradiction. For while during the 'golden age' of 'embedded liberalism' the growth – and parallel internationalization – of western capitalism had been dependent on domestic social compacts, in the era of 'disembedded liberalism' the 'ability of governments to live up to their side of the bargain' is wearing precariously thin ... despite the continued relevance of borders and national institutional settings as 'filters' of globalisation process, it can be argued that the nature and the role of the state is being transformed.[16]

An early study of welfare states by Myrdal also mentioned that western welfare states are protectionist and nationalistic. However, if western welfare states would like to achieve international stability and have external flexibility for their own sake, an attempt to go 'beyond the welfare state' is required. This is achieved by creating supranational regulations and common decision-making on a basis of solidarity with a more enlightened citizenry and universal brotherhood with a long-term view. Furthermore, Myrdal explained that, in order to achieve this stage, a different approach needs to be taken in developing countries than in developed countries. Namely the approach for developing countries should be connected with commercial and trading policies, and with concrete aid policies and support for self-independence so that these can mitigate the disparities.[17]

Though the topic of the issue of the relation between the EU and western welfare states is beyond the scope of this chapter, it should be stressed that some form of social governance dealing with global issues is increasingly required when faced with the limitations of the nation state and the phenomenon of borderless societies. However, this kind of framework of social governance is still very immature compared with the legal and institutional framework of economic or market governance. The creation of a framework of social governance and the enrichment of its substance have to be planned and promoted in positive terms. In this context, the challenge for the EU and the emerging new social sphere of the EU have to be accorded attention. Additionally, although the influence of 'globalisation' on social policy is still unclear and is often regarded in a negative light, it may act as a trigger for the development of alternative approaches to and implementation of social policy.[18] The phenomenon and discourse of globalisation have to be consciously and intentionally used for creating better social governance that provides better living standards for all people. It means social governance has to respect the diversity of nations and areas, cultures and people.

Conclusions

If the idea of European integration, aiming at peace and sustainable economy, is really possible while increasing wealth based on market integration, the effectiveness of EU countries will be increased. However, it can be said that individual citizens of the EU are likely to face the economic and social risks of the Single Market without the benefits of the implementation of certain areas of social policy at the EU level. 'The third way', which ensures both high standards of social protection and freedom of individuals, can be realised with the formation of a multi-tiered social policy participated in by multifarious organisations including the EU. In this respect, taking account of the interrelated situation of the world today, the international or external dimensions of EU social policy cannot be neglected.

Considering both EU internal and external social policy, and the emerging new sphere arising from these, it can be said that a new way of social governance involving regulatory and networking governance at the EU level has been created through the formation of a multi-layered/multi-tiered polity. Attempts by the EU to implement various innovative ideas and social actions are required, and some have already been proposed, as discussed so far, in order to deal with socio-economic issues and needs in the globalised society. Depending on its nature, this sphere may offer possibilities for the promotion of welfare for people both within and outside the EU. The role of the nation, which has protected its own citizens with certain social standards especially after the Second World War, but which excludes outsiders, might be changed. At the moment, the contents of the social sphere, such as what will be the European and international core social and labour standards, how these will be realised and what the rules of the private use of international standards are, are questions which require wide-ranging discussion rather than political integration and social intervention at the EU level. Last but not least, the newly emerging social sphere of the EU and some innovative legal and institutional systems within it have the potential to provide a number of crucial ideas for further development of a more comprehensive global social governance and for pursuing international common social interests in the shared world.

Notes

1   Swaan, Abram de (1992) *Perspectives for Transnational Social Policy, Government and Opposition*, London, Winter, 27: 33–52; Hantrais, Linda (1995) *Social Policy in the European Union*. London: Macmillan Press Ltd, pp. 1–17.
2   Leibfried, Stephan and Pirson, Paul (1995) 'Semisovereign Welfare State: Social Policy in a Multi-tiered Europe', in Leibfried, S. and Pirson, P. (eds) *European Social Policy: Between Fragmentation and Integration*. Washington: Brookings, p. 44.
3   See Fink, Janet, Lewis, Gail and Clarke, John (2001) 'Transitions and Trajectories in European Welfare', in Fink, Janet, Lewis, Gail and Clarke, John (eds) *Rethinking European Welfare: Transformations of Europe and Social Policy*, London: SAGE, pp. 1–25; Kleinman, Mark (2001) *A European Welfare State? European Union Social Policy in Context*. Hampshire: Palgrave, pp. 1–7.
4   Falkner, Gerda (1999) 'European Social Policy: Towards Multi-level and Multi-actor Governance', in Kohler-koch, B. and Eising, R. (eds). *The Transformation of Governance in the European Union*. London: Routledge, p. 84.
5   Kleinman, Mark and Piachaud, David (1992) *European Social Policy: Models and Rationales*. London: STICERD, p. 16.
6   Moravcsik, Andrew (1993) 'Preference and Power in the European Community: A Liberal Intergovernmentalist Approach', *Journal of Common Market Studies*, 31, 4: 473–524.
7   Haas, Ernst. B. (1958) *The Uniting of Europe: Political, Social and Economical Forces 1950-1957*. London: Stevens & Son.
8   Streeck, Wolfgang and Schmitter, Philippe C. (1992). 'From National Corporation to Transitional Pluralism: Organized Interests in the Single European Market', in Streeck, Wolfgang (eds) *Social Institutions and Economic Performance: Studies of Industrial Relations in Advanced Capitalist Economics*. London: SAGE, pp. 197–231.
9   Jansen, Carsten Strøby (2000) 'Neofunctionalist Theories and the Development of European Social and Labour Market Policy', *Journal of Common Market Studies*, 38, 1: 71–92; Lindberg, Leon N. and Scheingold, Stuart, A. (1970) *Europe's Would-Be Polity: Patterns of Change in the European Community*. Englewood Cliffs, NJ: Prentice Hall; Lindberg, Leon N. and Scheingold, Stuart, A. (eds) (1971) *Regional Integration: Theory and Research*. Cambridge, MA: Harvard University Press.
10 Pirson, Paul (1996) 'The Path to European Integration: A Historical Institutionalist Analysis', *Comparative Political Studies*, 20, 2: 27–57.
11 Steiner, Josephine (1992) *Textbook on EEC Law*, 3rd edn. London: Blackstone, 14.
12 Fukuda, Koji (2002) 'Contemporary International Theory and European Integration', *The Doushisha Law Review*, 282: 218–65.
13 Falkner, Gerda (1999) op. cit. p. 93.
14 Szyszczak, Erika (2001) 'The New Paradigm for Social Policy: A Virtuous Circle?', *Common Market Law Review*, 38: 1125–9.
15 Room, Graham (1991) *Towards a European Welfare State?* Bristol: SAUS, pp. 1–14.
16 Rhodes, Martin (1996) 'Globalization and West European Welfare States: A Critical Review of Recent Debates', *Journal of European Social Policy*, 6(4): 306–12.
17 Myrdal, G. (1960) *Beyond the Welfare State: Economic Planning in the Welfare States and its International Implications*. Yale University Press (reprinted 1961, London, Gerald Duckworth & Co. Ltd), pp. 117–214.
18 Kleinman, Mark (2001) op. cit. pp. 59–81; Sykes, Robert, Palier, Bruno and Prior, Pauline M. (eds), (2001) *Globalization and European Welfare States: Challenge and Change*. Hampshire: Palgrave, pp. 1–16.

7 Hopes and fears for EU membership

The case of Poland

Takayuki Ito

> For Poles the European Union is an imposer of effectiveness and further
> modernization on their country, much like an enlightened despot. The
> appeal to the European Tribunal in Strasbourg enjoys, therefore, enorm-
> ous support among them, as if it were the true court at last.
>
> (Kolarska-Bobinska, 2001)

Introduction

It is widely assumed that Central and Eastern Europeans want to join the
European Union. Whether the European Union expands eastward or not
is seen to depend only on the EU itself, and the agreement of Central and
Eastern Europeans is taken for granted. Conventional wisdom holds that
the Danes can afford to hesitate before joining the EU, and the Swiss even
to refuse, but that for Central and Eastern Europeans there is no option
other than to accept membership due to the gravity of their economic
problems and the instability of their political systems.

But do Central and Eastern Europeans really want to join the European
Union? This chapter examines the question, not on the basis of common
opinion but rather on that of polling data and political analysis, with a
particular focus on the case of Poland.

Let us begin by looking at public opinion. The data in Table 7.1 are
from an opinion poll that has been conducted in Poland every few
months since 1994 on the following question: How would you vote if a referendum on Poland's membership in the European Union were to be
held today? Respondents were able to answer "yes," "no," or "difficult to
say." The results reflect a clear trend: enthusiasm for EU membership
peaked in May 1996, when 80 percent of respondents answered "yes," but
support for joining the EU has declined steadily since then. In July 2001,
support reached an all-time low of 53 percent. In contrast, opposition to
EU membership was insignificant early in the period when this poll was
taken – only 6 percent in June 1994 – but it increased steadily until March

Table 7.1 How would you vote in a referendum on EU membership?

If the referendum on Poland's membership in the European Union were to take place today, you would vote:	Indications of respondents according to the timing of poll (%)																	
	VI	V	V	III	IV	VIII	V	VIII	XII	V	XI	II	V	IX	III	V	VI	VII
	1994	1995	1996	1997	1997	1997	1998	1998	1998	1999	1999	2000	2000	2000	2001	2001	2001	2001
For Poland's membership in the European Union	77	72	80	72	72	72	66	63	64	55	59	55	59	55	55	55	54	53
Against Poland's membership in the European Union	6	9	7	12	11	12	19	19	19	26	26	26	25	26	30	28	29	25
Difficult to say	17	19	13	16	18	15	15	18	17	19	15	19	16	19	15	17	17	22

Source: CBOS, "Poglądy na temat integracji z Unia Europejska," in fttp://www.cbos.pl (September 9, 2001).

Note
See *Actual Problems and Events* (134), conducted on July 6–9, 2001, for a representative probe of 1,015 random sampled adult inhabitants of Poland.

2001, when it reached 30 percent. Opposition has since declined by five points, but nonetheless, the overall trend is clear. Though supporters still constitute an absolute majority for the present, opponents may overtake them sometime in the future.

Of course, Poles cannot speak for all Central and Eastern Europeans on the question of joining the EU. Czechs and Hungarians may be more solid supporters of membership. Unfortunately, I was only able to process pertinent materials written in Polish, and few sources in English, French, or German were available to me at the time this chapter was written. However, I suspect that other Central and Eastern Europeans betray similar tendencies to that of the Poles, and in any case Poles constitute the largest nation in Central and Eastern Europe, with a population (38 million) greater than all of the other candidate-nations combined. An explanation for the trend of declining Polish support for EU membership thus may well have relevance for the entire region.

Regarding the origins of the topic, the method, and sources of this chapter, my research has focused on possible outcomes of the referendum. A referendum is a mechanism through which the citizens of a nation raise their voices in the ultimate determination of the course for their country to take. In a democracy, not all political decisions are taken through this mechanism; even in Switzerland, where the referendum has played an important role in political life since the mid-nineteenth century, other (often elitist) mechanisms such as consociational democracy or corporatism have proved to be more decisive. Under the current Polish constitution, the referendum plays only a minor role. Only once since the systemic change in 1989 has a referendum been held – on the issue of adopting a new constitution in 1997. No referendum was held, for example, on the decision to join NATO. Nonetheless, for good or ill, EU membership is a matter to be decided by referendum.[1] I believe that this Polish referendum has relevance for other Central and Eastern European countries as well.

When a referendum is held, the citizens of a nation are called on to vote, and their voting behavior in the referendum can be gauged in advance by opinion polls. However, it is a rather less straightforward task to assess what motivates citizens in making their decisions. The rational-choice school assumes that actors choose what they consider to be most conducive to their interests. Yet the citizens of a country are not always in a position to calculate costs and benefits. Moreover, they do not always know what their interests are. Their choices are often swayed by emotions, unfounded expectations, advice heard just before voting, the charisma of their leaders as well as other factors.

On the other hand, citizens are not invariably prisoners of irrational feelings. They do have notions of their rational interests, however vague these notions may be, and citizens are capable of anticipating what will advance their interests and what will not. Thus, it is often said that every public decision produces winners and losers, and everyone tries to end up on the side of the winners. It is impossible to know with certainty who will win or lose, but it is quite possible to find out what people think about their choices subjectively. This task is central to the purpose of this chapter.

In contrast to the general public, the elite of a nation know more or less where their interests lie. They are usually more capable of calculating the costs and benefits of public decisions with accuracy. If they were not thus capable, they would be unable to formulate or execute policy, which is their usual domain of activity. The assumptions of the rational-choice school therefore apply better to the elite than to other sections of society. Yet the concept of an elite is a broad and relative one. For instance, only a handful of politicians will be personally responsible for facilitating the decision on Poland's accession to the European Union: the President, the Premier, the Foreign Minister, and certain other members of the cabinet; these constitute a political elite with direct influence on this political decision. Around this narrow core of decision-makers stands a wider circle of people who can influence the decision indirectly – leaders of political parties, businessmen, journalists, army officers, religious leaders, and representatives of various interest groups; this wider circle comprises the elite of the groups or organizations which they are supposed to represent.

In dealing with possible outcomes of the Polish referendum on EU membership, this chapter does not focus on the elite as such, nor does it focus on the general public independent of its elite. My interest is in the mechanism of interaction between the elite and the public as regards the question of EU membership.

Three layers of society can be distinguished in this interaction: the political class, intermediary groups, and the general public. I agree with most specialists on political culture that political opinion diffuses from top to bottom, that is, from the elite to the citizenry, particularly during phases of transformation.[2] It is, therefore, quite important in a referendum, for instance, to know the views of the elite, as they presumably influence the voting behavior of the public. However, the Polish case shows that the public is not always susceptible to the influence of the elite. Since the great upheaval of 1989, Poland has been ruled without interruption by pro-integrationist governments. To some extent, Poles have been influenced by these governments to adopt relatively pro-integrationist attitudes, at least in comparison with the Communist period. The opinion poll cited above, however, reveals a trend contrary to this influence. It is unclear whether the Polish people will even become involved in a referendum when they have not yet been fully convinced to support it by their elite.

EU studies have become something of a boom industry in Poland. Specialists have done a great deal of research on various aspects of Poland's accession to the European Union, including its history, the process of negotiations surrounding it, economic conflicts that it may engender, security implications, incipient identity crises, and resulting social problems.[3] Institutes and journals dedicated to addressing the problems of European integration have been founded,[4] and every several months symposia or study meetings are convened on some aspect of the subject. As a result, there is no shortage of studies on related topics, and I have made use of these as far as possible. As far as I know, however, little political science analysis has yet been conducted, particularly analysis of the impact of European integration on the political system in Poland and vice versa. A huge amount of sociological data has been accumulated, however, by a number of competing polling organizations, and much of this data is available over the Internet;[5] I make use of some of it here.

Euro-enthusiasts versus Euro-sceptics

Pasierbinska, Turyk, Kubicki, and Galent have constructed an informative map of Polish hopes and fears concerning EU membership, based on responses to polls conducted in March 1998 on opinions regarding the costs and benefits of membership (Table 7.2). These researchers classify the hopes and fears of respondents into four groups: high politics, social policy, the economy, and culture. Unfortunately, this map does not make clear the intensity of hopes and fears in these areas, how they are related to each other, or what kind of people share them.

The Center for Public Opinion Polling (known by its Polish acronym, CBOS), conducted a poll in August 1996 on the potential consequences of Poland's accession to the EU that affords more specific insight into what Poles think of the possible costs and benefits of EU membership (see Table 7.3). To Poles, European integration clearly means changes mainly in the broadly understood economic sphere, and not in the spheres of high politics, social policy, or culture, as categorized in Table 7.2. This is not surprising, as high politics and culture are concerns of the elite, and it is difficult for the public to associate EU membership with social policy issues. Poles have a clearer idea of benefits in these three areas than of costs; indeed, it is difficult to characterize the narrow group of potential outcomes that Poles regard as costs of integration, since 36 percent of the respondents found it difficult to answer at all.[6]

Table 7.2 List of fears and hopes about EU membership

	Fears	Hopes
High politics	– loss of sovereignty – interference of EU states in Polish military policy – loss of the national Polish currency – subordination of weaker states to stronger states – influx of immigrants – exodus of specialists	– security – possibility of appeal to EU law organizations – freedom of movement
Social policy	– loss of social benefits – decay of state safety nets – decay of health service – spread of social pathology	– guarantee by the EU of suitable pensions – more efficient health service and social care – improvement of natural environment
Economy	– disintegration of monopolistic state enterprises – increase of zloty's significance – opening of the market – decline of exports – increase of imports – foreign ownership of land – fear of foreign corporations – mass dismissals – increase in unemployment – deterioration of economic conditions – decline of unspecialized, unprofitable agricultural units – increase in bankruptcies – tightening of access to loans and credits – subordination and economic exploitation of Poland by EU states – "farmerization" of agriculture	– restructuring of the state economy – credits and loans not requiring repayment – influx of capital – opening of markets – new opportunities for work – improvement of material conditions – increase of economic efficiency and entrepreneurship – mechanization and specialization in agriculture – new technology
Culture	– influx of foreign cultural elements – decline of Polish culture – Westernization of culture – decline of traditional Polish family and religious values.	– development of cultural and scientific positions – increase in belief in education – advance in civilization.

Source: Zuzanna Pasierbinska, Ewa Turyk, Pawel Kubicki, and Marcin Galent, "Interesy, szanse i zagrozenia a integracja europejska," in Macha, 1998, pp. 86–7.

Table 7.3 Costs and benefits of integration

	Percentage	Benefits of integration
1	31	Favorable changes in the economy, strengthening of zloty, and influx of foreign capital
2	19	Improvement of economic conditions of life, higher salaries
3	15	Stimulation of foreign trade
4	11	Decrease in unemployment
5	8	Influx of new technology
6	6	Free movement across borders, opening to the world
7	5	Greater security for the country
8	4	Hopes of a better life in general
9	3	Improvement of Poland's image abroad
10	3	Benefits for agriculture
11	3	Financial aid from the West and freezing of debts
12	2	Adaptation of laws to EU requirements
13	2	Better access to culture
14	9	Overall benefits (protection of environment, changes of attitudes, legal job prospects in the West, support from Western countries in general, and so on)
15	3	Lack of benefits
16	24	Difficult to say

	Percentage	Costs of integration
1	9	Difficulties adapting the Polish economy to EU requirements
2	9	Competition from Western commodities
3	8	Difficulties for agriculture
4	8	Financial losses for the state
5	7	Loss or limitation of autonomy
6	4	Increase of criminality
7	3	Ownership of property by foreigners
8	3	Difficulties of adapting Polish norms, prescriptions, and laws to EU obligations
9	3	Increase of unemployment
10	2	Economic exploitation by stronger states with inexpensive labor resources
11	2	Decline of living standards
12	2	"It will be hard for us" in general
13	2	Difficulties in mental adaptation
14	9	Overall problems (diseases of civilization, narcotics, unfavorable changes in the sphere of customs and mentality, loss of national identity, mass influx of foreigners, and so on)
15	9	Neither losses nor problems
16	36	Difficult to say

Source: CBOS, "Ocena niektorych konsekwencji przystapienia Polski do UE, sierpien 1996," cited in: Pasierbinska *et al.*, *Interesy*, pp. 88–90. An opinion poll on a similar topic is conducted every year, but it is rather difficult to track changes over time precisely, as polling conditions change frequently (for instance, the wording of questionnaires may change). For the most recent poll (July 2001), see CBOS, "Poglady na temat integracji z Unia Europejska," in fttp://www.cbos.pl (July 26, 2001). For the present, it suffices to say that economic motivations dominate throughout the polls.

Let us now consider which sections of the Polish public fear EU membership, and which have high hopes for it. First, those who fear joining the EU have been called "Euro-sceptics," "Euro-realists," or simply "Nationalists." Those who expect benefits to come from integration have been called "Euro-enthusiasts," or simply "Europeans," or "Cosmopolitans."

Most observers agree that four factors are the most important indicators of whether a particular Pole will be a Euro-sceptic or a Euro-enthusiast: generation, geography, education, and social/economic status. Most pro-Europeans are youths, ranging in age from twenty to twenty-six (64 percent), whereas most anti-Europeans are over sixty (21 percent). Those over sixty are also most likely to answer "difficult to say": 39 percent.[7]

Turning to geography, inhabitants of Poland's Western and Northern regions (including Lower and Upper Silesia) are most likely to expect benefits from integration. In contrast, inhabitants of the so-called "Eastern Wall" regions – that is, Poland's Eastern and Central regions (including Galicia) – have the greatest fear of integration. In particular, inhabitants of the Eastern regions express fears about their places of work three times more frequently than inhabitants of the Western regions. It is unclear why this is so; geographical proximity to the West, economic prosperity, density of population, and the presence of major cities are all possible explanations for this geographic bias, but there are facts contradicting each of these factors as simple explanations. This problem merits further investigation by Polish sociologists.[8]

Education is also an important variable indicating attitudes towards the integration process. In general, the higher one's level of education, the greater one's support for integration. However, there are exceptions to this rule; some respondents with higher levels of education are pessimistic about Poland's EU membership, as they have a heightened sensitivity toward the challenges that integration will pose. Moreover, some Poles with lower education levels welcome EU membership, perhaps in keeping with the observation that a lack of information often encourages optimism. Typical of this group are the unemployed, who hope that EU membership will change their fortune for the better.[9] In general, however, those with higher education are for the most part pro-European (74 percent). As the level of education rises, the number of respondents who answer "difficult to say" decreases.[10]

Perhaps the most important variable in determining attitudes toward EU membership, however, is social/economic status. In general, those who possess higher social statuses and who view their economic situation favorably tend to expect benefits from EU integration. In contrast, those whose social status is lower and who currently fare poorly in economic terms tend to expect their situations to deteriorate if Poland joins the

EU.[11] In present-day Poland, the socially and economically well situated include private entrepreneurs, organizational leaders and managers, professionals, intellectuals, and students, all of whom tend to be Euro-enthusiasts. At the other end of the spectrum, peasants, unskilled workers, and retirees are included among those whose social/economic status is low at present; and these groups tend to be Euro-sceptics. All other strata of Polish society can be located between these two poles.

Thus, Pasierbinska offers the following model of social attitudes toward Poland's accession to the EU in an attempt to arrange the main social strata of Polish society on a single scale ranging from Euro-enthusiasm to Euro-scepticism:[12]

← Support for EU integration			Opposition to EU integration →
Private entrepreneurs			
Organizational leaders and managers			
Professionals	White-collar workers		
Intellectuals	Housewives		
Students		Blue-collar workers	
Schoolboys		Small entrepreneurs	Small landholders
			Large landholders
Intelligent Euro-enthusiast	Not sufficiently informed Euro-enthusiast	Moderate Euro-sceptic	Categorical Euro-sceptic

Figure 7.1 Poland's social groups on EU membership.

Let us consider further the last of the four factors discussed above – social/economic status – singling out representative groups for close analysis, in an attempt to understand why some strata of Polish society tend to be Euro-enthusiasts and others Euro-sceptics.

Potential winners versus potential losers

Let us begin with Poland's peasants, by far the nation's most numerous and influential group of Euro-sceptics. Before considering their attitudes toward EU membership, let us first briefly survey the state of Polish agriculture today.

Miklaszewski identifies seven key features of Polish agriculture, summarized as follows.

1   A relatively high percentage of the population (38 percent) inhabits the countryside, and consequently agriculture employs as much as 27 percent of the working population and accounts for an even larger segment of the unemployed population (48 percent).

2   Only 47 percent of peasant holdings (*gospodarstwa*) produce goods for the market, and only 12 percent of peasants make their living exclusively from agriculture; this clearly indicates an unusually low level of commercialization.

3   The average peasant holding is about eight hectares in size (in contrast to eighteen hectares in the EU); 13.9 percent are holdings of one to two hectares, 29.7 percent two to five hectares, and 28.1 percent five to ten hectares.

4   The productivity of Polish agriculture is low: as many as twenty-nine workers are required to produce 100,000 ecus worth of agricultural goods in contrast to five to seven workers in the European Union.

5   The significance of pensions as sources of income for the rural population has increased (the number of retirees doubled between 1985 and 1995) even as over half of the unemployed have lost the right to social benefits; overall, transfers of income through pensions, annuities, and social benefits currently constitute the basis of existence for about five million people in the rural population, or more than 30 percent.

6   Only 15.4 percent of the rural population complete a middle school education (compared with 34.5 percent of the urban population), and only 1.9 percent pursue higher education (compared with 9.7 percent of the urban population).

7   In 1996, 59 percent of those engaged in agriculture finished only an agricultural course of training or learned on the job without formal training.[13]

Given these conditions, it is quite understandable that Polish peasants are not very enthusiastic about EU membership, though their reasons for this may be obscured by the huge amount of aid from the EU and other international institutions for which Poland's backward agriculture sector will be eligible as an EU member. Even before Poland joins the EU, it is entitled to receive so-called "pre-accession aid," and specialists have been busy calculating how much Poland should ultimately receive. From the three pre-accession aid programs – PHARE 2000, ISPA (Instrument for Structural Pre-accession Policies), and SAPARD (Support for Pre-accession Measures for Agriculture and Rural Development) – the total amount for which Poland is eligible over the years is 3.12 billion euro. These funds are distributed on the basis of four criteria: agricultural population, size of arable lands, per capita GDP, and specific territorial situations. Based on these criteria, Poland can expect to receive as much as 40 percent of all the aid earmarked for candidate-states (620 million euro) annually. These funds began to flow in 2000.

Furthermore, after joining the EU, Poland will be entitled to receive additional subsidies from the so-called "Structural Fund." These funds were set up to equalize economic disparities between EU Member States and their regions. Until now, Southern European countries like Spain, Portugal, Greece, and Italy have been their main beneficiaries, but when the countries of Central and Eastern Europe join the EU, they will also claim shares of the available subsidies, as most of these countries have per capita GDPs below 75 percent of the EU average, and are therefore eligible. Miklaszewski estimates that if Poland joins the EU in 2003, her share of these funds will amount to about 4 billion euro in the first year, and will soar up to 7.2 billion euro in 2006, peaking at 8.5 billion euro sometime in between. Altogether, Poland is projected to receive approximately 21 billion euro from the EU budget between 2003 and 2006.[14]

However, although these figures might be expected to console Polish peasants, one must bear in mind that such calculations are not their concern; calculating such figures and trying to persuade the nation of the advantages of EU membership is rather the job of the elite. Peasants themselves have different concerns. First of all, Poland's low productivity is due to rural overpopulation. If Poland is to approach EU productivity standards, the rural population must be reduced to one-quarter of its present size. That is, three out of four peasants must disappear, a fact that offers no consolation to the people concerned. If these people had somewhere to go, serious problems might be avoided, but given their extremely low levels of education, it will be difficult for them to find ways to support themselves outside of agriculture.

As shown in Table 7.4, those who believe that EU membership will have a positive effect on individual peasants dwindled from 40 percent in June 1994 to 17 percent in May 1999. The rate has recovered since then, though weakly, rising to 19 percent in May 2000. Those who believe that it will have a negative effect on individual peasants increased from 24 percent in June 1994 to 61 percent in May 1999. The rate has declined since then, but again only weakly, decreasing to 60 percent in May 2000. In retrospect, 1994 proved to be the year when the greatest optimism prevailed about the prospects for Polish agriculture within the EU. Respondents' views on the outlook for agriculture coincided almost perfectly with their prognoses for living standards.

Poles also have little confidence that Polish agriculture will be able to compete on an equal footing with European agriculture. In an opinion poll conducted in March 1998, a majority of respondents maintained that, after joining the EU, Poland would be flooded with agricultural products from Western Europe (58 percent). Only about one-third of respondents

Table 7.4 Opinions on the influence of EU membership on the industrial sector

In your opinion, will the association or integration of Poland with the European Union have a positive or negative effect on:	Positive effect (%)						Negative effect (%)						No influence (%)					
	VI '94	V '96	IV '97	IV '98	V '99	V '00	VI '94	V '96	IV '97	IV '98	V '99	V '00	VI '94	V '96	IV '97	IV '98	V '99	V '00
The state of the Polish economy?	–	–	–	57	51	50	–	–	–	23	28	28	–	–	–	4	5	6
Private enterprises?[a]	67	67	51	56	48	49	6	7	15	16	21	21	9	11	8	7	7	8
State enterprises?[a]	32	34	35	38	30	27	37	37	29	37	42	43	10	11	7	5	5	8
Individual farms in Poland?[a]	40	37	29	26	17	19	24	32	37	54	61	60	13	11	7	4	5	4
Your farm or place of work?[b]	–	–	26	29	26	25	–	–	17	18	25	24	–	–	29	23	27	26

Source: CBOS, "Opinie o skutkach integracji Polski z Unią Europejską i przebiegu negocjacji akcesyjnych," in fttp://www.cbos.pl (September 15, 2001).

Notes

The answer "Difficult to say" has been omitted.

a In the years 1994–6 the question concerning these spheres of life was worded as follows: "The association or integration of Poland with the European Union may affect various areas of life in Poland. In your opinion will it contribute to the development or rather the decline of state enterprises and factories, private enterprises and factories, or individual farms?"

b Opinions of professionally active persons.

(35.7 percent) believed that Polish peasants could withstand the competition. Those who expressed the greatest fear of agricultural competition, including villagers and peasants themselves, were also the least educated.[15]

Yet not all peasants are Euro-sceptics. Those who have relatively greater knowledge of the integration process and own well-organized, large, and more specialized holdings tend neither to reject the idea of integration nor to fear foreign buy-outs of Polish lands or European competition. In Poland's accession to the European Union, such peasants see valuable benefits for their own "economies." Younger peasants furthermore tend to see opportunities in EU membership.

Nonetheless, a majority of Polish peasants think that the stronger EU Member States want to subordinate the weaker in order to exploit them and make them economically dependent. The majority fear "farmerization," that is, the adoption of a system of large-scale agriculture with farming entrepreneurs hiring workers and producing goods for the market, that they believe will ensue after the sale of Polish lands to foreigners. Such fears are expressed most frequently by peasants who are older, less educated, own smaller and less mechanized holdings, and fear that they will not be able to withstand Western competition.[16]

Unskilled workers comprise the next largest group of Euro-sceptics. Workers expect to lose more personally than they gain from integration, and they suspect the EU of harboring negative motivations in offering the prospect of membership to Poland. Workers, both skilled and unskilled, are also the social–professional group that suffered the most severe loss of privilege and prestige due to the systemic transformation from Communism to the present system. Unfortunately, Polish sociologists have largely neglected the resulting problems that workers have faced.[17]

Many retirees also tend to be Euro-sceptics, because they fear the weakening of paternalistic state policies on which they depend. Most, however, are indifferent, either because they are ignorant or because they do not believe that they personally will suffer adverse consequences due to integration.[18]

Other groups are smaller, but are nonetheless politically significant. As shown in Table 7.4, it is widely believed that private enterprises will be winners in European integration, yet not all entrepreneurs are Euro-enthusiasts. Small-scale, private entrepreneurs who do not feel that their businesses are competitive tend to be Euro-sceptics, and such entrepreneurs are legion. It is also believed that state enterprises will be losers in integration; for as long as polls have been taken, more people have held that European integration will have a negative effect on state enterprises than have held the opposite view. In May 2000 the gap between the rates at which people held these divergent opinions peaked at 43 percent versus 27 percent, respectively. It is little wonder that industrialists from large state firms tend to be Euro-sceptics.[19]

On the other hand, the more successful or confident private entre-preneurs are undoubtedly the most important Euro-enthusiasts. In general, the Polish public believes that entrepreneurs will be beneficiaries of European integration, and most entrepreneurs agree. These opinions are reported in almost all polls on these topics. Pasierbinska *et al.* wonder whether these views are a result of rational judgments or a vestige of socialist convictions.[20]

Organizational leaders, managers, and professionals – for example, dir-ectors, department heads, scientists, doctors, and teachers – are typically well-informed Euro-enthusiasts. They consider both the positive and negative results of integration in forming their opinions, and thus they are the enthusiasts with the fullest knowledge of the integration process. Most support Poland's accession to the EU within five years, expecting integra-tion to spur entrepreneurship and efficiency, and recognizing the integra-tion process as the engine propelling modernization in Poland. Nonetheless, many fear that the Polish economy will encounter difficulties in adapting, and assess Poland's geopolitical situation as an EU Member State rather pessimistically.[21]

Young people comprise another group of Euro-enthusiasts. Polish young people view the future with great optimism, and take little notice of any obstacles on the road to joining the EU on an equal footing with other member countries. A total of 64.5 percent believe that Poland's accession to the EU will be beneficial, particularly in the long term; only 3 percent disagree with this view. The higher the educational institutions attended, the more likely the young people are to support integration. Almost all university and gymnasium students are Euro-enthusiasts, but youths who attend vocational schools or do not attend school at all have limited knowledge and often answer "difficult to say" on opinion polls. In general, the more knowledge young people have of integration, the more likely they are to support it.[22]

Let us consider two additional social groups that may influence public opinion on the question of Poland joining the EU: Catholic priests and army officers. First, the Catholic hierarchy in Poland has expressed clear support for European integration in official documents of the Polish Episcopacy. In 1995, Bishop Tadeusz Pieronek, Secretary-General of the Episcopacy, as well as Primate Jozef Glemp, declared that the entry of Poland into the EU threatens neither the national nor religious identity of Poles. In a poll conducted by CBOS in May 1998, nearly 80 percent of priests expressed positive attitudes toward European integration.[23] Is it possible to conclude on the basis of these data, however, that believers –

who constitute an overwhelming majority of Poles – support European integration?

Most Poles view themselves as deeply religious, and Europeans as more secularized. On the question of the religious effects of Poland's integration into secular Europe, the CBOS poll of May 1996 showed that 29 percent of respondents held that the religiousness of Poles would decrease as a result of European integration, while only 5 percent held the opposite view. Other CBOS polls show that respondents also view the consequences of integration for priests with little optimism: 23 percent believe that priests will fare better, 25 percent worse, and 28 percent anticipate no change. Pasierbinska *et al.* conclude from these data that Polish society is prepared to accept a less significant role for the Catholic Church in Poland.[24]

Interestingly, there is an inverse relationship between knowledge of the EU and frequency of church visits: the more often one visits church, the less one knows about the EU. Of those who attend church several times a week, 21 percent have not heard of the EU, whereas among those who do not practice religion at all, only 5 percent have not heard of the EU. There is reason to doubt, therefore, whether priests truly support integration, since frequent church visitors, among whom they enjoy greatest authority and who are most eager to listen to them, do not hear much about integration.[25]

Military officers are important to the question of EU membership, not only as wielders of Poland's military power, but also as opinion leaders and information providers for their conscripted soldiers, in relation to whom they stand much as priests do to frequent church visitors. According to an opinion poll 86 percent of military officers supported Poland's membership in the EU. The percentage of supporters has declined slightly since, with the decline beginning in 1996. However, asked about the benefits of Poland's integration into Europe, 33 percent answer "Difficult to say," suggesting that support for integration is fluid and unrelated to knowledge of the issue.

Military officers fall into three groups on the question of EU membership:

1   Euro-progressives, who tend to accept the idea of a united Europe, support maximal European disarmament, and offer the most cosmopolitan arguments for membership;
2   Euro-pragmatists, who believe in striking a balance between maintaining state sovereignty and unifying Europe, and who view the possibilities of a united Europe with moderate optimism; and
3   National-conservatives, who do not want to sacrifice national (state)

sovereignty for the sake of the EU, and are pessimistic about integration and the prospects for permanent detente in Europe.

Young officers tend to adopt Euro-progressive positions, whereas middle-aged officers most often present national-conservative postures.[26]

The political elite

Let us turn finally to the elite, limiting ourselves here to the inner circle, that is, the leaders of political parties both inside and outside of the parliament. The role of political parties is much greater in Poland than in the Western countries or Japan, because the civil service and interest groups remain underdeveloped. Macieja estimates that the 200,000 most important posts in the government are controlled by Poland's political parties.[27] As most party leaders in Poland are members of the parliament – with the exception only of leaders whose parties were unable to gain seats due to the 5 percent threshold – let us furthermore limit discussion to parliamentarians.

The Polish parliament elected in 1997 was composed of five groupings: *AWS* (*Akcja Wyborcza Solidarnosc*, or Solidarity Electoral Action), *SLD* (*Sojusz Lewicy Demokratycznej*, or Alliance of the Democratic Left), *PSL* (*Polskie Stronnictwo Ludowe*, or Polish Peasant Party), *UW* (*Unia Wolnosci*, or Union of Freedom), and *UP* (*Unia Pracy*, or Union of Labor). A coalition government led by Jerzy Buzek as premier was formed by *AWS* and *UW*, but in June 1999 – when *UW* broke out of the coalition – the Buzek government became a minority government. All five parties represented in the parliament, including both government and opposition parties, were committed to Poland's accession to the European Union, though subtle nuances distinguished their positions.

Why the political elite chooses this or that particular orientation is an important question, but one that lies beyond the purposes of this chapter. The political elite has its own priorities which are not merely reflections of the public mood, and hence this question must be approached by methods other than public opinion polls. The statements and writings of political leaders, and if possible interviews, would serve as better sources of information in such an investigation, but these would be suitable sources for a separate study; in this chapter, the orientations of the political parties are treated as given.

By the time that new parliamentary elections were scheduled for September 23, 2001, the map of the political landscape had undergone substantial changes. Leading up to the elections, nine major parties struggled for voters' favors rather than the five introduced above. On the right, *AWS* split into *AWSP* (*AWS Prawicy*, or *AWS* of the Right), *PiS* (*Prawo i Sprawiedli-wosc*, or Law and Justice), and the more radical *LPR* (*Liga Polskich Rodzin*, or League of Polish Families). On the left, the *SLD–UP* electoral coalition and *PSL* remained more or less intact. A new grouping, *PO* (*Platforma Oby-watelska*, or Civic Platform) appeared in the center. In addition to *LPR*, two other radical groupings also appeared: *Samoobrona* (*Samoobrona Rzeczy-pospolitej Polskiej*, or Self-Defense of the Polish Republic), and *Alternatywa* (*Ruch Spoleczny "Alternatywa,"* or Social Movement "Alternative"). As all election forecasts indicated, the left coalition *SLD–UP* emerged from the elections as winners.

As far as the issue of Poland's accession to the European Union is con-cerned, however, it seems that little changed in the political class. The two groupings most clearly committed to European integration, *SLD–UP* and *PO*, maintained a majority in the new parliament (53.72 percent; see Table 7.5). Some radical groupings made gains, but remained on the periphery of the Polish parliamentary scene. Nonetheless, there were important changes: two integrationist parties were eclipsed (*AWSP*, which had led the government for the previous four years; and *UW*, which had twice led the government), and radical parties emerged (*Samoobrona* and *LPR*; *Alternatywa* failed to win any seats).

Although all of the major parties have been more or less committed to European integration, *UW* is its most outspoken advocate, not only in offi-cial statements but also in the beliefs of its supporters. However, in a certain sense, *PO* has replaced *UW* as the leading advocate of integration. Among supporters of the major parties, supporters of *PO* would be the most likely to vote for Poland's accession to the European Union if a refer-endum were held today (see Table 7.6). Next most likely after *PO* sup-porters are those of *AWSP* (though it must be noted that *AWSP* failed to win any seats in the parliament), followed by *SLD*. *PiS* supporters would also vote for integration, but by a slimmer majority. *PSL* supporters would vote against it.

In any case, it is easy to ascertain how serious (or not) the political parties are about European integration on the basis of their electoral pro-grams. For instance, *PiS* agrees to Poland's joining the European Union, but insists that Poland should remain a strong, unitary nation state; *PiS* resolutely defends Poland's national interests but shows little concern for the country's date of entry into the EU, an event the party does not seem to view as real.[28] It is clear that *PiS* sees little chance of Poland's joining the EU in the near future, and assigns a higher priority to the integrity of the nation state than to European integration.

PSL also agrees that membership in the EU should be a goal of Poland's foreign policy, but blames the *AWS* government for misguided

Table 7.5 Changes in support for political parties (February to September 2001)

	II '01	III '01 (1)	III '01 (2)	IV '01 (1)	IV '01 (2)	V '01 (1)	V '01 (2)	VI '01 (1)	VI '01 (2)	VII '01 (1)	VII '01 (2)	VII '01 (3)	VIII '01 (1)	VIII '01 (2)	VIII '01 (3)	VIII '01 (4)	IX '01 (1)	IX '01 (2)	IX '01 (3)	IX '01 (4)	IX '01 (5)	Final
SLD–UP (L. Miller)	40	43	42	46	43	38	41	50	45	44	47	46	47	47	47	50	52	50	52	48	43	41.04
PSL (J. Kalinowski)	12	11	12	12	13	14	13	12	11	15	13	12	14	12	12	12	9	12	10	11	12	8.98
PO (A. Olechowski, M. Płażyński, D. Tusk)	21	18	19	14	16	19	18	13	18	16	14	13	12	13	13	12	14	12	14	14	15	12.68
PiS (L. Kaczyński)	–	–	–	–	–	–	10	10	8	7	6	7	7	6	8	8	8	8	7	8	7	9.50
AWSP	–	–	–	–	–	–	8	6	5	6	10	7	7	8	8	8	8	7	5	7	4	5.60
UW (B. Geremek)	4	4	4	5	5	4	4	4	3	5	4	4	7	4	4	4	4	4	3	2	4	3.10
Samoobrona (A. Lepper)	2	2	3	2	3	4	2	2	4	2	2	1	1	3	2	2	2	4	5	5	9	10.20
LPR (M. Kotlinowski)	–	–	–	–	–	–	–	–	–	1	1	1	1	2	3	3	3	3	3	5	5	7.87
Alternatywa (J. Kraus)	–	–	–	–	–	0	0	0	1	0	0	2	0	0	0	0	0	0	1	0	1	0.42

Source: OBOP, "Preferencje wyborcze Polaków 2000/2001," in: ftp://www.obop.pl, September 28, 2001. The data for the last two polls, conducted on September 13–14, 2001, and September 20, 2001, were published just before the elections and caused a sensation. See Życie, September 18, and September 21, 2001, respectively. For the final results of the elections of September 23, 2001, see Państwowa Komisja Wyborcza, "Wybory do Sejmu: wyniki gosowania na listy komitetów wyborczych w skali kraju," in ftp://www.pwk.gov.pl (September 29, 2001), or Gazeta Wyborcza (September 27, 2001). The turnout rate was 46.29 percent.

Notes

SLD: Sojusz Lewicy Demokratycznej (Alliance of the Democratic Left)
UP: Unia Pracy (Union of Labor)
PSL: Polskie Stronnictwo Ludowe (Polish Peasant Party)
PO: Platforma Obywatelska (Civic Platform)
PiS: Prawo i Sprawiedliwość (Law and Justice)
AWSP: Akcja Wyborcza Solidarność Prawicy (Solidarity Electoral Action of the Right)
UW: Unia Wolności (Union of Freedom)
Samoobrona: Samoobrona Rzeczypospolitej Polskiej (Self-Defense of the Polish Republic)
LPR: Liga Polskich Rodzin (League of Polish Families)
Alternatywa: Ruch Społeczny "Alternatywa" (Social Movement "Alternative")

Table 7.6 Voting behavior in a referendum according to political parties

Potential voters by political groupings[a]	Would vote:[b]	
	for Poland's accession to the European Union (%)	against Poland's accession to the European Union (%)
PO	81	12
AWSP	58	25
SLD–UP	58	26
PiS	44	12
PSL	32	44
Not yet decided	53	25
No intention of voting	46	24

Source: CBOS, "Poglady na temat integracj z Unia Europejska," in fttp://www.cbos.pl (September 14, 2001).

Notes

a Parties whose electorates are too small have not been taken into consideration to preserve the credibility of reported data.

b The answer "Difficult to say" has been omitted.

EU policies that, in its view, favor the EU states at the expense of Poland. The *PSL* website decribes how "foreign firms have taken control of strategic segments of the Polish economy, a huge foreign trade deficit has accumulated, and a powerful lobby has developed to promote the interests of foreign companies."[29] Of course, these conditions are the norm in many EU Member States, and if *PSL* cannot accept such a state of affairs, it is not yet ready for integration.

More alarming in general, and to Euro-enthusiasts in particular, is the rise of the radical parties, *Samoobrona, LPR,* and *Alternatywa.* Respectively, *Samoobrona* represents rural radicalism, *LPR* Catholic–conservative radicalism (if such a formulation is permissible), and *Alternatywa* urban radicalism. What is common to each of these parties, however, is strong nationalism. *Samoobrona* and *Alternatywa* have long led a peripheral existence in Polish politics; *LPR* has played a more central role, with party leaders such as Jan Olszewski and Antoni Macierewicz having formed a government in the early 1990s, later joining *AWSP,* and eventually setting up their new, radical right-wing party. It had been believed that none of the radical parties would be able to overcome the 5 percent threshold in the 2001 elections, but according to opinion polls, *Samoobrona* and *LPR* became increasingly popular in the last phase of the 2001 election campaign (see Table 7.5). Ultimately, *Samoobrona* won 10.2 percent of the ballot cast, well ahead of its mother party, *PSL,* which won only 8.98 percent. LPR won 7.87 percent, also ahead of its mother party, *AWSP,* which won only 5.6 percent, far less than the 8 percent it needed to enter the parliament as an electoral coalition composed of more than three parties.

On the question of EU membership, the radical parties take somewhat different positions. *Somoobrona* is a rather inward-looking party, with a clear domestic program but an as-yet underdeveloped foreign policy. It is ostensibly not opposed to joining the EU, but at the same time it proposes "making borders waterproof (*uszczelnienie granic*)" to protect domestic agriculture and to prevent smuggling.[30] In its programmatic declaration, *Independence for Poland! Work, Bread, and Housing for the Poles!*, LPR asks rhetorically, "Do we import unemployment, eat foreign bread, and live on the streets in the framework of the European Union or another contemporary Tower of Babel?" and answers "Let us choose independence and sovereignty for Poland!"[31] This shows that *LPR* is manifestly opposed to EU membership. *Alternatywa* has developed a detailed foreign policy. Specifically, *Alternatywa* takes a Gaullist position, "Europe of Fatherlands," rejecting all integrationist measures taken by the government to date as violations of national sovereignty.[32] In any case, the chances of *Alternatywa* entering the parliament were not great in the last phase of the 2001 election campaign, and indeed it did not win any seats.

For some time, diplomatic negotiations have been underway in Brussels between the European Commission and the Polish government on the conditions of Poland's entry into the EU. Poland has taken an unusually hard stance in these negotiations; of the thirty-one items on the agenda, Poland agrees with the European Commission on only sixteen, and of all the current candidate states, Poland has made the slowest progress in negotiations with the Commission.[33]

From the Polish point of view, the most difficult issue is the right of foreigners to purchase land. Poles are fearful that their lands will be bought up by foreigners, particularly Germans, if they grant them this right. Poles are therefore insisting on an unusually long transition period of eighteen years before granting this right to foreigners, while the European Commission proposes a compromise of seven years. Regarding this issue, most Poles consider some kind of transition necessary, but not as long a period as their government proposes (see Table 7.7).

From the EU's point of view, on the other hand, the free flow of labor comprises the greatest obstacle to Poland's membership. The Europeans are fearful that their job markets will be flooded with cheap labor from Poland. They therefore propose a transition period of seven years, while Poland insists on the free flow of labor from the first day of membership. On this issue, most Poles agree with their government that no transitional measures are justified, and that their government should not compromise

Table 7.7 Acceptance of a transition period for foreigners' rights to purchase land

How long a transitional period is necessary in your opinion?	Poles (N= 637) (%)	Czechs (N= 609) (%)
1–5 years	20	19
6–10 years	36	37
11–15 years	9	3
16–20 years	14	5
21 years or more	5	22
Difficult to say	16	14

Source: CBOS, "Poglady na temat integracj z Unia Europejska," in ftp://www.cbos.pl (September 14, 2001).

Note
Percentages are based on the total number of respondents for each nationality who think that a transition period is necessary.

on this point (see Tables 7.8 and 7.9). Do Poles intend to go job-hunting en masse in the West if and when they are allowed to? This is highly unlikely because of language barriers, housing problems, family ties, and so on. Even if they want to, the fact that the possibility is always open will make them reconsider, as several polls report. For this reason, Poles find the European position unnecessary and perceive it as discriminatory. Public opinion on this issue at home seems to be shared by Poland's negotiators in Brussels. It is worth noting that there are no substantial differences between Poles and Czechs on either the right of foreigners to buy land or the free flow of labor vis-à-vis the EU (see Tables 7.8 and 7.9).

Table 7.8 Level of acceptance of a transition period for freedom of work

In countries of the European Union and also in the European Commission, proposals have appeared requiring that citizens of candidate states are not allowed to work for seven years on the territory of current member countries. Do you think that this transition period is:	Poles (%)	Czechs (%)
adequate?	6	7
a little longer than necessary?	6	17
much longer than necessary?	15	18
not necessary?	57	45
difficult to say?	16	13

Source: CBOS, "Poglady na temat integracj z Unia Europejska," in ftp://www.cbos.pl (September 14, 2001).

Table 7.9 Should the government accept a transition period for freedom of work?

Do you think that the Polish (Czech) government should accept a seven-year transition period during which Poles (Czechs) would not be allowed to work in other countries of the European Union even after Poland (Czechoslovakia) had joined the EU?	Poles (%)	Czechs (%)
Definitely yes	3	2
Probably yes	8	13
Probably no	26	32
Definitely no	47	37
Difficult to say	16	16

Source: CBOS, "Poglady na temat integracj z Unia Europejska," in fttp://www.cbos.pl (September 14, 2001).

Conclusions

For the present, the political scene in Poland continues to be dominated by Euro-enthusiasts, but a cloud of Euro-scepticism looms on the horizon. Despite the great success of the *SLD–UP* in the 2001 elections, this grouping failed to secure an absolute majority in the *Sejm* (the lower house of the parliament). It is almost inconceivable that this Euro-enthusiastic grouping will form a ruling coalition with another Euro-enthusiastic grouping, *PO*, because the *SLD–UP* is a successor to the Communist party, whereas *PO* is staunchly anti-Communist. It is more likely that *SLD–UP* will instead be forced to form a minority government that will face incessant attacks from the noisy anti-EU radical parties now represented in the parliament. In the near future, it will become extremely difficult for *SLD–UP* to dissolve the parliament, as the new government will have to adopt strict belt-tightening policies in response to the grave conditions of state finances. Hence, the Polish government will continue to pursue pro-integrationist policies, but it is doomed to instability.

In the final analysis, Poles do not know concretely what European integration means for them. Their opinions are not based on solid knowledge, and their mood can change swiftly. The higher their social status and the better they fare economically, the more likely they are to welcome European integration, and to believe that they will be winners in post-integration Poland. Yet Poles of lower social/economic status outnumber those of higher status who are closer to the political elite. Such higher status Poles constitute intermediary groups between the political elite and the public. If things go well, the public will adopt their values in time. If

not, the public will look for other values. Since 1989, Poland has been
ruled by Euro-enthusiasts, and the public has been subjected without
interruption to political socialization from above. Now, a new Euro-scepti-
cal elite has appeared that has begun to catch the public imagination. It is
no longer certain how a referendum on Poland's membership in the EU
will turn out.

Notes

The author completed writing this chapter at the end of September 2001 when
the Polish parliamentary elections were held. Since that time there has been a new
development in Polish politics: *SLD–UP* made a coalition with *PSL* to form a
government, with *Samoobrona* supporting it outside the cabinet. Immediately after
the government was launched, there was a clash between the government coalition
and *Samoobrona*. Now the government must defend itself against Euro-enthusiatic
but staunchly anti-Communist *PO*, Euro-sceptic *PiS*, and two radical Euro-sceptic
parties: *LPR* and *Samoobrona*. Inside the government, *PSL* is notoriously Euro-
sceptic. It will not be easy for the government to uphold a consistent pro-integrationist policy.

 1 K. Bachmann, a journalist for the weekly Polityka, questions the wisdom of
   such a referendum and warns that it will result in an even more serious fiasco
   than the one in Ireland. Klaus Bachmann (2001) "Tygrys uciekl, zostal kot,"
   Polityka, 27 (2305), 7 July: 34–6.
 2 For example, William Zimmerman (1994) "Markets, Democracy and Russian
   Foreign Policy," *Post-Soviet Affairs*, Vol. 10, No. 2 (April–June): 103–26.
 3 See the literature listed in the Further Reading list below.
 4 The journals *Studia Europejskie* and *Przeglad Europejski* offer two examples.
 5 For instance, see CBOS, OBOP, PBS, and Central and Eastern Eurobarometer.
 6 Zuzanna Pasierbinska, Ewa Turcyk, Pawel Kubicki, and Marcin Galent (1998)
   "Interesy, szanse i zagrozenia a integracja europejska," in Mach (ed.), pp.
   89–90. See also Zdsislaw Mach (1998) "Podsumowanie," in Mach (ed.), pp.
   142–3.
 7 Magdalena Gora, Renata Gora, and Rafa Pieprzyk (1998) "Wiedza o Unii
   Europejskiej," in Mach (ed.), p. 26. See also Elzbieta Mach, "Polacy wobec integracji europejskiej," in Mach (ed.), pp. 127–33.
 8 Pasierbinska *et al.* "Interesy," pp. 96, 122. See also Gora *et al.*, "Wiedza," p. 21,
   and Zdzislaw Mach, "Podsumowanie," p. 143.
 9 Pasierbinska *et al.*, "Interesy," p. 85.
10 Gora *et al.*, "Wiedza," p. 26.
11 Pasierbinska *et al.*, "Interesy," p. 122.
12 Ibid., p. 119.
13 Stanislaw Miklaszewski (1999) "Polityka rolna i regionalna jako podstawowe
   kwestie sporne w negocjaciach Polski i Unii Europejskiej," in Dach (ed.), pp.
   147–8. See also Jan Siekierski (1999) "Koszty i korzysci integracji polskiego rol-
   nictwa z Unia Europejska," in Dach (ed.), pp. 28–130.
14 Miklaszewski, "Polityka," p. 154.
15 Pasierbinska *et al.*, "Interesy," p. 100. This observation is based on data up to
   1996. See also Gora *et al.*, "Wiedza," pp. 34–6.
16 Pasierbinska *et al.*, "Interesy," pp. 114–15.

17 Ibid., pp. 119, 123.
18 Ibid., p. 118.
19 Ibid., pp. 115–16.
20 Ibid., pp. 103–4. See also Table 7.4.
21 Pasierbinska *et al.*, "Interesy," p. 118.
22 Ibid., p. 117.
23 Joanna Karmowska and Grzegorz Pozarlik (1998) "Polak – Europejczyk. Odmienne stany swiadomosci," in Mach (ed.), p. 73. For more on the fact that Catholic priests are not always optimistic about EU integration, see a thoughtful interview with Bishop Tadeusz Pieronek and Roland Freudenstein, "Kosiciol – Unia – Obawy," *Gazeta Wyborcza*, September 22–3, 2001.
24 Pasierbinska *et al.*, "Interesy," pp. 93, 111. See also Miroslaw Natanek and Dariusz Niedzwiedzki (1998) "Kulturowe kompetencje Polakow a integracja europejska," in Mach (ed.), pp. 53–4, 57–8.
25 Gora *et al.*, "Wiedza," pp. 13, 18, 28.
26 Gora *et al.* "Wiedza," pp. 31–3. See also Karmowska and Pozarlik, "Polak," pp. 73–4.
27 Dorota Macieja (2001) "Rzeczpospolita nomenklaturowa," *Wprost*, No. 31 (975), August 5: 26–8.
28 "Program wyborczy Prawa i Sprawiedliwosci," in fttp://www.pis.org.pl (September 14, 2001).
29 "Deklaracja wyborcza Polskiego Stronnictwa Ludowego," in fttp://www.psl.org.pl (September 16, 2001). For other parties, see their respective Internet home pages.
30 "Tezy programowe," in fttp://www.samoobrona.org.pl (September 14, 2001).
31 "Polsce – Niepodleglosc. Polakom – Praca, Chleb, Mieszkania," in fttp://www.lpr.org.pl (September 14, 2001).
32 "Program Ruchu Spolecznego 'Alternatywa'," in fttp://www.alternatywa.org.pl (September 14, 2001).
33 *Gazeta Wyborcza*, July 3, 2001.

Reference

Lena Kolarska-Bobinska, "Nie liczymy na pieniadze. Raport Polska – Unia Europejska (We do not count on money. Report on Poland – the European Union)," *Gazeta Wyborcza*, July 12, 2001.

Further reading

The following is a list of literature on related topics that the author obtained during a stay in Warsaw from July to August 2001:

For political science studies, see Zbigniew Drozdowicz and Zdzislaw W. Puslecki (eds) *Adaptacja przez transformacje* (Poznan: Fundacja Humaniora, 2001); Zdsislaw Mach and Dariusz Niedzwiedzki (eds) *Polska lokalna wobec integracji europejskiej* (Krakow: Uniwersytet Jagiellonski, 2001).

  For sociological studies, see Lena Kolarska-Bobinska (ed.) *Polacy wobec wielkiej zmiany. Integracja z Unia Europejska* (Warszawa: Instytut Spraw Publlicznych, 2001); Renata Suchocka, *Integracja europejska w polskiej perspektywie* (Poznan: Wyd.

Naukowe UAM, 2000); Zdzislaw Mach (ed.) Integracja europejska w oczach Polakow (Krakow: Fundacja "Miedzynarodowe Centrum Rozwoju Demokracji," 1998); Bogdan W. Mach, Wojciech Zaborowski, Kazimierz M. Slomczynski, Elzbieta Skotnicka-Illasiewicz, and Hanna Palska, *Polacy wobec integracji Polski z Unia Europejska. Trwalosc i zmiana postaw spolecznych wobec integracji Polski z Unia Europejska* (Warszawa: Centrum Stosunkow Miedzynarodowych, 1998); Katarzyna Glabicki (ed.) *Spoleczne skutki integracji Polski z Unia Europejska* (Warszawa: Wyzsza Szkola Pedagogiczna, 1999).

For international relations studies, see Janusz Stefanowicz (ed.) *Miedzy tozsamoscia i wspolnota. Wspolczesne wyznaczniki polityki zagranicznej panstw europejskich* (Warszawa: ISP PAN, 1996); Elzbieta Kawecka-Wyrzykowska, *Stosunki Polski ze Wspolnotami Europejskimi od 1989 roku* (Warszawa: SGH, 1997); Tomasz Otlowski, *Polska w prozesie integracji z NATO i Unia Zachodnioeuropejska 1991–1998* (Torun: Adam Marszalek, 1999); Stanislaw Miklaszewski (ed.) *Polska w Unii Europejskiej* (Krakow: Meritum, 1999); Maria Marczewska-Rytko (ed.) *Polska miedzy Zachodem a Wschodem w dobie integracji europejskiej* (Lublin: Wyd. Uniwersytet Marii Curii-Sklodowskiej, 2001); Krzysztof Jazwinski (ed.) *Polska w procesie integracji i bezpieczenstwa europejskiego* (Warszawa: Askon, 1999); Andrzej Karpinski, *Unia Europejska – Polska. Dylematy przyszlosci* (Warszawa: Elipsa, 1998); Helena Tendera-Wlaszczuk, *Rozszerzenie Unii Europejskiej na Wschod. Polska nat tle innych krajow* (Warszawa: PWN, 2001); Julian Kaczmarek, *Unia Europejska. Rozwoj i zagrozenia* (Wroclaw: Atla 2, 2000).

For international economics studies, see Zofia Dach (ed.) *Kontrowersje wokol korzysci i kosztow integracji Polski z Unia Europejska* (Chrzanow: Wyzsza Szkola Przedsiebiorczosci i Marketingu w Chrzanowie, 1999); Witold Orlowski, *Koszty i korzysci z czlonkostwa w Unii Europejskiej. Metody, modele, szacunki* (Warszawa: Centrum Analiz Spoleczno-Ekonomicznych, 2000); Stanislaw Miklaszewski (ed.) *Europa Srodkowo-Wschodnia w warunkach globalizacji handlu* (Krakow: Instytut Studiow Strategicznych, 2000).

Appendix Presidency conclusions

European Council meeting in Laeken, 14 and 15 December 2001

1 Just when the European Union is introducing its single currency, its enlargement is becoming irreversible and it is initiating an important debate on its future, the European Council meeting in Laeken on 14 and 15 December 2001 has provided fresh impetus to increase the momentum of its integration.

2 The European Council's discussions were preceded by an exchange of views with the President of the European Parliament, Mrs Nicole Fontaine, on the principal items on the agenda.

I The future of the Union

The Laeken declaration

3 Following the conclusions adopted in Nice, the European Council adopted the declaration set out in Annex I. That declaration and the prospects it opens mark a decisive step for the citizen towards a simpler Union, one that is stronger in the pursuit of its essential objectives and more present in the world. In order to ensure that preparation for the forthcoming Intergovernmental Conference is as broadly-based and transparent as possible, the European Council has decided to convene a Convention, with Mr V. Giscard d'Estaing as Chairman and Mr G. Amato and Mr J.L. Dehaene as Vice-Chairmen. All the candidate countries will take part in the Convention. In parallel with the proceedings of the Convention, a Forum will make it possible to give structure to and broaden the public debate on the future of the Union that has already begun.

4 In parallel with the proceedings of the Convention, a certain number of measures can already be taken without amending the Treaties. In this context, the European Council welcomes the Commission's white paper on governance and the Council Secretary-General's intention

of submitting, before the European Council meeting in Barcelona, proposals for adapting the Council's structures and functioning to enlargement. The European Council will draw the operational conclusions from it at its meeting in Seville. Finally, the European Council welcomes the final report by the High-Level Advisory Group ("Mandelkern Group") on the quality of regulatory arrangements and the Commission communication on regulatory simplification, which should lead to a practical plan of action in the first half of 2002.

Transition to the euro

5 The introduction of euro notes and coins on 1 January 2002 will be the culmination of a historic process of decisive importance for the construction of Europe. Every measure has been taken to ensure that the physical introduction of the euro is a success. The use of the euro on international financial markets should be easier as a result. The euro area now represents a pole of stability for those countries participating in it by protecting them from speculation and financial turmoil. It is strengthening the internal market and contributing to the maintenance of healthy fundamental figures, fostering sustainable growth. The euro is also helping to bring the citizens of the Union closer together by giving visible, concrete expression to the European design. In that regard, the European Council welcomes the recent adoption by the Council and the European Parliament of a Regulation intended to reduce substantially the cost of cross-border payments in euro.

The European security and defence policy

6 The European Council has adopted the declaration on the operational capability of the European security and defence policy set out in Annex II, as well as the Presidency report. Through the continuing development of the ESDP, the strengthening of its capabilities, both civil and military, and the creation of appropriate structures within it and following the military and police Capability Improvement Conferences held in Brussels on 19 November 2001, the Union is now capable of conducting some crisis-management operations. The Union is determined to finalise swiftly arrangements with NATO. These will enhance the European Union's capabilities to carry out crisis-management operations over the whole range of Petersberg tasks. In the same way, the implementation of the Nice arrangements with the Union's partners will augment its means of

conducting crisis-management operations. Development of the means and capabilities at its disposal will enable the Union progressively to take on more demanding operations.

Enlargement

7   The Commission document entitled "Making a success of enlargement", the regular reports and the revised partnerships for accession are a solid framework for the success of the accession process, which is now irreversible. The Berlin European Council established the financial framework permitting enlargement.

8   In recent months considerable progress has been made in the negotiations and certain delays have been made good. The European Union is determined to bring the accession negotiations with the candidate countries that are ready to a successful conclusion by the end of 2002, so that those countries can take part in the European Parliament elections in 2004 as members. Candidacies will continue to be assessed on their own merits, in accordance with the principle of differentiation. The European Council agrees with the report of the Commission, which considers that, if the present rate of progress of the negotiations and reforms in the candidate States is maintained, Cyprus, Estonia, Hungary, Latvia, Lithuania, Malta, Poland, the Slovak Republic, the Czech Republic and Slovenia could be ready. It appreciates the efforts made by Bulgaria and Romania and would encourage them to continue on that course. If those countries are to receive specific support, there must be a precise framework with a timetable and an appropriate roadmap, the objective being to open negotiations with those countries on all chapters in 2002.

9   The candidate countries must continue their efforts energetically, in particular to bring their administrative and judicial capabilities up to the required level. The Commission will submit a report on the implementation of the plan of action for strengthening institutions to the Seville European Council in June 2002.

10 The roadmap drawn up by the Nice European Council remains fully applicable. At the beginning of 2002 the Commission will propose common positions on the agriculture, regional policy and budgetary chapters on the basis of the present *acquis* and of the principles decided on in Berlin. Proceedings on the drafting of the accession treaties will begin in the first half of 2002.

11 The European Council welcomes the recent meetings between the leaders of the Greek and Turkish Cypriot communities and would encourage them to continue their discussions with a view to an overall

solution under the auspices of the United Nations consistent with the relevant resolutions of the United Nations Security Council.

12 Turkey has made progress towards complying with the political criteria established for accession, in particular through the recent amendment of its constitution. This has brought forward the prospect of the opening of accession negotiations with Turkey. Turkey is encouraged to continue its progress towards complying with both economic and political criteria, notably with regard to human rights. The pre-accession strategy for Turkey should mark a new stage in analysing its preparedness for alignment on the *acquis*.

II The Union's action following the attacks in the USA on 11 September

The Union's action in Afghanistan

13 The European Council welcomes the signing in Bonn on 5 December of the agreement defining the provisional arrangements applicable in Afghanistan pending the re-establishment of permanent State institutions. It urges all Afghan groups to implement that agreement.

14 The European Council has undertaken to participate in the efforts of the international community with a view to restoring stability in Afghanistan on the basis of the outcome of the Bonn Conference and the relevant resolutions of the United Nations Security Council. In that context, it encourages the deployment of an international security force, which would be mandated, on the basis of a resolution of the United Nations Security Council, to contribute to the security of the Afghan and international administrations established in Kabul and the surrounding areas and to the establishment and training of new Afghan security and armed forces. The Member States of the Union are examining their contributions to such a force. The participation of the Member States of the Union in that international force will provide a strong signal of their resolve to better assume their crisis-management responsibilities and hence help stabilise Afghanistan.

15 The urgent needs of the Afghan people mean that humanitarian aid continues to be an absolute priority. The delivery of such aid, inter alia for refugees and displaced persons, must be adapted to changes in the situation and must take place in as efficient and well-coordinated a manner as possible. The Union has already pledged or is ready to pledge a total of EUR 360 million for humanitarian aid, of which EUR 106 million will come from the Community budget.

16 More than twenty years of war and political instability have destroyed

the structures of Afghan society, completely disrupted the functioning of the public institutions and authorities and caused immense human suffering. The European Union will help the Afghan people and its new leaders rebuild the country and encourage as swift a return to democracy as possible. The situation of women will merit particular attention. Rehabilitation and reconstruction will require strong international cooperation and coordination. The European Union has appointed Mr Klaus-Peter Klaiber Special Representative in Afghanistan under the authority of the High Representative for the CFSP. On 21 December in Brussels, the Union will co-chair the first meeting of the steering group to support political renewal in Afghanistan and better coordinate donors' efforts with a view to the ministerial conference scheduled for January 2002 in Tokyo. At those meetings, the Union will undertake to help to cover the requirements, alongside the USA, the Arab countries and Japan, inter alia.

Combating terrorism

17   The European Union reaffirms its total solidarity with the American people and the international community in combating terrorism with full regard for individual rights and freedoms. The plan of action adopted on 21 September is being implemented in accordance with the timetable set. The progress which has been achieved indicates that the objectives will be met. Agreement on the European arrest warrant constitutes a decisive step forward. The common definition of terrorist crimes, the drawing up of lists of terrorists and terrorist organisations, groups and bodies, the cooperation between specialist services and the provisions concerning the freezing of assets which have been adopted following Resolution 1373 of the United Nations Security Council all constitute practical responses in the campaign against terrorism. The European Council invites the Council and the Commission to move swiftly towards finalising the programme to improve cooperation between Member States with regard to threats of the use of biological and chemical means; the work of the European Civil Protection Agency will provide the framework for such cooperation.

18   The European Union is committed to alleviating the consequences of the attacks of 11 September for the aviation sector with a view to ensuring a rapid and coordinated response from all Member States. The European Council welcomes the adoption of a common position of the Council on the Regulation on aviation security.

III Trends in the economic and social spheres and in sustainable development

General economic situation and prospects

19 The Union's economy is experiencing a period of slower growth and uncertainty under the combined impact of a global slowdown and a reduction in demand. Yet, present expectations are for a gradual recovery in the course of 2002. Disposable incomes are improving owing to diminishing inflation and tax cuts in several countries. Budgetary policy is geared to maintaining sound public finances. It has resulted in a reduction in long-term interest rates, which will help support demand. The progress already made in budgetary consolidation within the framework of the Stability and Growth Pact will enable budgetary policy to play a positive part in combating the slowdown with automatic stabilisers working while staying on the medium-term path of consolidation. Confidence must be based on the consistent implementation of the economic policy strategy as defined in the Broad Economic Policy Guidelines (BEPGs), the main axes of which are macroeconomic stability and structural reforms to enhance job creation and the Union's potential for growth. The European Council endorsed the report of the ECOFIN Council on the taxation of savings.

20 The European Council welcomes the outcome of the Ministerial Conference in Doha, which launched a new round of global trade negotiations based on an approach balanced equally between liberalisation and regulation, taking account of the interests of developing countries and promoting their capacity for development. The Union is determined to promote the social and environmental dimension of that round of negotiations.

The Lisbon strategy

21 At the Barcelona European Council on 15 and 16 March 2002 we will take stock of our progress towards the Lisbon strategic goal of becoming the most dynamic knowledge-based economy in the world, with full employment and increased levels of social cohesion, by 2010, and agree concrete steps on the priority actions we must take to deliver this strategy. The slowdown in growth makes it more important than ever to deliver the structural reforms agreed at Lisbon and Stockholm, and to demonstrate the continued relevance of our agenda for economic and social issues and sustainable development to Europe's

citizens and businesses. We should use the structural indicators we have agreed to assess our progress and focus our activity. In order to give the European Council a full picture of the situation and to ensure that its decisions are coherent, the various preparatory processes will have to converge on the spring European Council.

22 Progress has been made following the Stockholm European Council on the various aspects of the Lisbon strategy. After thirty years of discussion, agreement has been reached on the European Company. There have been agreements on the liberalisation of postal services and on the package of Directives concerning telecommunications. The adoption of a series of economic and social structural indicators, including as regards quality in work and the fight against poverty and social exclusion as well as key indicators for sustainable development, will make it possible to see more clearly how each Member State is performing. The Commission will use them as a basis when drawing up its summary report to be submitted in January 2002.

Employment

23 The aim of the Lisbon strategy is to enable the Union to regain the conditions for full employment. We must accelerate our efforts to achieve by 2010 the 70% employment rate agreed in Lisbon. That must be the first objective of the European Employment Strategy. At the social summit on 13 December 2001 the social partners expressed their willingness to develop social dialogue by jointly drawing up a multiannual work programme before the European Council at the end of 2002. They also stressed the need to develop and improve coordination of tripartite consultation on the various aspects of the Lisbon strategy. It was agreed that a social affairs summit of this kind would in future be held before each spring European Council.

24 The European Council endorses the agreement reached in the Council concerning the 2002 employment guidelines, the individual recommendations to the Member States and the joint report on the employment situation. These decisions bear witness to the Union's desire, despite the world economic slowdown, to persist in its efforts to reform the structure of the labour market and continue to pursue its objectives concerning full employment and quality in work.

Fleshing out the European social model

25 In the field of social legislation, the European Council welcomes the political agreement between the Council and the European Parlia-

ment on the Directive on informing and consulting workers and the political agreement by the Council on a common position on the Directive on the protection of workers in the event of the insolvency of their employer. It stresses the importance of preventing and resolving social conflicts, and especially transnational social conflicts, by means of voluntary mediation mechanisms concerning which the Commission is requested to submit a discussion paper.

26 The European Council welcomes the Council's conclusions and the joint Council and Commission report concerning services of general interest, which will be the subject of an assessment, at Community level, as to their performance and their effects on competition. The European Council encourages the Commission to set up a policy framework for State aid to undertakings entrusted with the provision of services of general interest.

27 The European Council notes with interest the consideration given to the principle of equality between men and women in the broad economic policy guidelines and in the Euro-Mediterranean partnership, and also the list of indicators of gender pay inequalities.

28 The first joint report on social inclusion and the establishment of a set of common indicators constitute important elements in the policy defined at Lisbon for eradicating poverty and promoting social inclusion, taking in health and housing. The European Council stresses the need to reinforce the statistical machinery and calls on the Commission gradually to involve the candidate countries in this process.

29 The European Council notes the political agreement on extending the coordination of social security systems to third-country nationals and calls on the Council to adopt the necessary provisions as soon as possible.

30 The European Council has noted the Joint Report on pensions drawn up by the Social Protection Committee and the Economic Policy Committee. The adequacy of pensions, the sustainability and modernisation of pension systems and the improvement of access to occupational pension schemes are all of particular importance for dealing with the increasing needs. The European Council calls on the Council to take a similar approach when preparing the report on health care and care for the elderly, in the light of the Commission communication. Particular attention will have to be given to the impact of European integration on Member States' health care systems.

Research and development

31 The Lisbon European Council drew attention to the importance of encouraging innovation, especially through the introduction of a Community patent, which should have been available at the end of 2001. The European Council asks the Internal Market Council to hold a meeting on 20 December 2001 in order to reach, in particular in the light of the Presidency document and of the other contributions of the Member States, agreement on a flexible instrument involving the least possible cost while complying with the principle of non-discrimination between Member States' undertakings and ensuring a high level of quality.

32 The European Council welcomes the adoption by the Council of a common position on the 6th Framework Programme for research and development, aimed at reinforcing the European Research Area.

33 The European Council reaffirms the strategic importance it attaches to the Galileo project and welcomes the decision of the European Space Agency taken in Edinburgh to grant finance to the amount of EUR 550 m. The European Council calls on the Council to continue its work with a view to taking a decision on the funding of the development phase by March 2002 and to decide on the Regulation by June 2002, taking account of the audit report by PriceWaterhouseCoopers.

Sustainable development and quality of life

34 The European Council welcomes the adoption by the Council of the key environmental indicators which supplement the social and economic structural indicators with a view to the forthcoming summary report by the Commission. The European Council will assess – on this basis, and for the first time – the implementation of the Sustainable Development Strategy at its next meeting in the spring in Barcelona.

35 The European Council welcomes the outcome of the Marrakesh Conference on Climate Change. The Union is determined to honour its commitments under the Kyoto Protocol and confirms its desire that the Protocol should come into force before the Johannesburg World Summit on Sustainable Development, where the European Union intends to be represented at the highest political level.

36 The European Union has sought to respond to people's expectations regarding health, consumer protection, safety and quality of life. The European Council especially welcomes the setting up of the European Food Safety Authority, the European Air Safety Agency and the European Maritime Safety Agency. The Commission will very shortly be

submitting a proposal for setting up a European Railway Safety Agency. The European Council notes the adoption of a number of texts seeking to increase consumer protection in the areas of product safety, indebtedness, the standards applicable to blood products and the prudent use of antimicrobial agents in human medicine.

IV   Strengthening the areas of freedom, security and justice

37   The European Council reaffirms its commitment to the policy guide-lines and objectives defined at Tampere and notes that while some progress has been made, there is a need for new impetus and guide-lines to make good delays in some areas. Holding Justice and Home Affairs sessions at shorter intervals will help speed work up. It is also important that decisions taken by the Union be transposed speedily into national legal systems and that conventions concluded since the Maastricht Treaty came into force be ratified as soon as possible.

A true common asylum and immigration policy

38   Despite some achievements such as the European Refugee Fund, the Eurodac Regulation and the Directive on temporary protection, progress has been slower and less substantial than expected. A new approach is therefore needed.

39   The European Council undertakes to adopt, on the basis of the Tampere conclusions and as soon as possible, a common policy on asylum and immigration, which will maintain the necessary balance between protection of refugees, in accordance with the principles of the 1951 Geneva Convention, the legitimate aspiration to a better life and the reception capacities of the Union and its Member States.

40   A true common asylum and immigration policy implies the establish-ment of the following instruments:

- the integration of the policy on migratory flows into the European Union's foreign policy. In particular, European readmission agree-ments must be concluded with the countries concerned on the basis of a new list of priorities and a clear action plan. The Euro-pean Council calls for an action plan to be developed on the basis of the Commission communication on illegal immigration and the smuggling of human beings;
- the development of a European system for exchanging informa-tion on asylum, migration and countries of origin; the implemen-tation of Eurodac and a Regulation for the more efficient

application of the Dublin Convention, with rapid and efficient procedures;
- the establishment of common standards on procedures for asylum, reception and family reunification, including accelerated procedures where justified. These standards should take account of the need to offer help to asylum applicants;
- the establishment of specific programmes to combat discrimination and racism.

41   The European Council asks the Commission to submit, by 30 April 2002 at the latest, amended proposals concerning asylum procedures, family reunification and the "Dublin II" Regulation. In addition, the Council is asked to expedite its proceedings on other drafts concerning reception standards, the definition of the term "refugee" and forms of subsidiary protection.

More effective control of external borders

42   Better management of the Union's external border controls will help in the fight against terrorism, illegal immigration networks and the traffic in human beings. The European Council asks the Council and the Commission to work out arrangements for cooperation between services responsible for external border control and to examine the conditions in which a mechanism or common services to control external borders could be created. It asks the Council and the Member States to take steps to set up a common visa identification system and to examine the possibility of setting up common consular offices.

Eurojust and judicial and police cooperation in criminal matters

43   The Decision setting up Eurojust and the setting up of the instruments needed for police cooperation – Europol, whose powers have been increased, the European Police College and the Police Chiefs Task Force – constitute significant progress. The Council is urged swiftly to examine the Commission Green Paper on the European Public Prosecutor, taking account of the diversity of legal systems and traditions. The European Council calls for a European network to encourage the training of magistrates to be set up swiftly; this will help develop trust between those involved in judicial cooperation.

Combating drug trafficking

44 The European Council notes the importance of intensifying the fight against drug trafficking and the urgency of adopting the Commission proposal on the subject by the end of May 2002. It reserves the right to take fresh initiatives in the light of the Commission's midterm report on the implementation of the European Union's Action Plan on Drugs.

Harmonisation of laws, mutual recognition of judgments and the European arrest warrant

45 The Framework Decision on combating trafficking in human beings, the European arrest warrant and the common definition of terrorist offences and of minimum sentences constitute important progress. Efforts to surmount the problems arising from differences between legal systems should continue, particularly by encouragement of recognition of judicial decisions, both civil and criminal. For example, the harmonisation of family law took a decisive step forward with the suspension of intermediate procedures for the recognition of certain judgments and especially for cross-border rights of access to children.

V External relations

The Middle East

46 The European Council adopted the Declaration set out in Annex III.

The Western Balkans

47 The European Union has taken a full role in encouraging and assisting the countries of the region to continue their efforts in the framework of the Stabilisation and Association Process. The prospect of accession and the assistance provided by the European Union are key elements in promoting that process, respecting human rights, democratic principles and internationally recognised frontiers. The European Council welcomes the appointment of Dr Erhard Busek as Special Coordinator of the Stability Pact and thanks his predecessor, Mr Bodo Hombach, for his major contribution to the stability of the region.

48 The Union will continue to contribute to the recovery and stability of the Former Yugoslav Republic of Macedonia, particularly by insisting

on full implementation of the Ohrid Agreement. The European Council welcomes the elections held in Kosovo on 17 November which launched the process of provisional self-government for the benefit of all communities and of stability in accordance with Resolution 1244 of the UN Security Council. It mandates the High Representative for the CFSP to encourage the dialogue between Belgrade and Podgorica with a view to reaching a negotiated solution for the status of a democratic Montenegro in a democratic Federal Republic of Yugoslavia.

Africa

49 The Euro-African ministerial meeting in October reaffirmed the Union's solidarity with the African continent and its attachment to the dialogue process initiated in Cairo in May 2000. The European Council welcomes with great interest the New Partnership for African Development, which was announced by several African Heads of State in July and testifies to their determination to integrate the principles of good governance, African ownership and human rights into African governments' development policies. In that connection, the European Council welcomes the results of the Conference.

50 The European Council reaffirms its full support for the Lusaka and Arusha Agreements, the only tools capable of bringing the countries of the region to a lasting understanding and to true stabilisation. In that context, it appreciates the Commission's undertaking to sign the National Indicative Programme for the Democratic Republic of the Congo in January 2002 in Brussels, with a view to the resumption of the inter-Congolese dialogue, thus sending a strong signal of the European Union's commitment on behalf of all Congolese.

51 The European Council reiterates its great concern at the deterioration of the situation in Zimbabwe and makes a pressing appeal to the Zimbabwean government to take all the action needed to improve the situation immediately, particularly with a view to the consultations to be held in the next few days on the basis of Article 96 of the Cotonou Agreement.

Russia

52 The Summit held in Brussels on 3 October 2001 established important guidelines for the practical implementation of the strategic partnership between the Union and Russia: elaborating the concept of a Common European Economic Area; stepping up the energy dia-

logue; the specific situation of Kaliningrad, in particular questions concerning the movement and transit of persons; trade questions, including Russia's accession to the World Trade Organisation. The European Union has undertaken to intensify its relations with Russia still further and looks forward to substantial progress on all these issues. The dialogue on political and security issues must be given more substance and yield concrete results. This should be reflected in joint initiatives on subjects of mutual interest (Western Balkans, Middle East). A structure should also be established for cooperation between the Union and Russia, on the basis of the Partnership and Cooperation Agreement in combating organised crime, drug trafficking, terrorism and illegal immigration.

Development cooperation

53 The European Union considers that better growth and development prospects may offer a more solid basis for peace and security. The European Council calls on the Commission and the Council to report on ways of improving the coordination of European and international policies to promote development, as a contribution to the Monterrey Conference and the Johannesburg World Summit.

54 The European Council notes with satisfaction the Council's undertaking to examine the means and the timeframe for each Member States' achievement of the UN official development aid target of 0.7% of GNP and its commitment to continuing its efforts to improve development cooperation instruments, particularly in the countries affected by crisis or conflict.

55 The European Council stresses the need to disburse as soon as possible the financial resources available for development aid. It invites the Council and the Commission to examine the setting up of a Euro-Mediterranean Development Bank.

56 The European Council expresses satisfaction at the organisation of a conference on 30 October 2001 on the effects of globalisation and the instructions issued to the Commission to analyse its financial aspects, and in particular debt reduction and alternative methods of financing development.

57 Pending overall agreement on the seats of certain agencies, the European Food Safety Authority and Eurojust will be able to begin operations in Brussels and The Hague respectively. If the institution of European Public Prosecutor is established, its seat will be determined in accordance with the provisions of the Decision of 8 April 1965.

VI   Miscellaneous decisions

58   The dramatic accident in St Gothard, following on the Mont-Blanc accident, demonstrates the urgency of measures to transfer goods haulage from road to rail. The Commission will submit its framework proposal on charging for the use of infrastructure and its proposal on tunnel safety as soon as possible. As an interim solution, the European Council asks the Commission to submit a proposal for an extension of the ecopoint system, as provided for in Protocol 9 to the Act of Accession of Austria in order to conclude the transport chapter in the accession negotiations before the end of the year.

59   The European Council undertakes to maintain a high level of nuclear safety in the Union. It stresses the need to monitor the security and safety of nuclear power stations. It calls for regular reports from Member States' atomic energy experts, who will maintain close contact with the Commission.

Ratification of the new Decision on own resources

60   The European Council notes with concern that in several Member States the new Decision on own resources has not yet been ratified. It stresses the importance of transposing the decisions of the Berlin European Council in good time and urgently requests the Member States to finalise their ratification procedures as soon as possible so that the new Decision on own resources can enter into force without delay.

61   The European Council took note of the documents and reports submitted to it and the conclusions adopted by the Council which they contain (see Annex IV). It calls upon the institutions to take operational action on them without delay, while taking full account, when appropriate, of the policy guidelines set out in these conclusions.

Annexes to Presidency conclusions

European Council meeting in Laeken, 14 and 15 December 2001

ANNEXES

ANNEX I

Laeken Declaration on the future of the European Union

I *Europe at a crossroads*

For centuries, peoples and states have taken up arms and waged war to win control of the European continent. The debilitating effects of two bloody wars and the weakening of Europe's position in the world brought a growing realisation that only peace and concerted action could make the dream of a strong, unified Europe come true. In order to banish once and for all the demons of the past, a start was made with a coal and steel community. Other economic activities, such as agriculture, were subsequently added in. A genuine single market was eventually established for goods, persons, services and capital, and a single currency was added in 1999. On 1 January 2002 the euro is to become a day-to-day reality for 300 million European citizens.

The European Union has thus gradually come into being. In the beginning, it was more of an economic and technical collaboration. Twenty years ago, with the first direct elections to the European Parliament, the

Community's democratic legitimacy, which until then had lain with the Council alone, was considerably strengthened. Over the last ten years, construction of a political union has begun and cooperation been established on social policy, employment, asylum, immigration, police, justice, foreign policy and a common security and defence policy.

The European Union is a success story. For over half a century now, Europe has been at peace. Along with North America and Japan, the Union forms one of the three most prosperous parts of the world. As a result of mutual solidarity and fair distribution of the benefits of economic development, moreover, the standard of living in the Union's weaker regions has increased enormously and they have made good much of the disadvantage they were at.

Fifty years on, however, the Union stands at a crossroads, a defining moment in its existence. The unification of Europe is near. The Union is about to expand to bring in more than ten new Member States, predominantly Central and Eastern European, thereby finally closing one of the darkest chapters in European history: the Second World War and the ensuing artificial division of Europe. At long last, Europe is on its way to becoming one big family, without bloodshed, a real transformation clearly calling for a different approach from fifty years ago, when six countries first took the lead.

The democratic challenge facing Europe

At the same time, the Union faces twin challenges, one within and the other beyond its borders.

Within the Union, the European institutions must be brought closer to its citizens. Citizens undoubtedly support the Union's broad aims, but they do not always see a connection between those goals and the Union's everyday action. They want the European institutions to be less unwieldy and rigid and, above all, more efficient and open. Many also feel that the Union should involve itself more with their particular concerns, instead of intervening, in every detail, in matters by their nature better left to Member States' and regions' elected representatives. This is even perceived by some as a threat to their identity. More importantly, however, they feel that deals are all too often cut out of their sight and they want better democratic scrutiny.

Europe's new role in a globalised world

Beyond its borders, in turn, the European Union is confronted with a fast-changing, globalised world. Following the fall of the Berlin Wall, it looked briefly as though we would for a long while be living in a stable world order, free from conflict, founded upon human rights. Just a few years later, however, there is no such certainty. The eleventh of September has brought a rude awakening. The opposing forces have not gone away: religious fanaticism, ethnic nationalism, racism and terrorism are on the increase, and regional conflicts, poverty and underdevelopment still provide a constant seedbed for them.

What is Europe's role in this changed world? Does Europe not, now that it is finally unified, have a leading role to play in a new world order, that of a power able both to play a stabilising role worldwide and to point the way ahead for many countries and peoples? Europe as the continent of humane values, the Magna Carta, the Bill of Rights, the French Revolution and the fall of the Berlin Wall; the continent of liberty, solidarity and above all diversity, meaning respect for others' languages, cultures and traditions. The European Union's one boundary is democracy and human rights. The Union is open only to countries which uphold basic values such as free elections, respect for minorities and respect for the rule of law.

Now that the Cold War is over and we are living in a globalised, yet also highly fragmented world, Europe needs to shoulder its responsibilities in the governance of globalisation. The role it has to play is that of a power resolutely doing battle against all violence, all terror and all fanaticism, but which also does not turn a blind eye to the world's heartrending injustices. In short, a power wanting to change the course of world affairs in such a way as to benefit not just the rich countries but also the poorest. A power seeking to set globalisation within a moral framework, in other words to anchor it in solidarity and sustainable development.

The expectations of Europe's citizens

The image of a democratic and globally engaged Europe admirably matches citizens' wishes. There have been frequent public calls for a greater EU role in justice and security, action against cross-border crime, control of migration flows and reception of asylum seekers and refugees from far-flung war zones. Citizens also want results in the fields of employment and combating poverty and social exclusion, as well as in the field of economic and social cohesion. They want a common approach on environmental pollution, climate change and food safety, in short, all transnational issues which they instinctively sense can only be tackled by working together. Just as they also want to see Europe more involved in foreign affairs, security and defence, in other words, greater and better coordinated action to deal with trouble spots in and around Europe and in the rest of the world.

At the same time, citizens also feel that the Union is behaving too bureaucratically in numerous other areas. In coordinating the economic, financial and fiscal environment, the basic issue should continue to be proper operation of the internal market and the single currency, without this jeopardising Member States' individuality. National and regional differences frequently stem from history or tradition. They can be enriching. In other words, what citizens understand by "good governance" is opening up fresh opportunities, not imposing further red tape. What they expect is more results, better responses to practical issues and not a European superstate or European institutions inveigling their way into every nook and cranny of life.

In short, citizens are calling for a clear, open, effective, democratically controlled Community approach, developing a Europe which points the way ahead for the world. An approach that provides concrete results in terms of more jobs, better quality of life, less crime, decent education and better health care. There can be no doubt that this will require Europe to undergo renewal and reform.

II   *Challenges and reforms in a renewed Union*

The Union needs to become more democratic, more transparent and more efficient. It also has to resolve three basic challenges: how to bring citizens, and primarily the young, closer to the European design and the European institutions, how to organise politics and the European political area in an enlarged Union and how to develop the Union into a stabilising factor and a model in the new, multipolar world. In order to address them a number of specific questions need to be put.

A better division and definition of competence in the European Union

Citizens often hold expectations of the European Union that are not always fulfilled. And vice versa – they sometimes have the impression that the Union takes on too much in areas where its involvement is not always essential. Thus the important thing is to clarify, simplify and adjust the division of competence between the Union and the Member States in the light of the new challenges facing the Union. This can lead both to restoring tasks to the Member States and to assigning new missions to the Union, or to the extension of existing powers, while constantly bearing in mind the equality of the Member States and their mutual solidarity.

A first series of questions that needs to be put concerns how the division of competence can be made more transparent. Can we thus make a clearer distinction between three types of competence: the exclusive competence of the Union, the competence of the Member States and the shared competence of the Union and the Member States? At what level is competence exercised in the most efficient way? How is the principle of subsidiarity to be applied here? And should we not make it clear that any powers not assigned by the Treaties to the Union fall within the exclusive sphere of competence of the Member States? And what would be the consequences of this?

The next series of questions should aim, within this new framework and while respecting the "acquis communautaire", to determine whether there needs to be any reorganisation of competence. How can citizens' expectations be taken as a guide here? What missions would this produce for the Union? And, vice versa, what tasks could better be left to the Member States? What amendments should be made to the Treaty on the various policies? How, for example, should a more coherent common foreign policy and defence policy be developed? Should the Petersberg tasks be updated? Do we want to adopt a more integrated approach to police and criminal law cooperation? How can economic-policy coordination be stepped up? How can we intensify cooperation in the field of social inclusion, the environment, health and food safety? But then, should not the day-to-day administration and implementation of the Union's policy be left more emphatically to the Member States and, where their constitutions so provide, to the regions? Should they not be provided with guarantees that their spheres of competence will not be affected?

Lastly, there is the question of how to ensure that a redefined division of competence does not lead to a creeping expansion of the competence of the Union or to encroachment upon the exclusive areas of competence of the Member States and, where there is provision for this, regions. How are we to ensure at the same time that the European dynamic does not come to a halt? In the future as well the Union must continue to be able to react to fresh challenges and developments and must be able to explore new policy areas. Should Articles 95 and 308 of the Treaty be reviewed for this purpose in the light of the "acquis jurisprudentiel"?

Simplification of the Union's instruments

Who does what is not the only important question; the nature of the Union's action and what instruments it should use are equally important. Successive amendments to the Treaty have on each occasion resulted in a proliferation of instruments, and directives have gradually evolved towards more and more detailed legislation. The key question is therefore whether the Union's various instruments should not be better defined and whether their number should not be reduced.

In other words, should a distinction be introduced between legislative and executive measures? Should the number of legislative instruments be reduced: directly applicable rules, framework legislation and non-enforceable instruments (opinions, recommendations, open coordination)? Is it or is it not desirable to have more frequent recourse to framework legislation, which affords the Member States more room for manoeuvre in achieving policy objectives? For which areas of competence are open coordination and mutual recognition the most appropriate instruments? Is the principle of proportionality to remain the point of departure?

More democracy, transparency and efficiency in the European Union

The European Union derives its legitimacy from the democratic values it projects, the aims it pursues and the powers and instruments it possesses. However, the European project also derives its legitimacy from democratic, transparent and efficient institutions. The national parliaments also contribute towards the legitimacy of the European project. The declaration on the future of the Union, annexed to the Treaty of Nice, stressed the need to examine their role in European integration. More generally, the question arises as to what initiatives we can take to develop a European public area.

The first question is thus how we can increase the democratic legitimacy and transparency of the present institutions, a question which is valid for the three institutions.

How can the authority and efficiency of the European Commission be enhanced? How should the President of the Commission be appointed: by the European Council, by the European Parliament or should he be directly elected by the citizens? Should the role of the European Parliament be strengthened? Should we extend the right of co-decision or not? Should the way in which we elect the members of the European Parliament be reviewed? Should a European electoral constituency be created, or should constituencies continue to be determined nationally? Can the two systems be combined? Should the role of the Council be strengthened? Should the Council act in the same manner in its legislative and its executive capacities? With a view to greater transparency, should the meetings of the Council, at least in its legislative capacity, be public? Should citizens have more access to Council documents? How, finally, should the balance and reciprocal control between the institutions be ensured?

A second question, which also relates to democratic legitimacy, involves the role of national parliaments. Should they be represented in a new institution, alongside the Council and the European Parliament? Should they have a role in areas of European action in which the European Parliament has no competence? Should they focus on the division of competence between Union and Member States, for example through preliminary checking of compliance with the principle of subsidiarity?

The third question concerns how we can improve the efficiency of decision-making and the workings of the institutions in a Union of some thirty Member States. How could the Union set its objectives and priorities more effectively and ensure better implementation? Is there a need for more decisions by a qualified majority? How is the co-decision procedure between the Council and the European Parliament to be simplified and speeded up? What of the six-monthly rotation of the Presidency of the Union? What is the future role of the European Parliament? What of the future role and structure of the various Council formations? How should the coherence of European foreign policy be enhanced? How is synergy between the High Representative and the competent Commissioner to be reinforced? Should the external representation of the Union in international fora be extended further?

Towards a Constitution for European citizens

The European Union currently has four Treaties. The objectives, powers and policy instruments of the Union are currently spread across those Treaties. If we are to have greater transparency, simplification is essential.

Four sets of questions arise in this connection. The first concerns simplifying the existing Treaties without changing their content. Should the distinction between the Union and the Communities be reviewed? What of the division into three pillars?

Questions then arise as to the possible reorganisation of the Treaties. Should a distinction be made between a basic treaty and the other treaty provisions? Should this distinction involve separating the texts? Could this lead to a distinction between the amendment and ratification procedures for the basic treaty and for the other treaty provisions?

Thought would also have to be given to whether the Charter of Fundamental Rights should be included in the basic treaty and to whether the European Community should accede to the European Convention on Human Rights.

The question ultimately arises as to whether this simplification and reorganisation might not lead in the long run to the adoption of a constitutional text in the Union. What might the basic features of such a constitution be? The values which the Union cherishes, the fundamental rights and obligations of its citizens, the relationship between Member States in the Union?

III Convening of a convention on the future of Europe

In order to pave the way for the next Intergovernmental Conference as broadly and openly as possible, the European Council has decided to convene a Convention composed of the main parties involved in the debate on the future of the Union. In the light of the foregoing, it will be the task of that Convention to consider the key issues arising for the Union's future development and try to identify the various possible responses.

The European Council has appointed Mr V. Giscard d'Estaing as Chairman of the Convention and Mr G. Amato and Mr J.L. Dehaene as Vice-Chairmen.

Composition

In addition to its Chairman and Vice-Chairmen, the Convention will be composed of 15 representatives of the Heads of State or Government of the Member States (one from each Member State), 30 members of national parliaments (two from each Member State), 16 members of the European Parliament and two Commission representatives. The accession candidate countries will be fully involved in the Convention's proceedings. They will be represented in the same way as the current Member States (one government representative and two national parliament members) and will be able to take part in the proceedings without, however, being able to prevent any consensus which may emerge among the Member States.

The members of the Convention may only be replaced by alternate members if they are not present. The alternate members will be designated in the same way as full members.

The Praesidium of the Convention will be composed of the Convention Chairman and Vice-Chairmen and nine members drawn from the Convention (the representatives of all the governments holding the Council Presidency during the Convention, two national parliament representatives, two European Parliament representatives and two Commission representatives).

Three representatives of the Economic and Social Committee with three representatives of the European social partners; from the Committee of the Regions: six representatives (to be appointed by the Committee of the Regions from the regions, cities and regions with legislative powers), and the European Ombudsman will be invited to attend as observers. The Presidents of the Court of Justice and of the Court of Auditors may be invited by the Praesidium to address the Convention.

Length of proceedings

The Convention will hold its inaugural meeting on 1 March 2002, when it will appoint its Praesidium and adopt its rules of procedure. Proceedings will be completed after a year, that is to say in time for the Chairman of the Convention to present its outcome to the European Council.

Working methods

The Chairman will pave the way for the opening of the Convention's proceedings by drawing conclusions from the public debate. The Praesidium will serve to lend impetus and will provide the Convention with an initial working basis.

The Praesidium may consult Commission officials and experts of its choice on any technical aspect which it sees fit to look into. It may set up *ad hoc* working parties.

The Council will be kept informed of the progress of the Convention's proceedings. The Convention Chairman will give an oral progress report at each European Council meeting, thus enabling Heads of State or Government to give their views at the same time.

The Convention will meet in Brussels. The Convention's discussions and all official documents will be in the public domain. The Convention will work in the Union's eleven working languages.

Final document

The Convention will consider the various issues. It will draw up a final document which may comprise either different options, indicating the degree of support which they received, or recommendations if consensus is achieved.

Together with the outcome of national debates on the future of the Union, the final document will provide a starting point for discussions in the Intergovernmental Conference, which will take the ultimate decisions.

Forum

In order for the debate to be broadly based and involve all citizens, a Forum will be opened for organisations representing civil society (the social partners, the business world, non-governmental organisations, academia, etc.). It will take the form of a structured network of organisations receiving regular information on the Convention's proceedings. Their contributions will serve as input into the debate. Such organisations may be heard or consulted on specific topics in accordance with arrangements to be established by the Praesidium.

Secretariat

The Praesidium will be assisted by a Convention Secretariat, to be provided by the General Secretariat of the Council, which may incorporate Commission and European Parliament experts.

ANNEX II

Declaration on the operational capability of the Common European Security and Defence Policy

A   At Nice and Göteborg, the European Council undertook to make the European Union quickly operational in this field and to take a decision to that end no later than at the European Council in Laeken. The extraordinary European Council meeting on 21 September 2001 reaffirmed the objective: "it is by developing the Common Foreign and Security Policy (CFSP) and by making the European Security and Defence Policy (ESDP) operational at the earliest opportunity that the Union will be most effective."

Through the continuing development of the ESDP, the strengthening of its capabilities, both civil and military, and the creation of the appropriate EU structures, the EU is now able to conduct some crisis-management operations. The Union will be in a position to take on progressively more demanding operations, as the assets and capabilities at its disposal continue to develop. Decisions to make use of this ability will be taken in the light of the circumstances of each particular situation, a determining factor being the assets and capabilities available.

B   Such a capability to act results from the substantial progress that has been accomplished since the European Councils in Cologne and Helsinki.

Capabilities

The conferences on military and police capabilities have enabled progress to be made towards the achievement of the capability objectives. The Member States have made voluntary contributions on the basis of national decisions. The development of military capabilities does not imply the creation of a European army. Non-EU European Member States of NATO and other candidates for accession to the European Union have made highly valuable additional military and police contributions, with the aim of enhancing European capabilities.

Structures and procedures

On the basis of the approved exercise policy and programme, the Union has begun to test its structures and procedures relating to civilian and military crisis-management operations. The European Union has established crisis-management structures and procedures which enable it to analyse and plan, to take decisions and, where NATO as such is not involved, to launch and carry out military crisis-management operations.

Arrangements between the European Union and NATO

The Union's crisis-management capability has been strengthened by the development of consultations, cooperation and transparency between the two organisations in crisis management in the Western Balkans.

Arrangements with its partners

The implementation of the arrangements with the non-EU European Member States of NATO and other candidates for accession to the European Union and with Canada, Russia and the Ukraine has been taken further.

C   To enable the European Union to carry out crisis-management operations over the whole range of Petersberg tasks, including operations which are the most demanding in terms of breadth, period of deployment and complexity, substantial progress will have to be made.

Balanced development of military and civilian capabilities

The balanced development of military and civilian capabilities is necessary for effective crisis management by the Union: this implies close coordination between all the resources and instruments both civilian and military available to the Union.

The strengthening of military capabilities in accordance with the European Action Plan to remedy shortcomings identified and the implementation of the exercise policy will be necessary to enable the Union progressively to carry out more complex operations. The importance of adopting the planned mechanism for the development of military capabilities should be emphasised, in particular to avoid all unnecessary duplication and, for the Member States concerned, to take into account NATO's defence planning process and the planning and review process of the Partnership for Peace (PARP).

The Police Action Plan will be implemented to enable the Union to be capable in the near future of carrying out police operations. The Union will continue its efforts to develop means of rapidly achieving and implementing concrete targets in the following priority areas: rule of law, civilian administration and civil protection.

To achieve these objectives, the Union, and in particular the Ministers responsible, will seek solutions and new forms of cooperation in order to develop the necessary capabilities, in accordance with this report, making optimum use of resources.

Finalisation of the arrangements with NATO

The Union intends to finalise the security arrangements with NATO and conclude the agreements on guaranteed access to the Alliance's operational planning, presumption of availability of pre-identified assets and capabilities of NATO and identification of a series of command options made available to the Union. These agreements are essential for the ESDP and will substantially increase the Union's available capabilities.

Implementation of the arrangements with its partners

The full and complete implementation of the Nice arrangements with the 15 and the 6, their additional contribution to the civilian and military capabilities and their participation in a crisis-management operation in accordance with those arrangements (in particular by setting up a Committee of Contributors in the event of an operation) will appreciably strengthen crisis-management operations carried out by the European Union.

ANNEX III

Declaration on the situation in the Middle East

The extreme gravity of the situation in the Middle East requires each side to face up to its responsibilities: it is imperative to put an end to the violence.

The only basis for peace is UN Resolutions 242 and 338 and:

- reaffirmation and full recognition of Israel's inalienable right to live in peace and security within internationally recognised borders;
- the establishment of a viable, independent and democratic Palestinian state and an end to the occupation of Palestinian territories.

Israel needs the Palestinian Authority and its elected President, Yasser Arafat, as a partner to negotiate with, both in order to eradicate terrorism and to work towards peace. Its capacity to fight terrorism must not be weakened. The European Union renews its appeal to the Palestinian Authority to do everything to prevent acts of terrorism.

The European Union would remind the parties of the pledges demanded of them:

- The Palestinian Authority: the dismantling of Hamas' and Islamic Jihad's terrorist networks, including the arrest and prosecution of all suspects; a public appeal in Arabic for an end to the armed intifada.
- The Israeli Government: withdrawal of its military forces and a stop to extrajudicial executions; the lifting of closures and of all the restrictions imposed on the Palestinian people; a freeze on settlements and an end to operations directed against Palestinian infrastructures.

Implementation of these commitments requires resolute action by both the Palestinian Authority and Israel.

Immediate and unconditional implementation of the Tenet cease-fire plan and the Mitchell Committee recommendations remains the only way to resume political dialogue.

The European Union remains convinced that setting up a third-party monitoring mechanism would serve the interests of both parties. It is prepared to play an active role in such a mechanism.

Resolute and concerted action by the European Union, the United Nations, the United States, the Russian Federation and the Arab countries most concerned is essential and urgent. The European Council has mandated High Representative Javier Solana to continue appropriate contacts to this end.

The Union attaches great importance to an economic recovery programme focused on Palestine as a way of encouraging peace.

The European Union will continue its efforts to ensure that both States, Israel and Palestine, can live side by side in peace and security.

Peace in the Middle East can be comprehensive only if it includes Syria and Lebanon.

ANNEX IV

Documents submitted to the Laeken European Council

- Strategy paper and Commission Report on the progress towards accession by each of the candidate countries (14117/01)
- Conclusions of the Council (General Affairs) of 10 December 2001 on enlargement (15059/01 + REV 1 (en))
- Report from the Presidency on European Union action following the attacks in the United States (14919/1/01 REV 1)
- Report from the Presidency on ESDP (15193/01 + COR 1 (de) + COR 2 (en))
- Report from the Presidency on evaluation of the implementation of the Tampere conclusions (14926/01 + COR 1 (fr) + COR 2 (it))
- Commission communication on the biannual update of the scoreboard to review progress on the creation of an area of freedom, security and justice in the European Union (second half of 2001) (13554/01)
- Conclusions of the Council (Internal Market, Consumer Affairs and Tourism) on services of general interest (14866/01)
- Commission Report on Services of General Interest (13235/01)
- Report from the Presidency on the internal market in electricity and gas (14943/01 + COR 1 (fr es))
- Report from the Council (ECOFIN) on the economic situation (15232/01)
- Report from the Council (ECOFIN) to the European Council on the taxation of savings (15325/01 + COR 1 (fr) + COR 2 (de) + COR 3 (en))
- Council conclusions on environment-related headline indicators for sustainable development with a view to monitoring progress in the implementation of the EU Sustainable Development Strategy (14589/01 + COR 1 (en))
- Conclusion of the Council (Environment) on the strategy for sustainable development (follow-up of the environment-related aspects of Götenborg) (15280/01)
- Conclusions of the Council (Environment) on international environmental governance (15281/01)
- Joint Employment Report (Council/Commission) 2001 (13421/01)

- Council (Employment and Social Policy) Decision on Guidelines for Member States' employment policies for the year 2002 (14912/01 + COR 1(en))
- Commission Recommendation for a Council Recommendation on the implementation of Member States' employment policies (14911/01)
- Conclusions of the Council (Employment and Social Policy): Employment and social policies: a framework for investing in quality (Indicators of quality in work) (14913/01 + ADD 1)
- Commission Communication: Employment and social policies: a framework for investing in quality – Report by the Employment Committee (14263/01)
- Joint Report from the Social Protection Committee and the Economic Policy Committee on objectives and working methods in the area of pensions (14098/01 + COR 1 (nl))
- Commission communication on future trends in social protection in the long term: safe and sustainable pensions (10672/01)
- Report from the Social Protection Committee on indicators in the field of poverty and social exclusion (13509/01 + ADD 1 REV 2)
- Joint Report from the Commission and the Council on Social Inclusion (15223/01 + COR 1 (it) + COR 2 (fr) + COR 3 (fi) + ADD 1 + ADD 2)
- Conclusions of the Council (Employment and Social Policy) on the proposal for a Regulation on the coordination of social security systems: Parameters for the modernisation of Regulation (EEC) No 1408/71 (15045/01 + COR 1 (en))
- Conclusions of the Council (Employment and Social Policy) on the proposal for a Regulation on the coordination of social security systems: extension of Regulation (EEC) No. 1408/71 to third-country nationals (legal basis) (15056/01)
- Commission communication: Article 299(2): Implementation of the sustainable development strategy for the outermost regions – Progress report and work programme with a provisional timetable (15246/01)
- Report from the Mandelkern Group on Better Regulation (14654/01)
- Commission communication: Simplifying and improving the regulatory environment (15225/01)
- Commission report: Better law making 2001 (15181/01)
- Preparing the Council for enlargement: Interim report from the Secretary-General/High Representative (15100/01)
- Report from the Council (General Affairs) on the implementation of the Common Strategy of the European Union on the Ukraine (15195/01)

Index

Note: page numbers in italics denote figures or tables

For Product Safety Concerns and Information please contact our EU
representative GPSR@taylorandfrancis.com
Taylor & Francis Verlag GmbH, Kaufingerstraße 24, 80331 München, Germany

9 781138 993600